DIVINITY

MATT KINDT | TREVOR HAIRSINE | RYAN WINN | DAVID BARON

CONTENTS

Collection Cover Art: Jelena Kevic-Djurdjevic

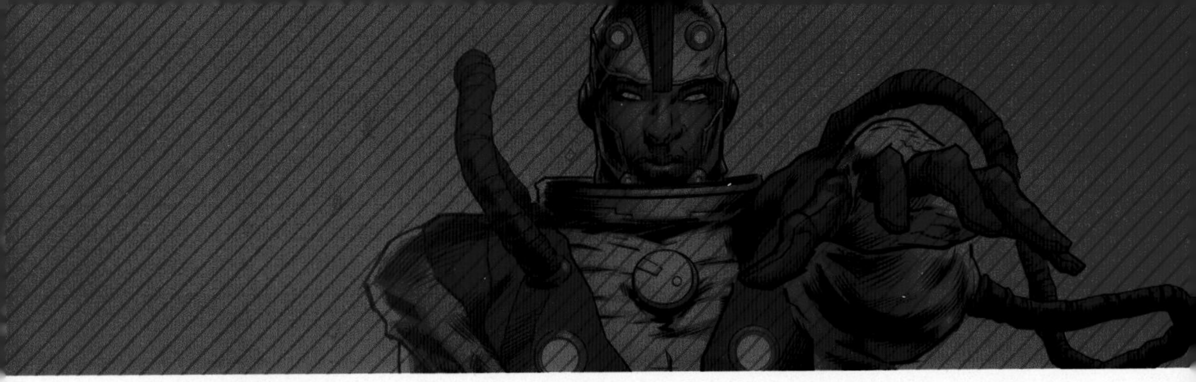

Associate Editor: Kyle Andrukiewicz
Editor: Warren Simons

VALIANT.

Peter Cuneo
Chairman

Dinesh Shamdasani
CEO & Chief Creative Officer

Gavin Cuneo
Chief Operating Officer & CFO

Fred Pierce
Publisher

Warren Simons
VP Editor-in-Chief

Walter Black
VP Operations

Hunter Gorinson
Director of Marketing,
Communications & Digital Media

Atom! Freeman
Matthew Klein
Andy Liegl
Sales Managers

Josh Johns
Digital Sales & Special Projects Manager

Travis Escarfullery
Jeff Walker
Production & Design Managers

Alejandro Arbona
Editor

Kyle Andrukiewicz
Tom Brennan
Associate Editors

Peter Stern
Publishing & Operations Manager

Chris Daniels
Marketing Coordinator

Danny Khazem
Operations Coordinator

Ivan Cohen
Collection Editor

Steve Blackwell
Collection Designer

Rian Hughes/Device
Trade Dress & Book Design

Russell Brown
President, Consumer Products,
Promotions and Ad Sales

Jason Kothari
Vice Chairman

Divinity™. Published by Valiant Entertainment LLC. Office of
Publication: 424 West 33rd Street, New York, NY 10001. Compilation
copyright ©2015 Valiant Entertainment LLC. All rights reserved.
Contains materials originally published in single magazine form as
Divinity #1-4. Copyright ©2015 Valiant Entertainment LLC. All rights
reserved. All characters, their distinctive likeness and related
indicia featured in this publication are trademarks of Valiant
Entertainment LLC. The stories, characters, and incidents featured
in this publication are entirely fictional. Valiant Entertainment does
not read or accept unsolicited submissions of ideas, stories, or
artwork. Printed in the U.S.A. Second Printing.
ISBN: 9781939346766.

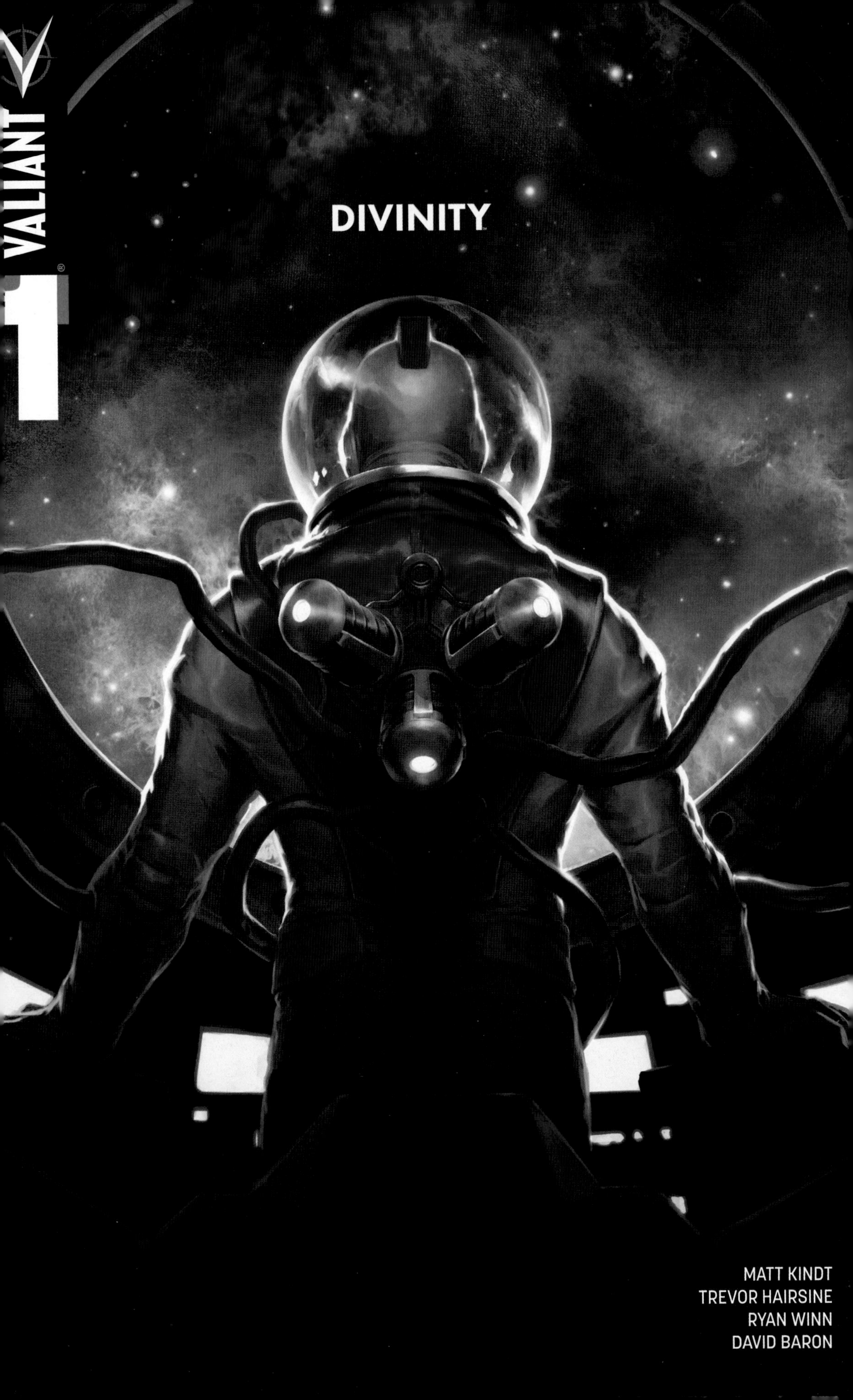
VALIANT
1
DIVINITY
MATT KINDT
TREVOR HAIRSINE
RYAN WINN
DAVID BARON

BOOK ONE

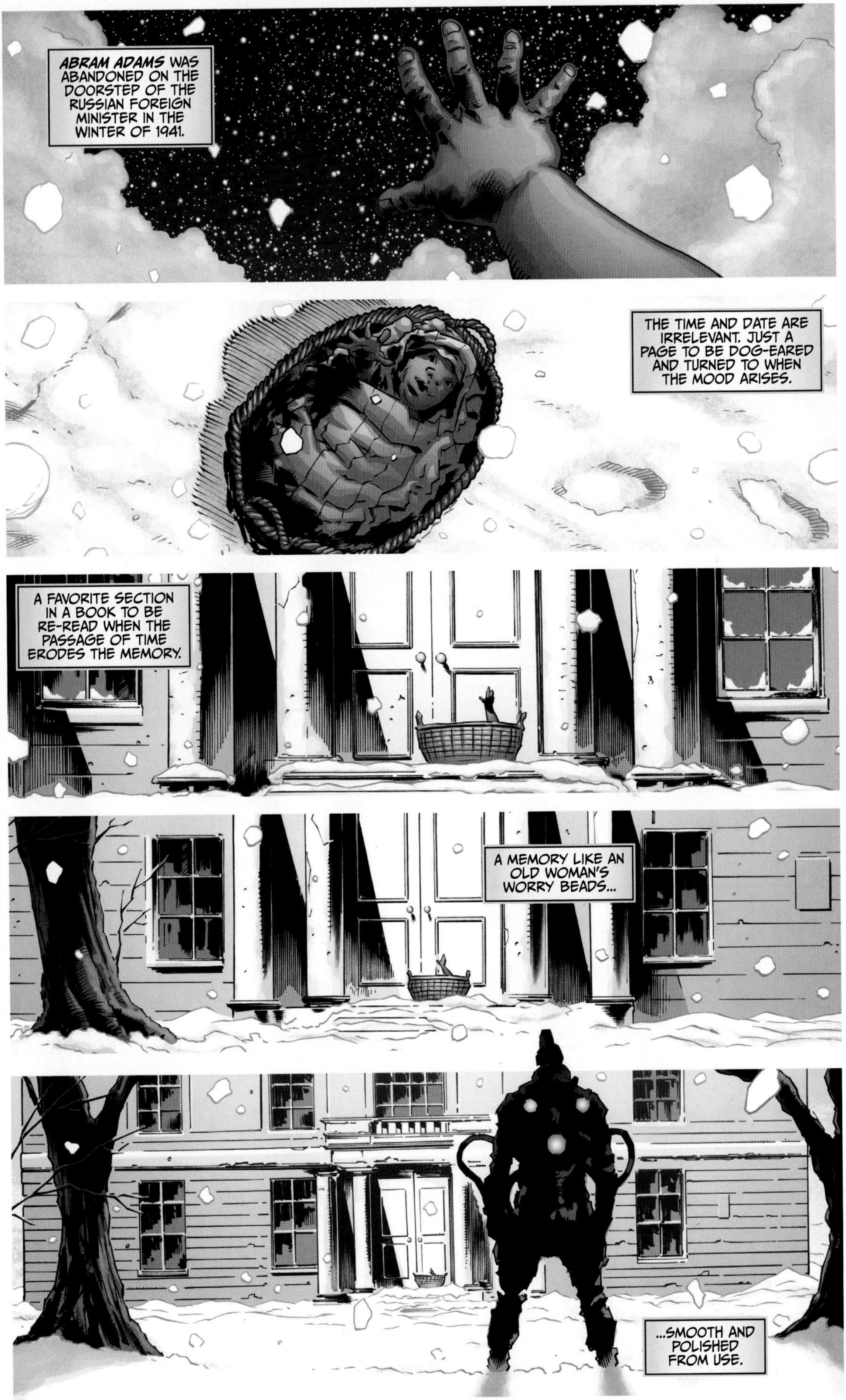

ABRAM ADAMS WAS ABANDONED ON THE DOORSTEP OF THE RUSSIAN FOREIGN MINISTER IN THE WINTER OF 1941.
THE TIME AND DATE ARE IRRELEVANT. JUST A PAGE TO BE DOG-EARED AND TURNED TO WHEN THE MOOD ARISES.
A FAVORITE SECTION IN A BOOK TO BE RE-READ WHEN THE PASSAGE OF TIME ERODES THE MEMORY.
A MEMORY LIKE AN OLD WOMAN'S WORRY BEADS...
...SMOOTH AND POLISHED FROM USE.

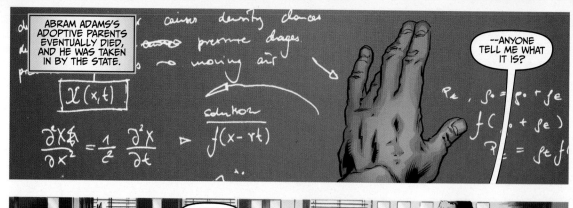

ABRAM ADAMS'S ADOPTIVE PARENTS EVENTUALLY DIED, AND HE WAS TAKEN IN BY THE STATE.

--ANYONE TELL ME WHAT IT IS?

YES, ABRAM?

HIS POTENTIAL WAS RECOGNIZED AND HE WAS GIVEN THE BEST THAT THE MOTHERLAND COULD OFFER.

"THE INDEFINITE CONTINUED PROGRESS OF EXISTENCE AND EVENTS IN THE PAST, PRESENT, AND FUTURE REGARDED AS A WHOLE."

HE WAS GROOMED BY THOSE IN POWER TO BE SOMETHING GREATER.

THE STATE SAW HIM AS A SYMBOL OF THE SOVIET UNION'S SUPERIORITY.

MORE RACE RIOTS IN THE UNITED STATES TODAY...

...AMERICAN POLICE TURNED RIOT DOGS ON THEIR OWN POPULACE...

YOU THINK YOU'LL GET PICKED FOR THE MISSION?

I DON'T KNOW. I HOPE SO.

ME TOO, COMRADE. YOU ARE THE SMARTEST OF ALL OF US. YOU DESERVE IT.

WE'LL SEE, NIKOLAI.

ABRAM WAS SLOW TO REALIZE ALL OF THIS.

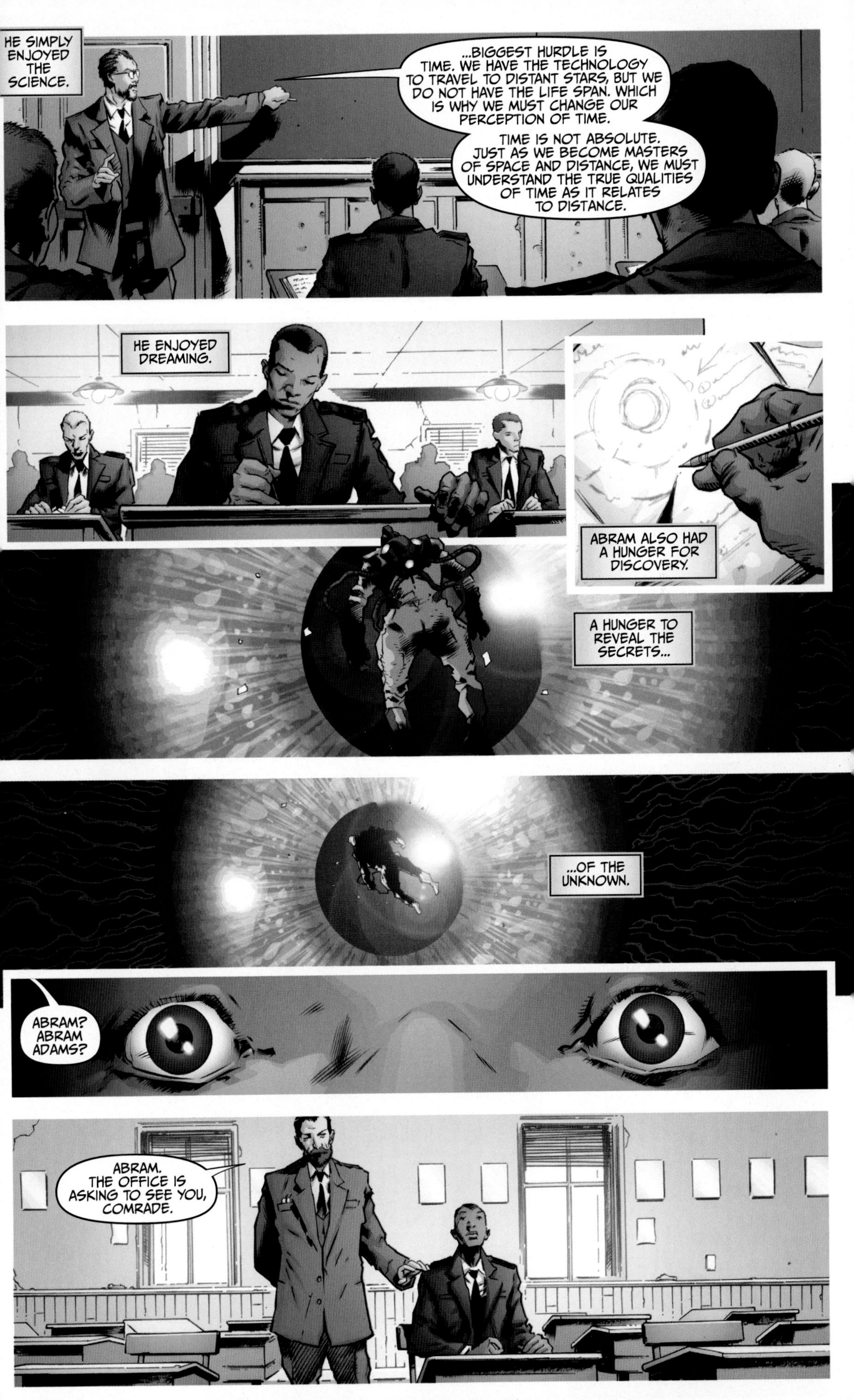
HE SIMPLY ENJOYED THE SCIENCE.
...BIGGEST HURDLE IS TIME. WE HAVE THE TECHNOLOGY TO TRAVEL TO DISTANT STARS, BUT WE DO NOT HAVE THE LIFE SPAN. WHICH IS WHY WE MUST CHANGE OUR PERCEPTION OF TIME.
TIME IS NOT ABSOLUTE. JUST AS WE BECOME MASTERS OF SPACE AND DISTANCE, WE MUST UNDERSTAND THE TRUE QUALITIES OF TIME AS IT RELATES TO DISTANCE.
HE ENJOYED DREAMING.
ABRAM ALSO HAD A HUNGER FOR DISCOVERY.
A HUNGER TO REVEAL THE SECRETS...
...OF THE UNKNOWN.
ABRAM? ABRAM ADAMS?
ABRAM. THE OFFICE IS ASKING TO SEE YOU, COMRADE.

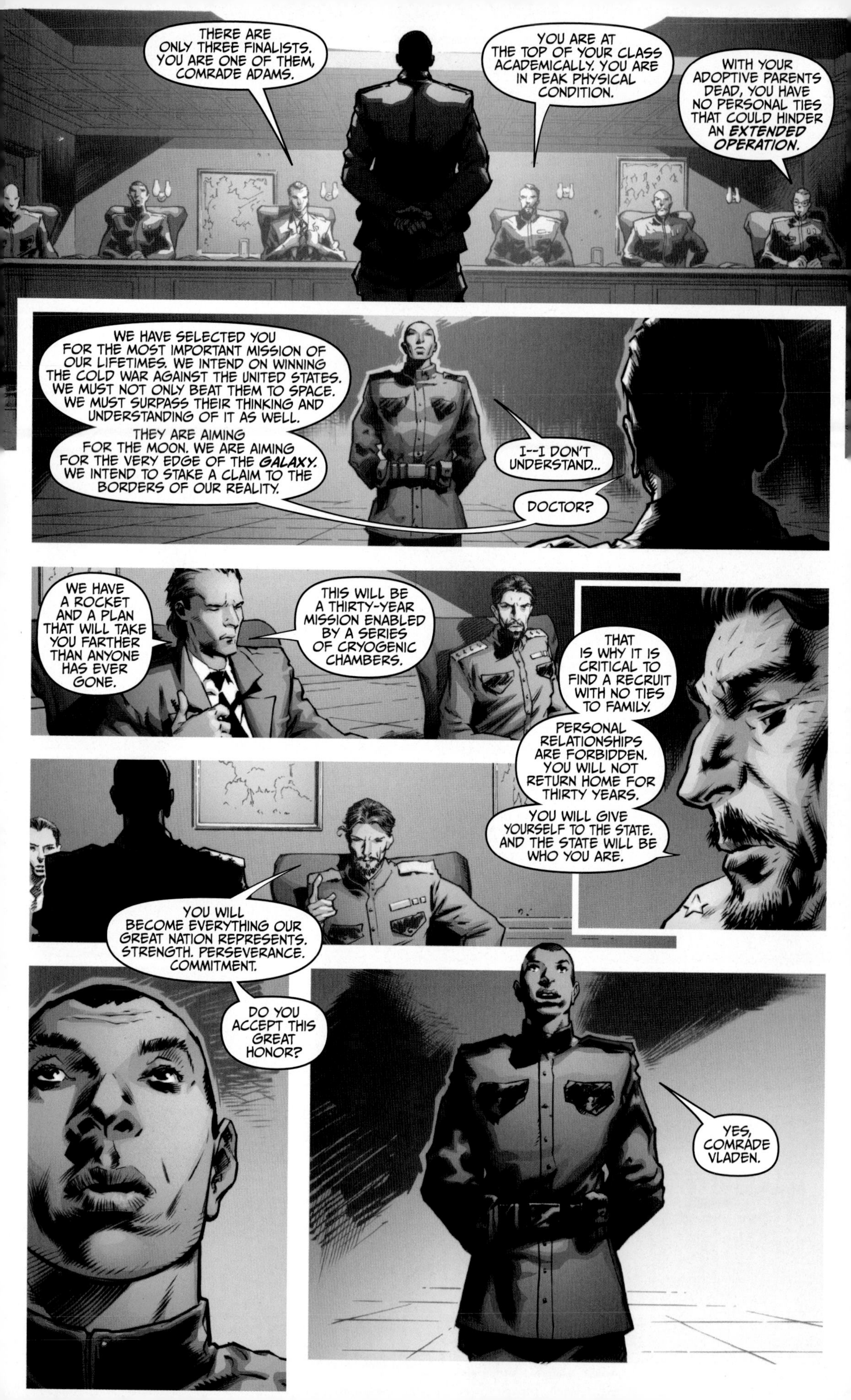
THERE ARE ONLY THREE FINALISTS. YOU ARE ONE OF THEM, COMRADE ADAMS.
YOU ARE AT THE TOP OF YOUR CLASS ACADEMICALLY. YOU ARE IN PEAK PHYSICAL CONDITION.
WITH YOUR ADOPTIVE PARENTS DEAD, YOU HAVE NO PERSONAL TIES THAT COULD HINDER AN EXTENDED OPERATION.
WE HAVE SELECTED YOU FOR THE MOST IMPORTANT MISSION OF OUR LIFETIMES. WE INTEND ON WINNING THE COLD WAR AGAINST THE UNITED STATES. WE MUST NOT ONLY BEAT THEM TO SPACE. WE MUST SURPASS THEIR THINKING AND UNDERSTANDING OF IT AS WELL.
THEY ARE AIMING FOR THE MOON. WE ARE AIMING FOR THE VERY EDGE OF THE GALAXY. WE INTEND TO STAKE A CLAIM TO THE BORDERS OF OUR REALITY.
I--I DON'T UNDERSTAND...
DOCTOR?
WE HAVE A ROCKET AND A PLAN THAT WILL TAKE YOU FARTHER THAN ANYONE HAS EVER GONE.
THIS WILL BE A THIRTY-YEAR MISSION ENABLED BY A SERIES OF CRYOGENIC CHAMBERS.
THAT IS WHY IT IS CRITICAL TO FIND A RECRUIT WITH NO TIES TO FAMILY.
PERSONAL RELATIONSHIPS ARE FORBIDDEN. YOU WILL NOT RETURN HOME FOR THIRTY YEARS.
YOU WILL GIVE YOURSELF TO THE STATE. AND THE STATE WILL BE WHO YOU ARE.
YOU WILL BECOME EVERYTHING OUR GREAT NATION REPRESENTS. STRENGTH. PERSEVERANCE. COMMITMENT.
DO YOU ACCEPT THIS GREAT HONOR?
YES, COMRADE VLADEN.

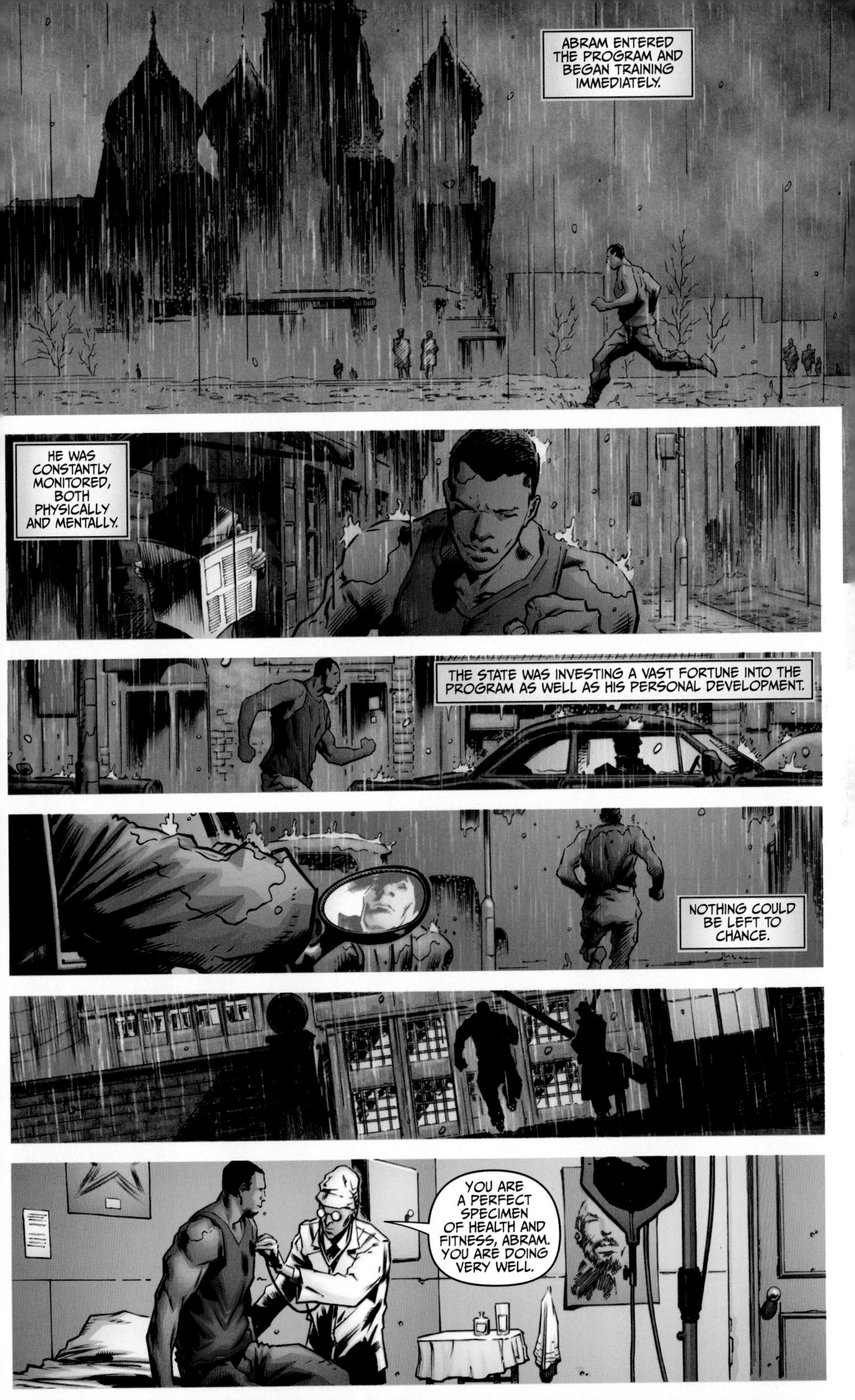
ABRAM ENTERED THE PROGRAM AND BEGAN TRAINING IMMEDIATELY.
HE WAS CONSTANTLY MONITORED, BOTH PHYSICALLY AND MENTALLY.
THE STATE WAS INVESTING A VAST FORTUNE INTO THE PROGRAM AS WELL AS HIS PERSONAL DEVELOPMENT.
NOTHING COULD BE LEFT TO CHANCE.
YOU ARE A PERFECT SPECIMEN OF HEALTH AND FITNESS, ABRAM. YOU ARE DOING VERY WELL.

ABRAM WAS SUBJECT TO A BATTERY OF EXPERIMENTAL VITAMIN AND DRUG REGIMENS DESIGNED TO KEEP HIS BODY IN PEAK CONDITION...

...AND TO INCREASE HIS IMMUNE SYSTEM'S ABILITY TO WITHSTAND THE RIGORS OF DEEP-SPACE TRAVEL.

YOU WON'T BE COMPLETELY UNDER. IT JUST SLOWS YOUR METABOLISM AND YOUR AGING.

YOU WILL REMAIN IN A SEMI-CONSCIOUS, DREAM-LIKE STATE SO THAT YOUR MIND CAN COPE WITH PROLONGED ISOLATION.

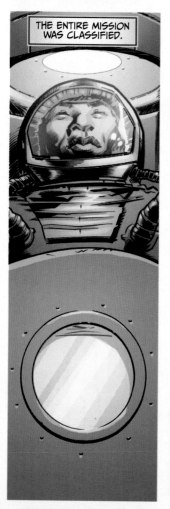

THE ENTIRE MISSION WAS CLASSIFIED.

GETTING CLOSE TO LAUNCH TIME. ARE YOU NERVOUS?

A LITTLE.

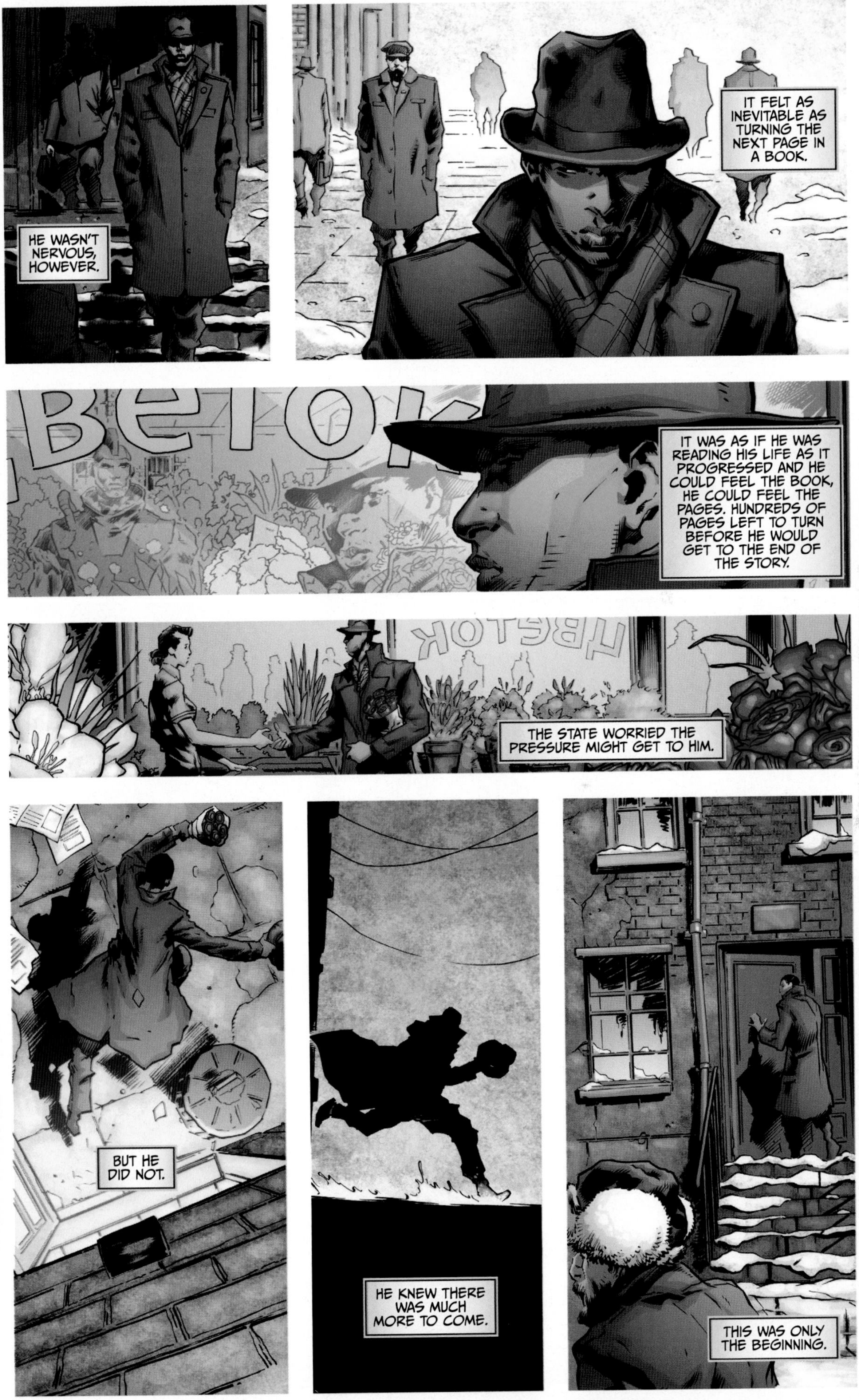
HE WASN'T NERVOUS, HOWEVER.
IT FELT AS INEVITABLE AS TURNING THE NEXT PAGE IN A BOOK.
IT WAS AS IF HE WAS READING HIS LIFE AS IT PROGRESSED AND HE COULD FEEL THE BOOK, HE COULD FEEL THE PAGES. HUNDREDS OF PAGES LEFT TO TURN BEFORE HE WOULD GET TO THE END OF THE STORY.
THE STATE WORRIED THE PRESSURE MIGHT GET TO HIM.
BUT HE DID NOT.
HE KNEW THERE WAS MUCH MORE TO COME.
THIS WAS ONLY THE BEGINNING.

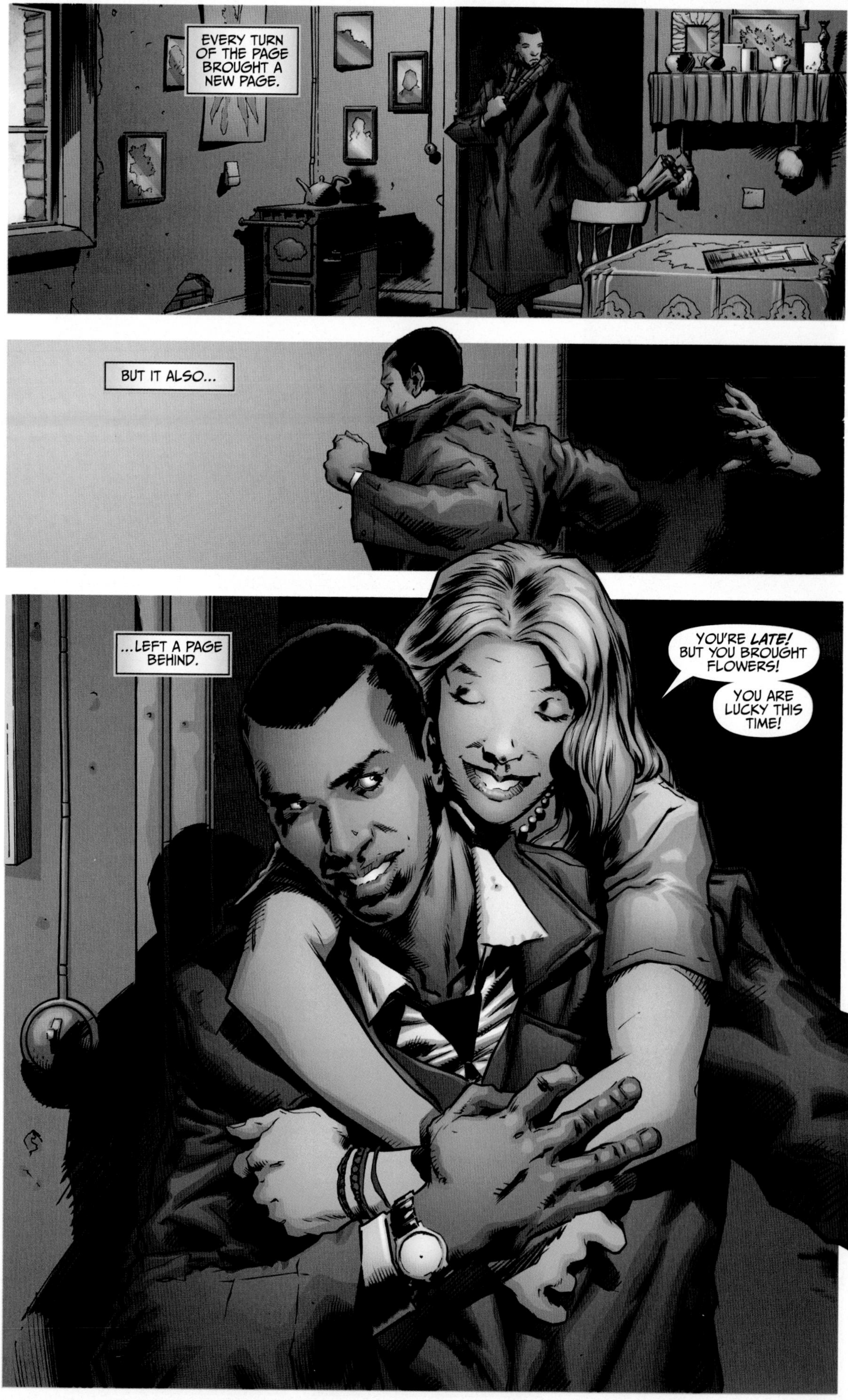
EVERY TURN OF THE PAGE BROUGHT A NEW PAGE.
BUT IT ALSO...
...LEFT A PAGE BEHIND.
YOU'RE *LATE!* BUT YOU BROUGHT FLOWERS!
YOU ARE LUCKY THIS TIME!

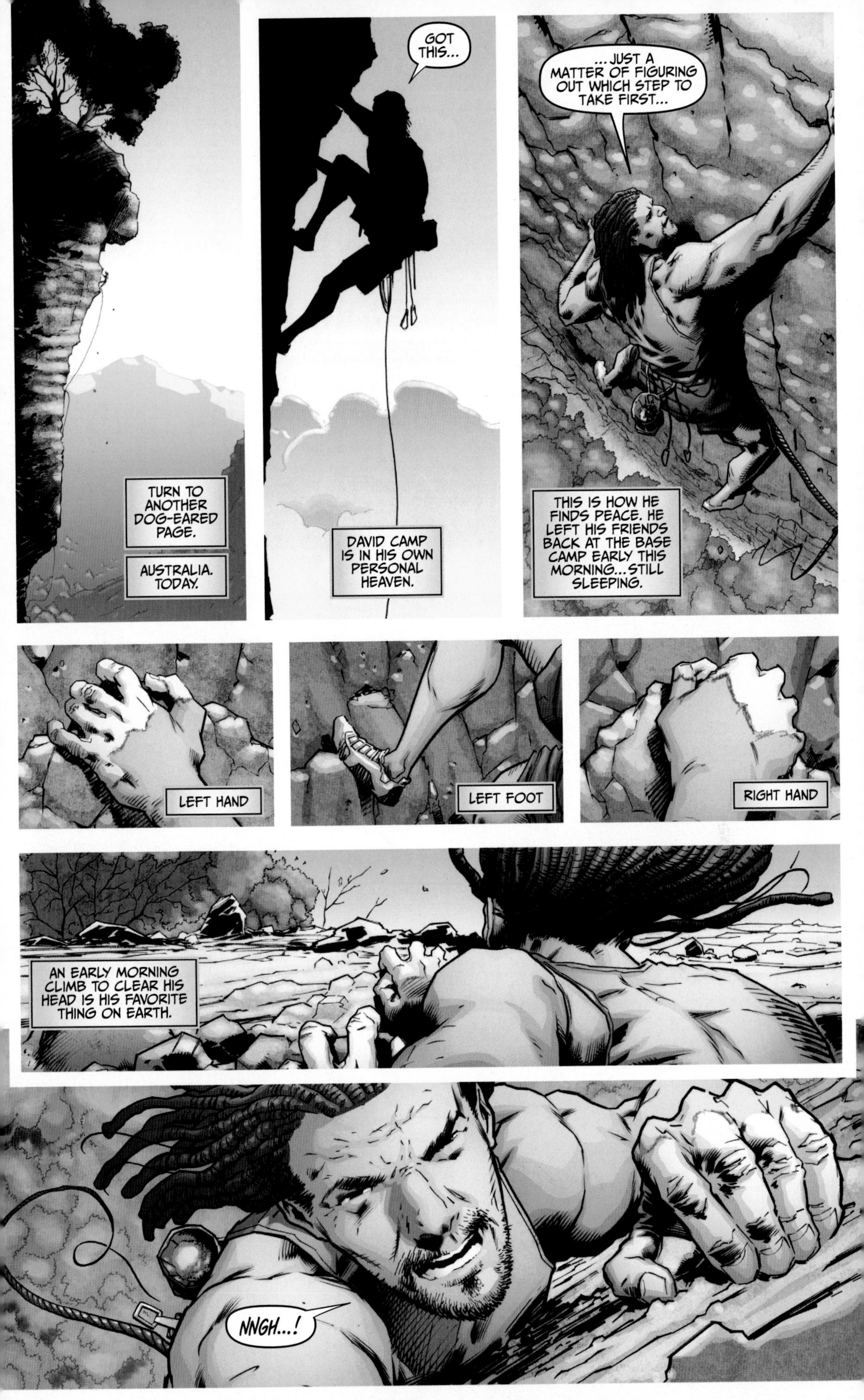
TURN TO ANOTHER DOG-EARED PAGE.
AUSTRALIA. TODAY.
GOT THIS...
DAVID CAMP IS IN HIS OWN PERSONAL HEAVEN.
...JUST A MATTER OF FIGURING OUT WHICH STEP TO TAKE FIRST...
THIS IS HOW HE FINDS PEACE. HE LEFT HIS FRIENDS BACK AT THE BASE CAMP EARLY THIS MORNING...STILL SLEEPING.
LEFT HAND
LEFT FOOT
RIGHT HAND
AN EARLY MORNING CLIMB TO CLEAR HIS HEAD IS HIS FAVORITE THING ON EARTH.
NNGH...!

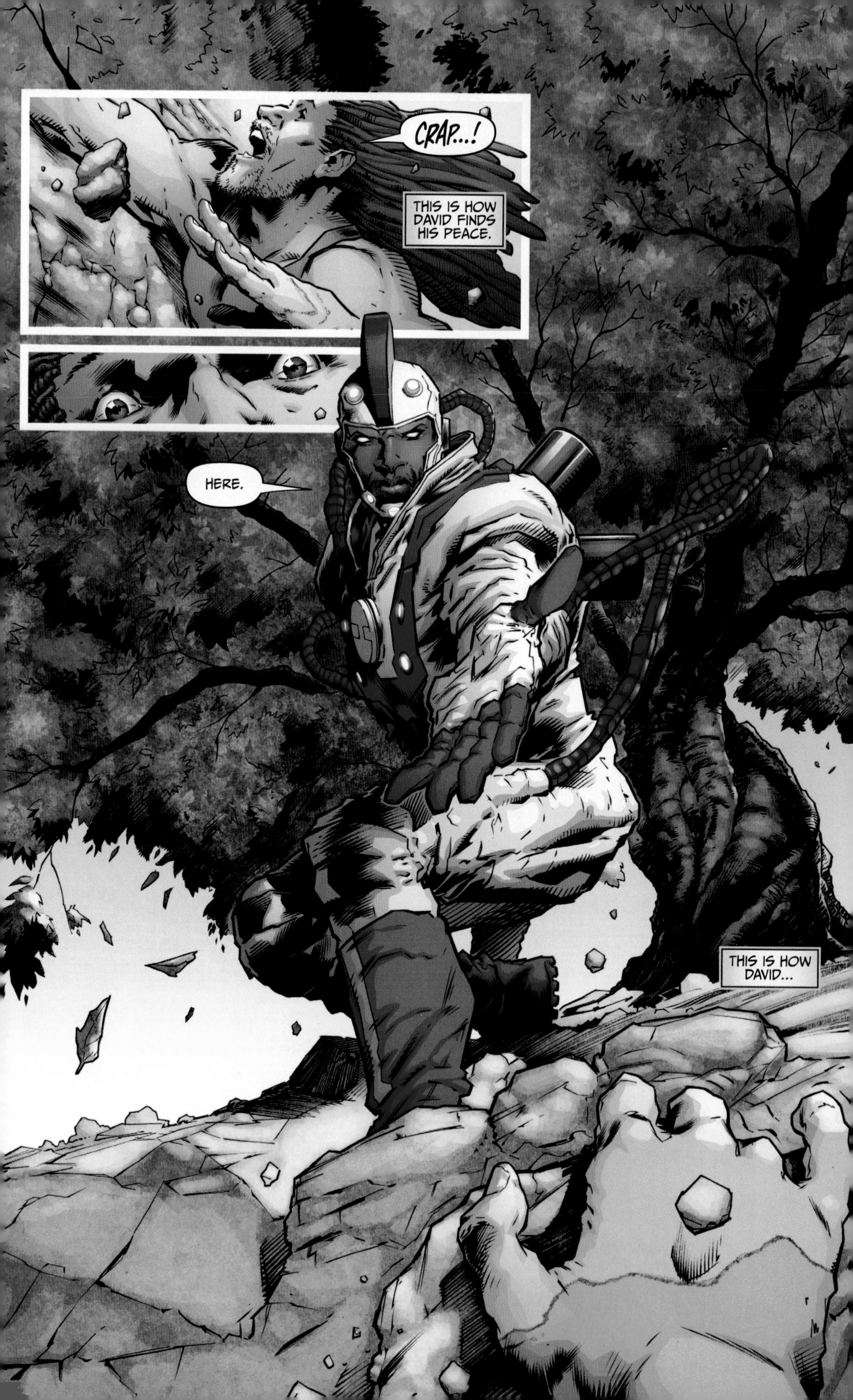
CRAP...!
THIS IS HOW DAVID FINDS HIS PEACE.
HERE.
THIS IS HOW DAVID...

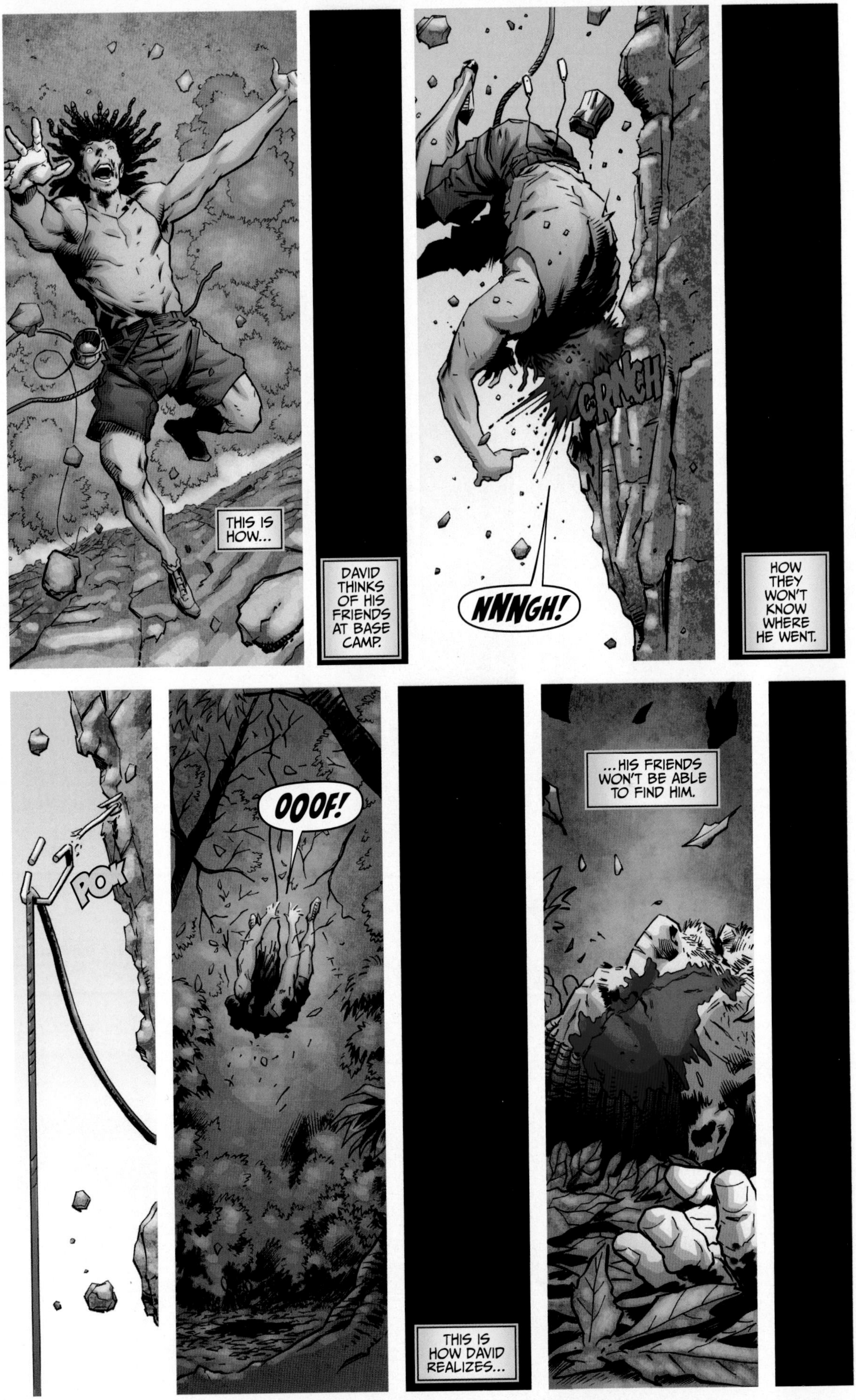
THIS IS HOW...
DAVID THINKS OF HIS FRIENDS AT BASE CAMP.
CRNCH
NNNGH!
HOW THEY WON'T KNOW WHERE HE WENT.
POK
OOOF!
THIS IS HOW DAVID REALIZES...
...HIS FRIENDS WON'T BE ABLE TO FIND HIM.

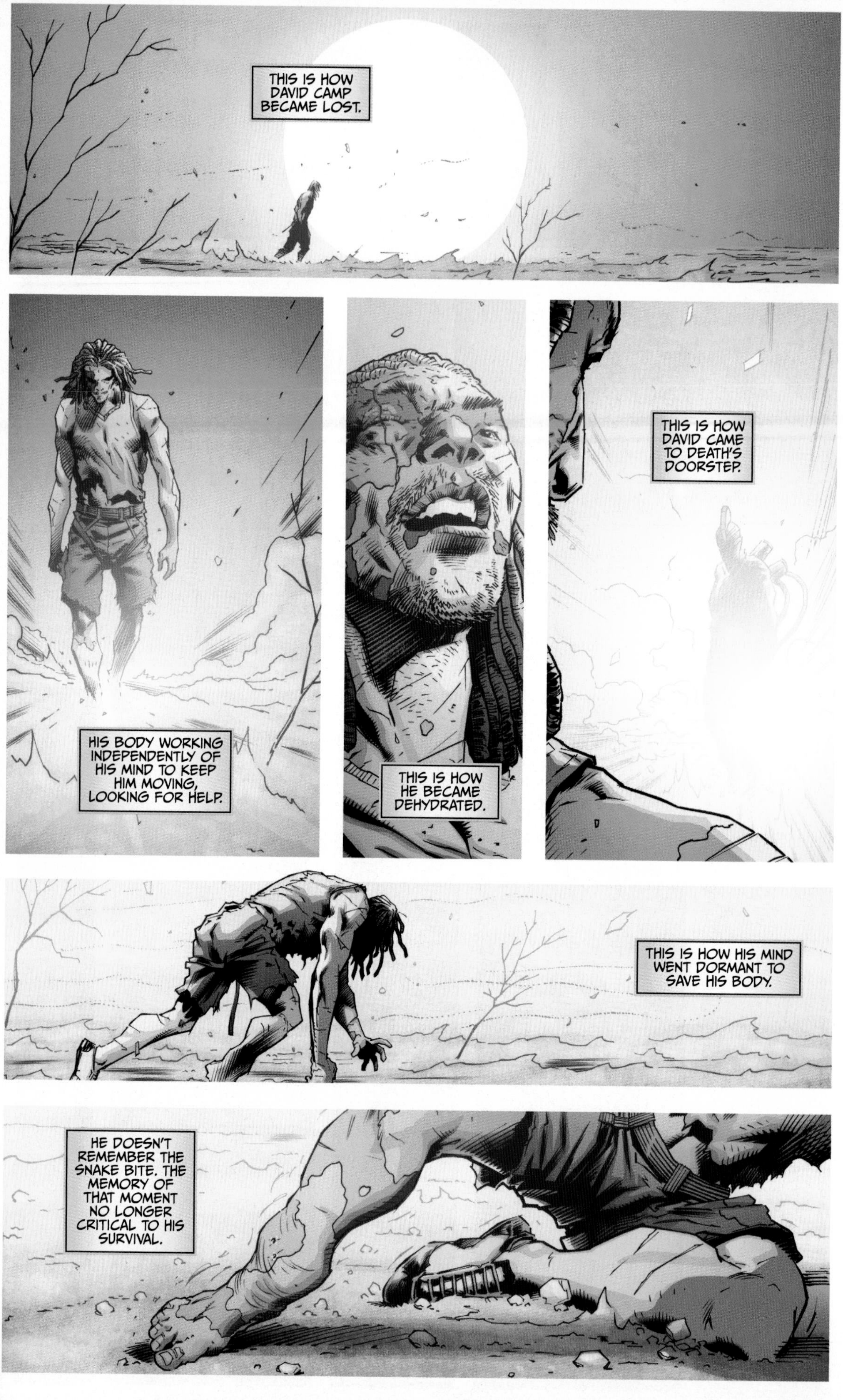
THIS IS HOW DAVID CAMP BECAME LOST.
HIS BODY WORKING INDEPENDENTLY OF HIS MIND TO KEEP HIM MOVING, LOOKING FOR HELP.
THIS IS HOW HE BECAME DEHYDRATED.
THIS IS HOW DAVID CAME TO DEATH'S DOORSTEP.
THIS IS HOW HIS MIND WENT DORMANT TO SAVE HIS BODY.
HE DOESN'T REMEMBER THE SNAKE BITE. THE MEMORY OF THAT MOMENT NO LONGER CRITICAL TO HIS SURVIVAL.

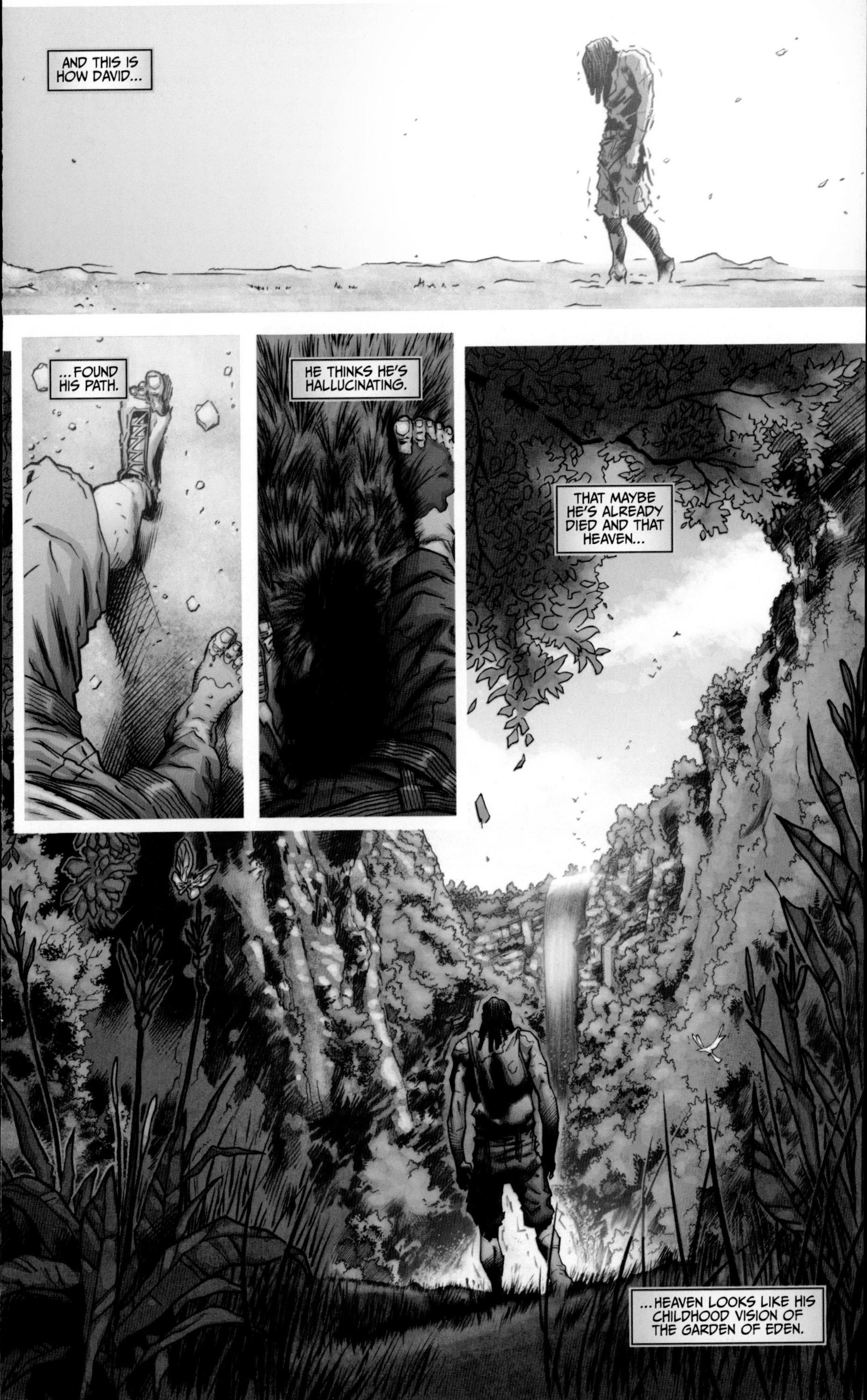
AND THIS IS HOW DAVID...
...FOUND HIS PATH.
HE THINKS HE'S HALLUCINATING.
THAT MAYBE HE'S ALREADY DIED AND THAT HEAVEN...
...HEAVEN LOOKS LIKE HIS CHILDHOOD VISION OF THE GARDEN OF EDEN.

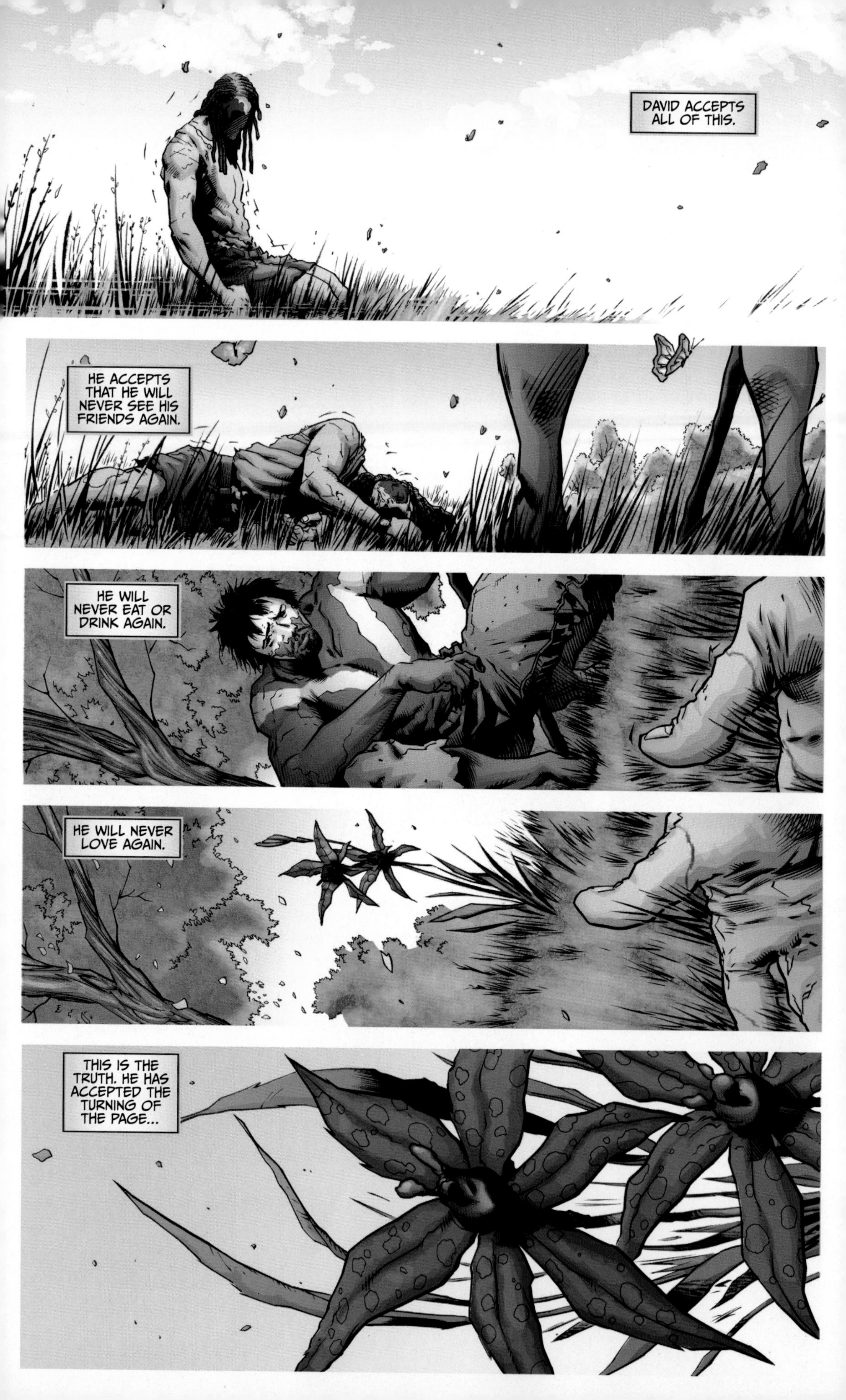
DAVID ACCEPTS ALL OF THIS.
HE ACCEPTS THAT HE WILL NEVER SEE HIS FRIENDS AGAIN.
HE WILL NEVER EAT OR DRINK AGAIN.
HE WILL NEVER LOVE AGAIN.
THIS IS THE TRUTH. HE HAS ACCEPTED THE TURNING OF THE PAGE...

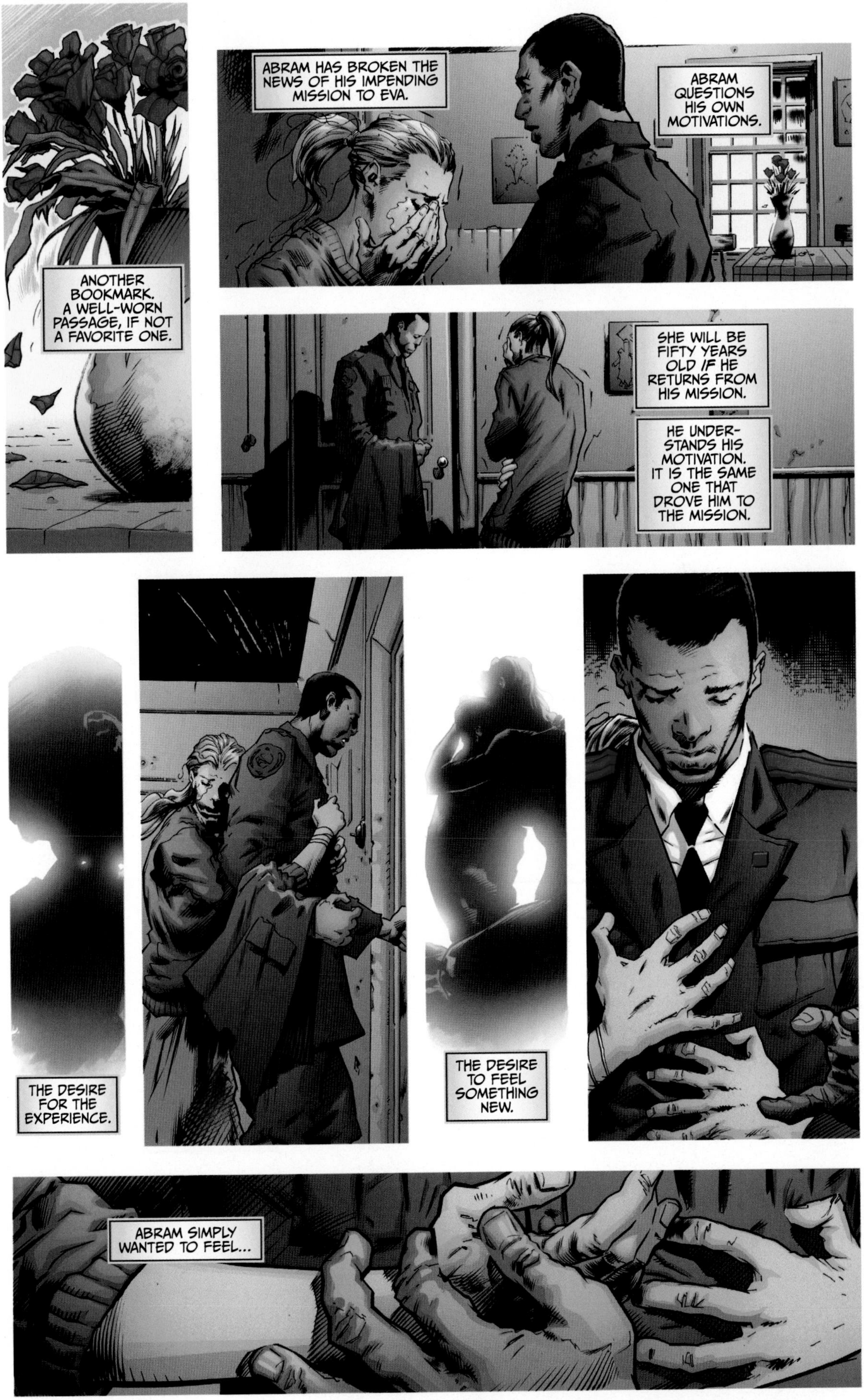
ABRAM HAS BROKEN THE NEWS OF HIS IMPENDING MISSION TO EVA.
ABRAM QUESTIONS HIS OWN MOTIVATIONS.
ANOTHER BOOKMARK. A WELL-WORN PASSAGE, IF NOT A FAVORITE ONE.
SHE WILL BE FIFTY YEARS OLD *IF* HE RETURNS FROM HIS MISSION.
HE UNDER-STANDS HIS MOTIVATION. IT IS THE SAME ONE THAT DROVE HIM TO THE MISSION.
THE DESIRE FOR THE EXPERIENCE.
THE DESIRE TO FEEL SOMETHING NEW.
ABRAM SIMPLY WANTED TO FEEL...

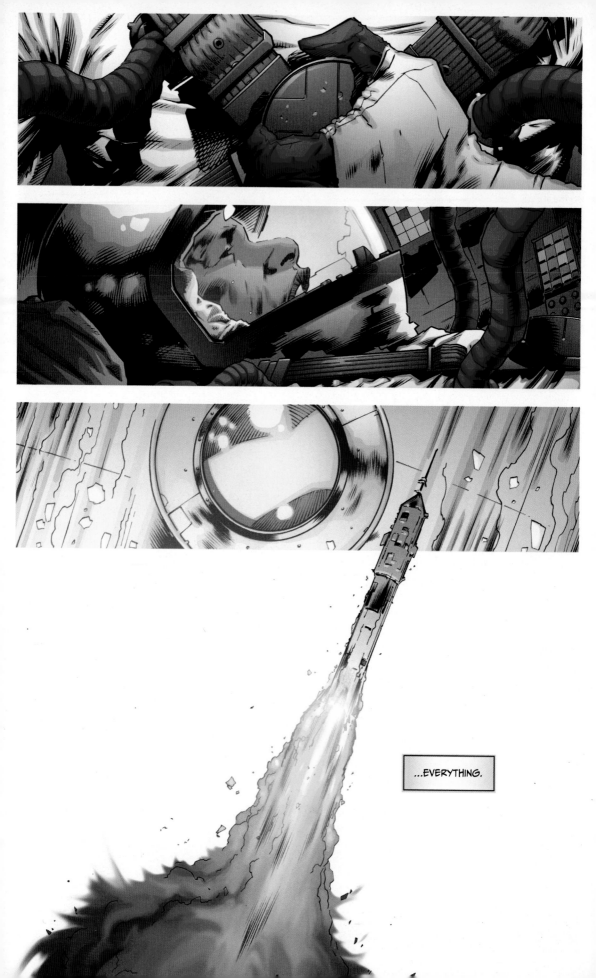

...EVERYTHING.

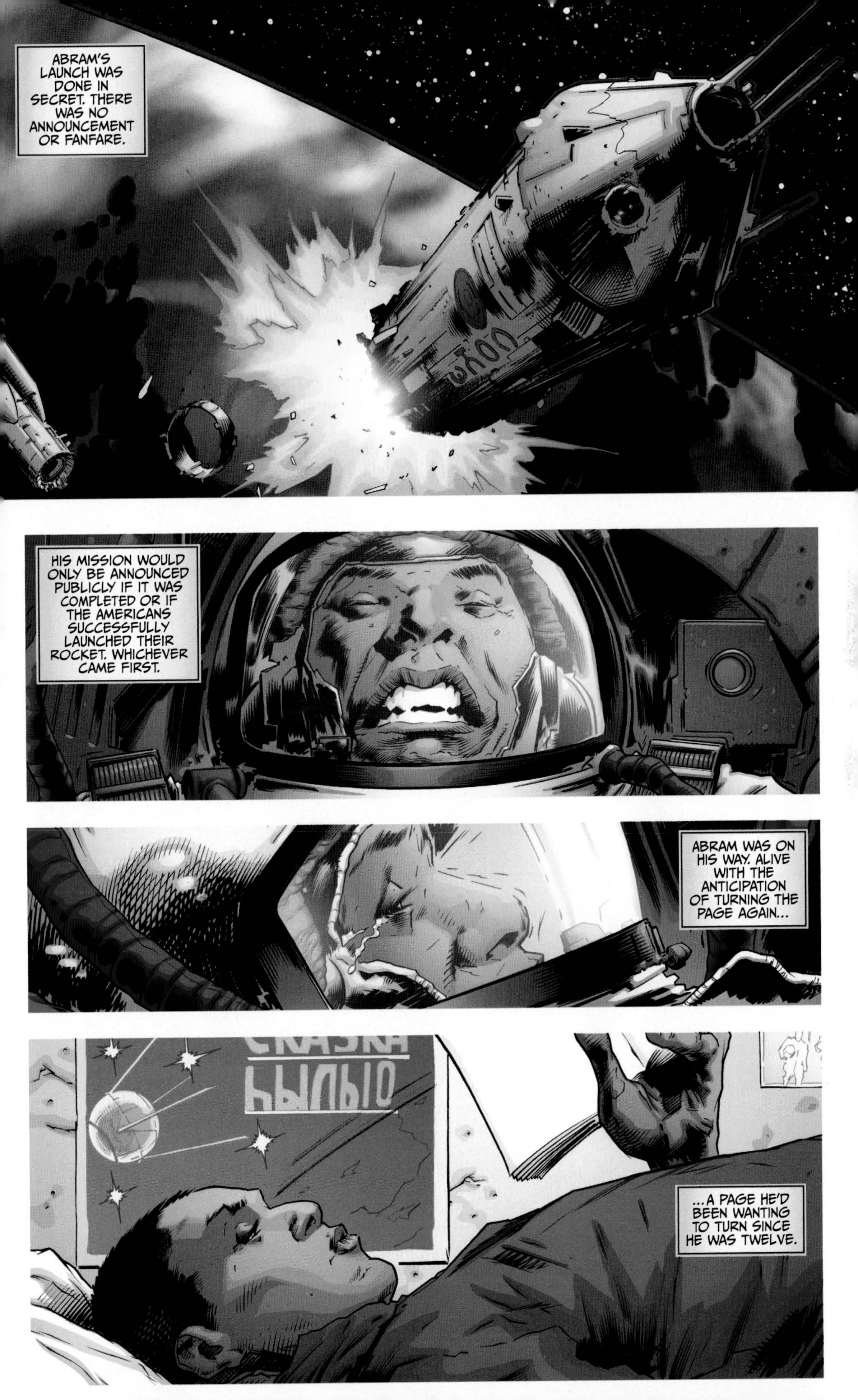
ABRAM'S LAUNCH WAS DONE IN SECRET. THERE WAS NO ANNOUNCEMENT OR FANFARE.
HIS MISSION WOULD ONLY BE ANNOUNCED PUBLICLY IF IT WAS COMPLETED OR IF THE AMERICANS SUCCESSFULLY LAUNCHED THEIR ROCKET. WHICHEVER CAME FIRST.
ABRAM WAS ON HIS WAY. ALIVE WITH THE ANTICIPATION OF TURNING THE PAGE AGAIN...
...A PAGE HE'D BEEN WANTING TO TURN SINCE HE WAS TWELVE.

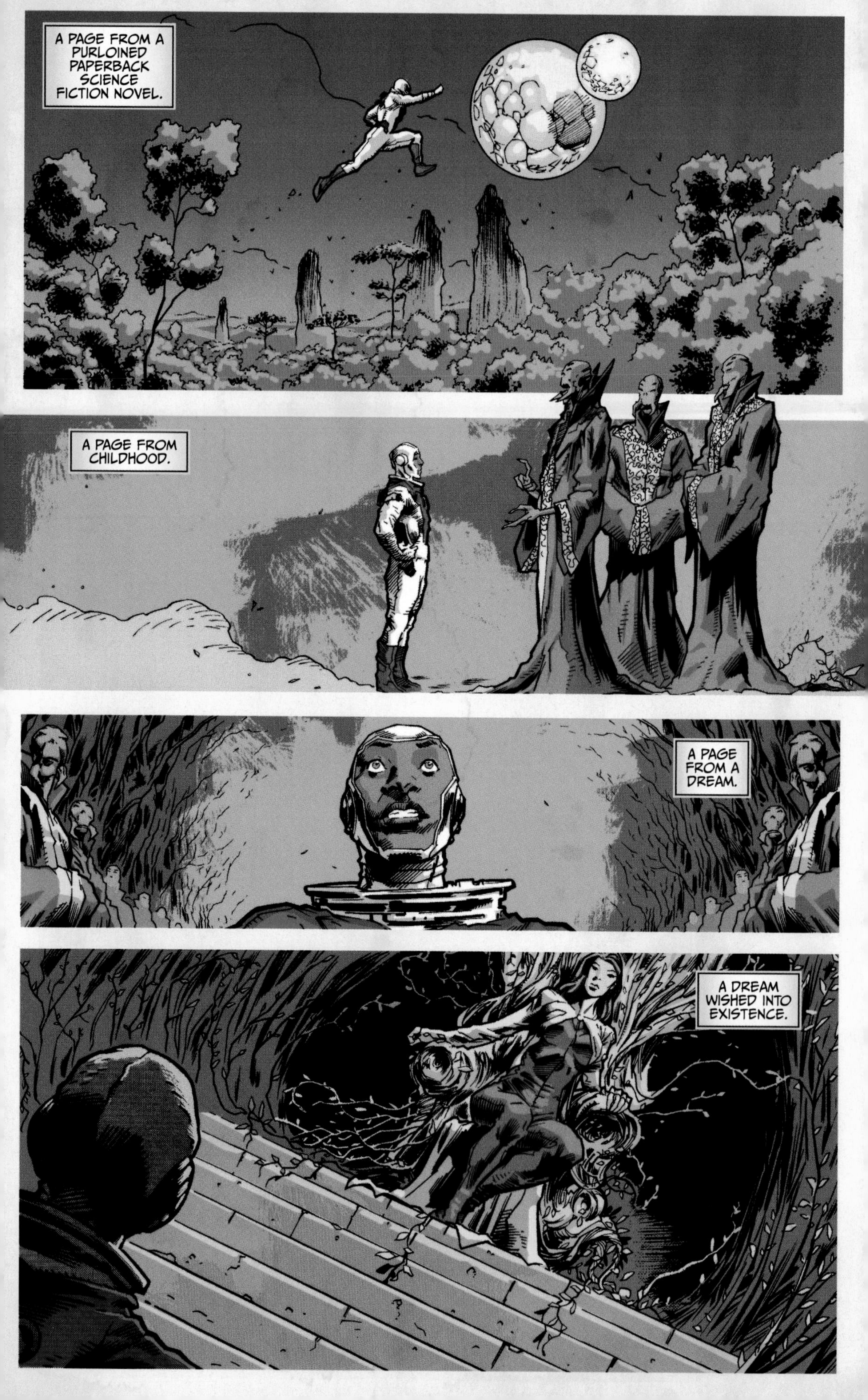
A PAGE FROM A PURLOINED PAPERBACK SCIENCE FICTION NOVEL.
A PAGE FROM CHILDHOOD.
A PAGE FROM A DREAM.
A DREAM WISHED INTO EXISTENCE.

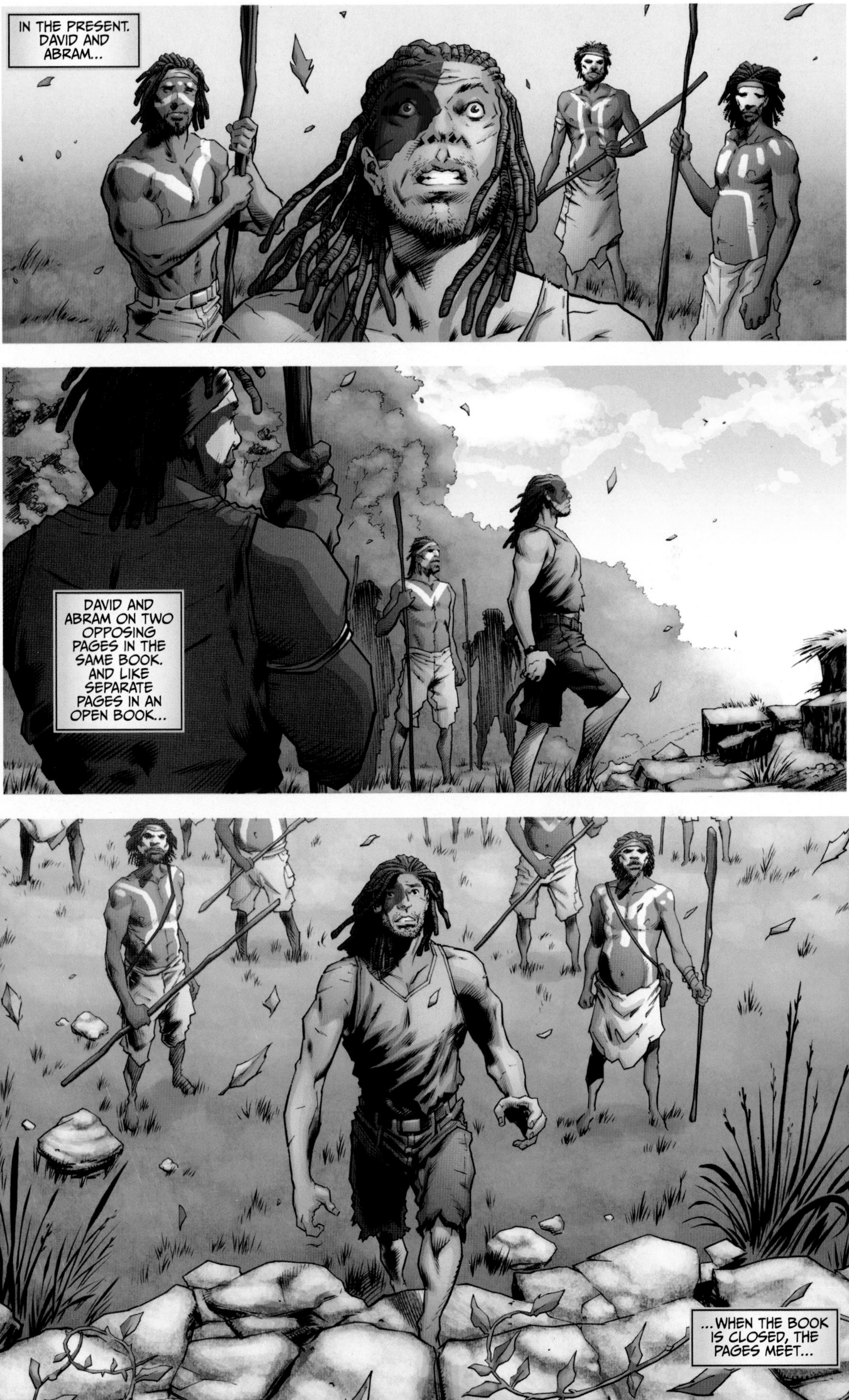
IN THE PRESENT. DAVID AND ABRAM...
DAVID AND ABRAM ON TWO OPPOSING PAGES IN THE SAME BOOK. AND LIKE SEPARATE PAGES IN AN OPEN BOOK...
...WHEN THE BOOK IS CLOSED, THE PAGES MEET...

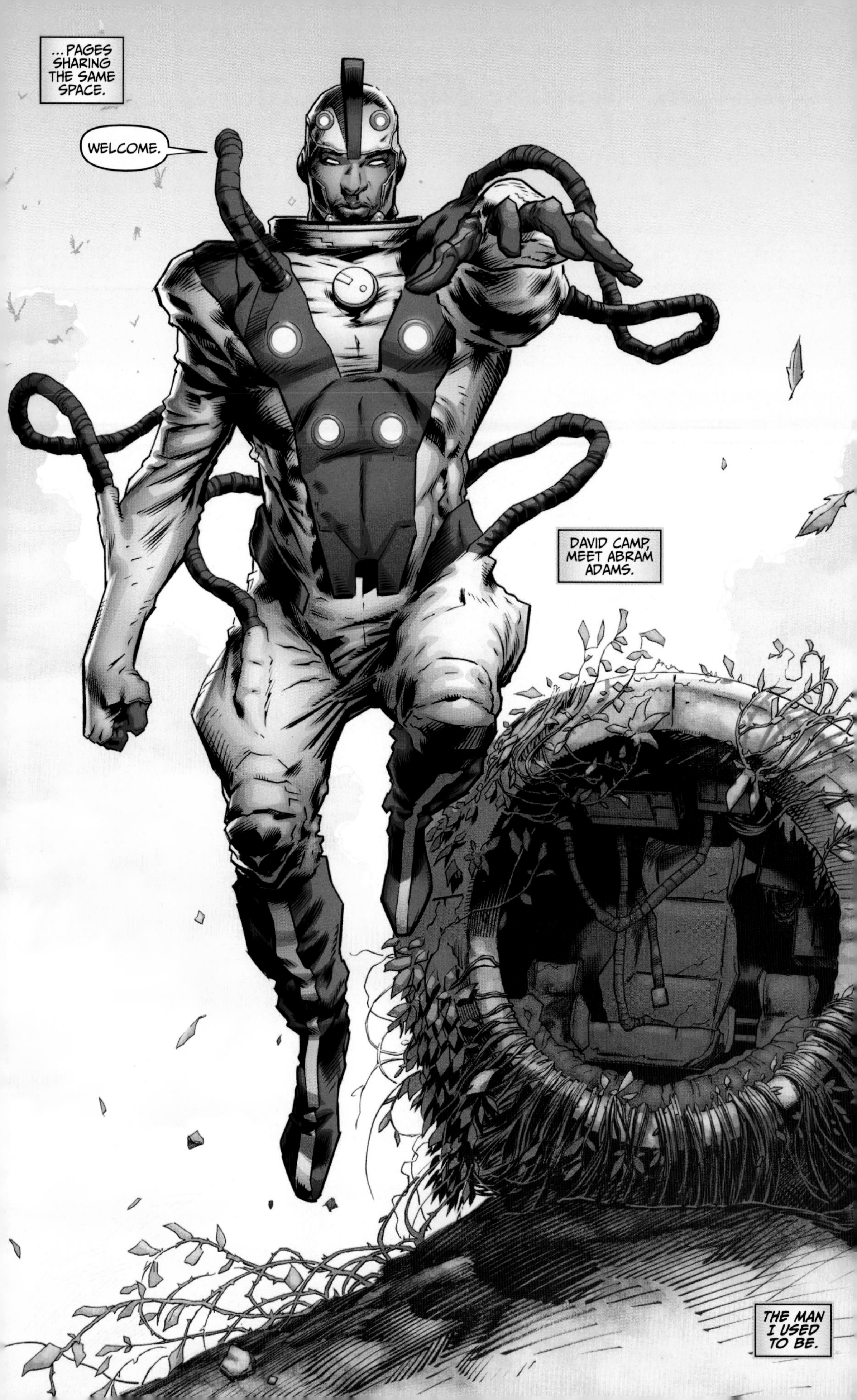
...PAGES SHARING THE SAME SPACE.
WELCOME.
DAVID CAMP, MEET ABRAM ADAMS.
THE MAN I USED TO BE.

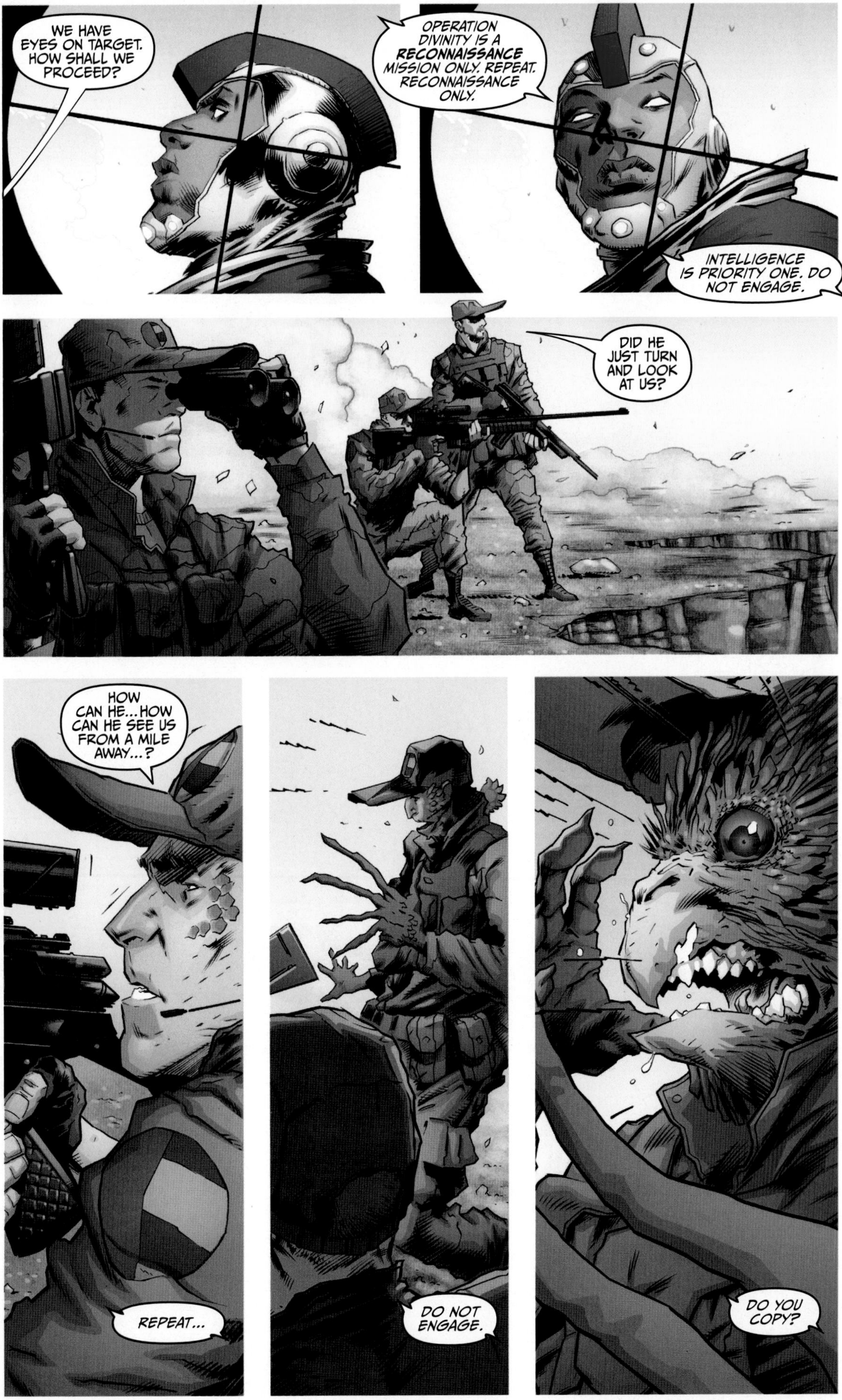
WE HAVE EYES ON TARGET. HOW SHALL WE PROCEED?
OPERATION DIVINITY IS A RECONNAISSANCE MISSION ONLY. REPEAT. RECONNAISSANCE ONLY.
INTELLIGENCE IS PRIORITY ONE. DO NOT ENGAGE.
DID HE JUST TURN AND LOOK AT US?
HOW CAN HE...HOW CAN HE SEE US FROM A MILE AWAY...?
REPEAT...
DO NOT ENGAGE.
DO YOU COPY?

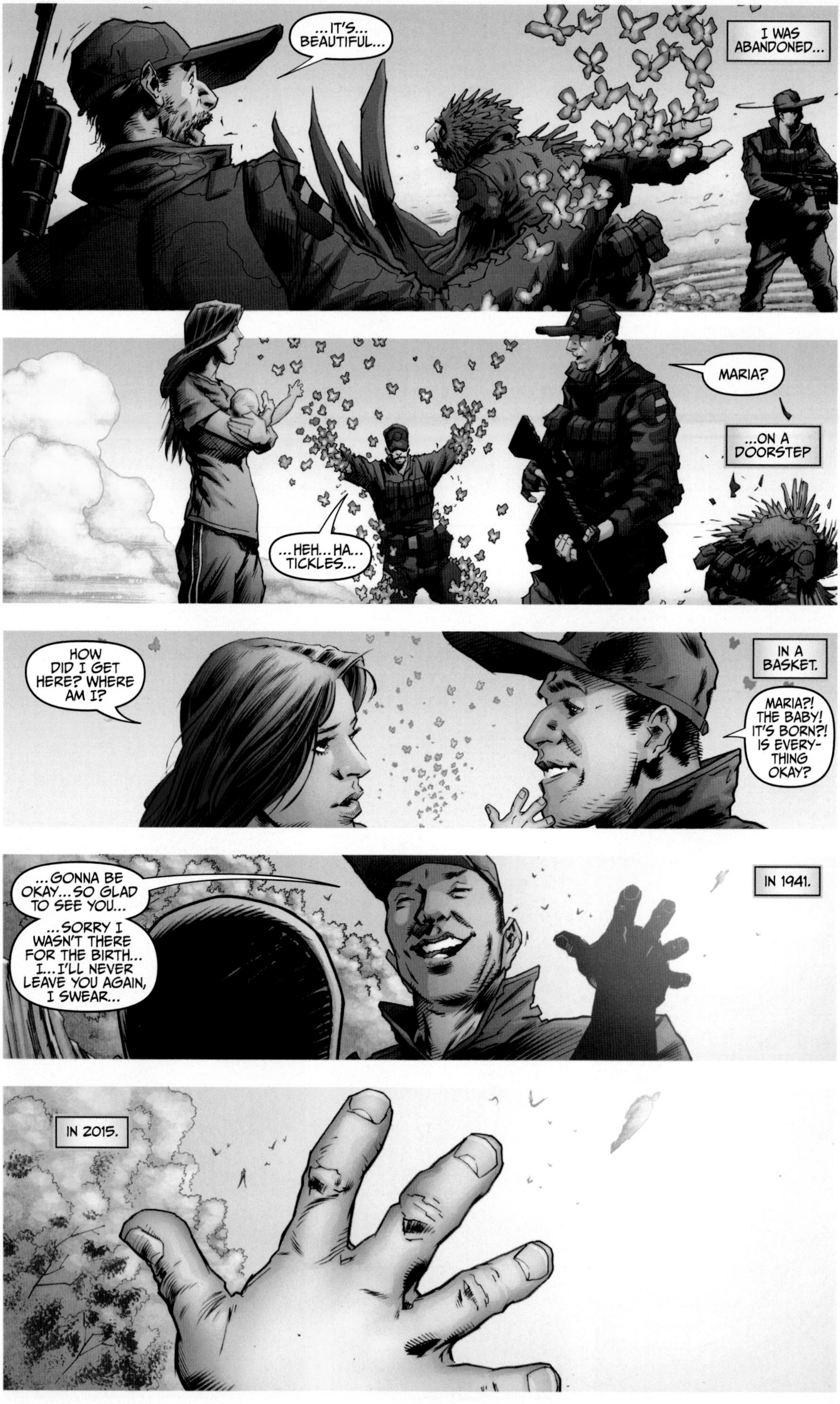
...IT'S... BEAUTIFUL...
I WAS ABANDONED...
MARIA?
...ON A DOORSTEP
...HEH...HA... TICKLES...
HOW DID I GET HERE? WHERE AM I?
IN A BASKET.
MARIA?! THE BABY! IT'S BORN?! IS EVERY-THING OKAY?
...GONNA BE OKAY...SO GLAD TO SEE YOU...
...SORRY I WASN'T THERE FOR THE BIRTH... I...I'LL NEVER LEAVE YOU AGAIN, I SWEAR...
IN 1941.
IN 2015.

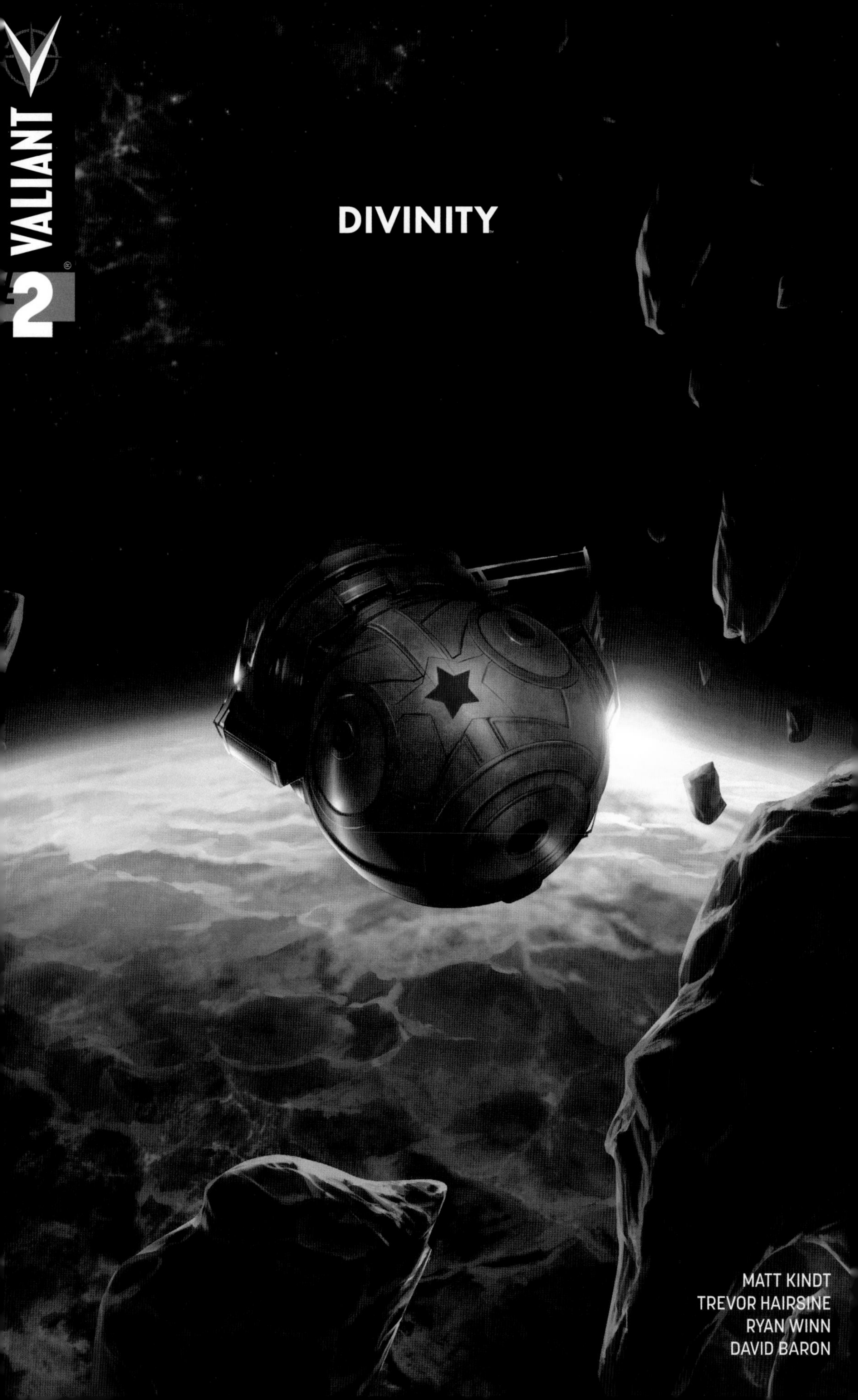
VALIANT
2
DIVINITY
MATT KINDT
TREVOR HAIRSINE
RYAN WINN
DAVID BARON

BOOK TWO

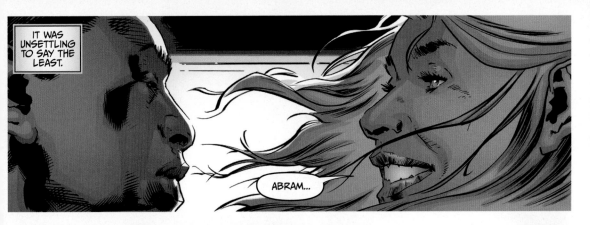

IT WAS UNSETTLING TO SAY THE LEAST.

ABRAM...

THE CLOSER I GOT TO HIM, THE MORE HE REVEALED HIMSELF.

THERE'S SOMETHING I HAVE TO TELL YOU...

HIS LIFE.

I'M PREGNANT.

HIS LOVE.

I...

AREN'T YOU HAPPY?

HIS REGRET.

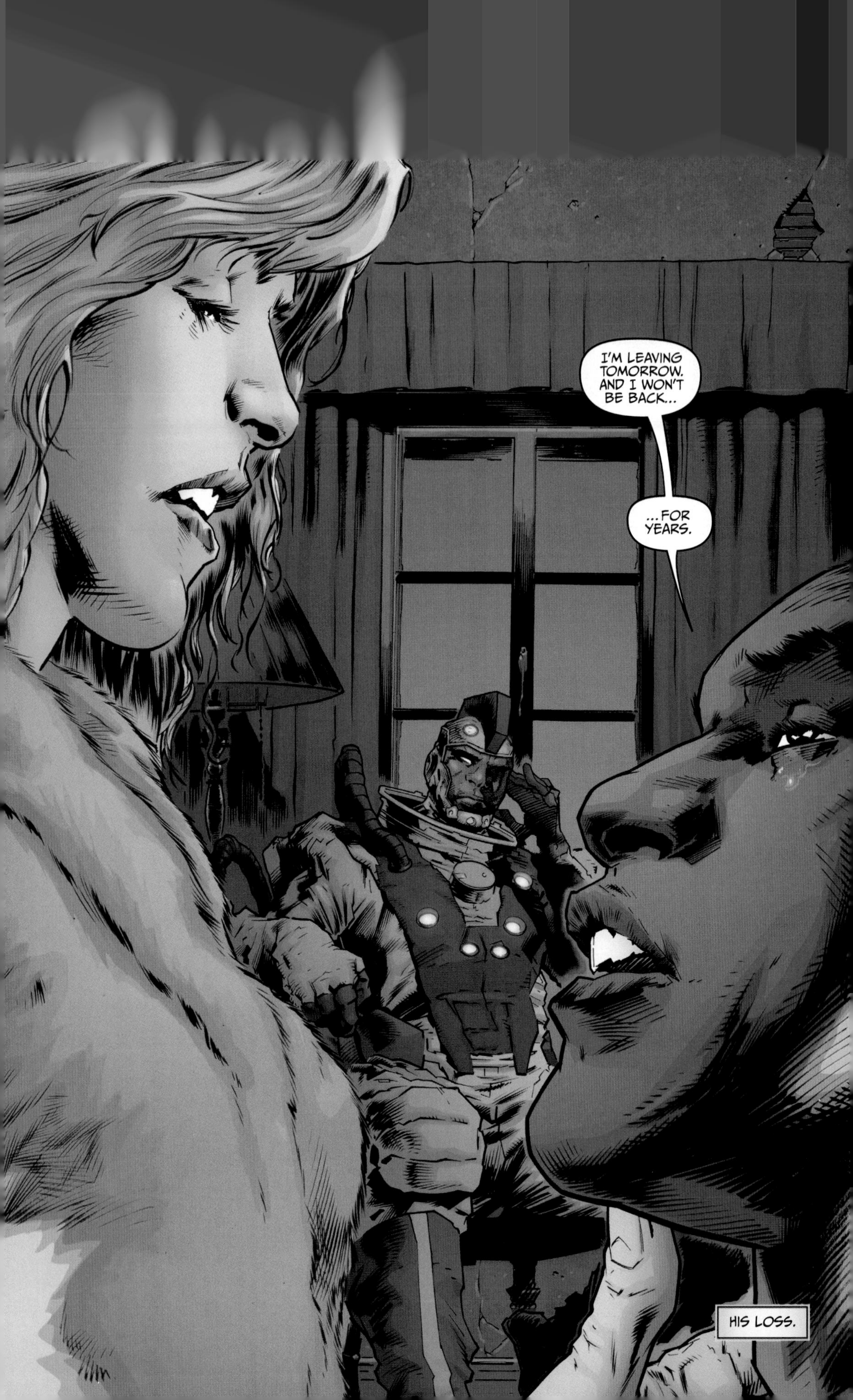
I'M LEAVING TOMORROW. AND I WON'T BE BACK...
...FOR YEARS.
HIS LOSS.

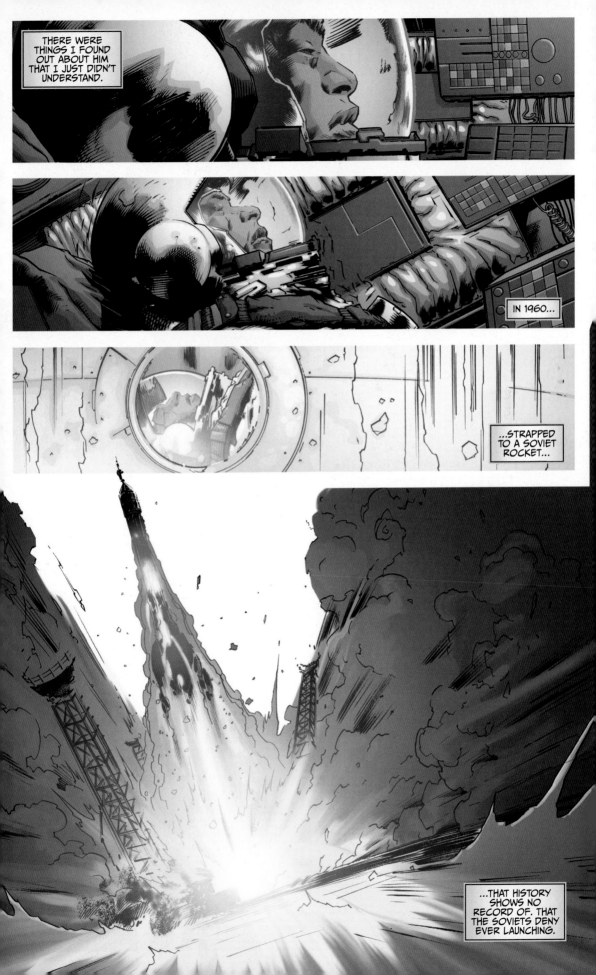

THERE WERE THINGS I FOUND OUT ABOUT HIM THAT I JUST DIDN'T UNDERSTAND.

IN 1960...

...STRAPPED TO A SOVIET ROCKET...

...THAT HISTORY SHOWS NO RECORD OF. THAT THE SOVIETS DENY EVER LAUNCHING.

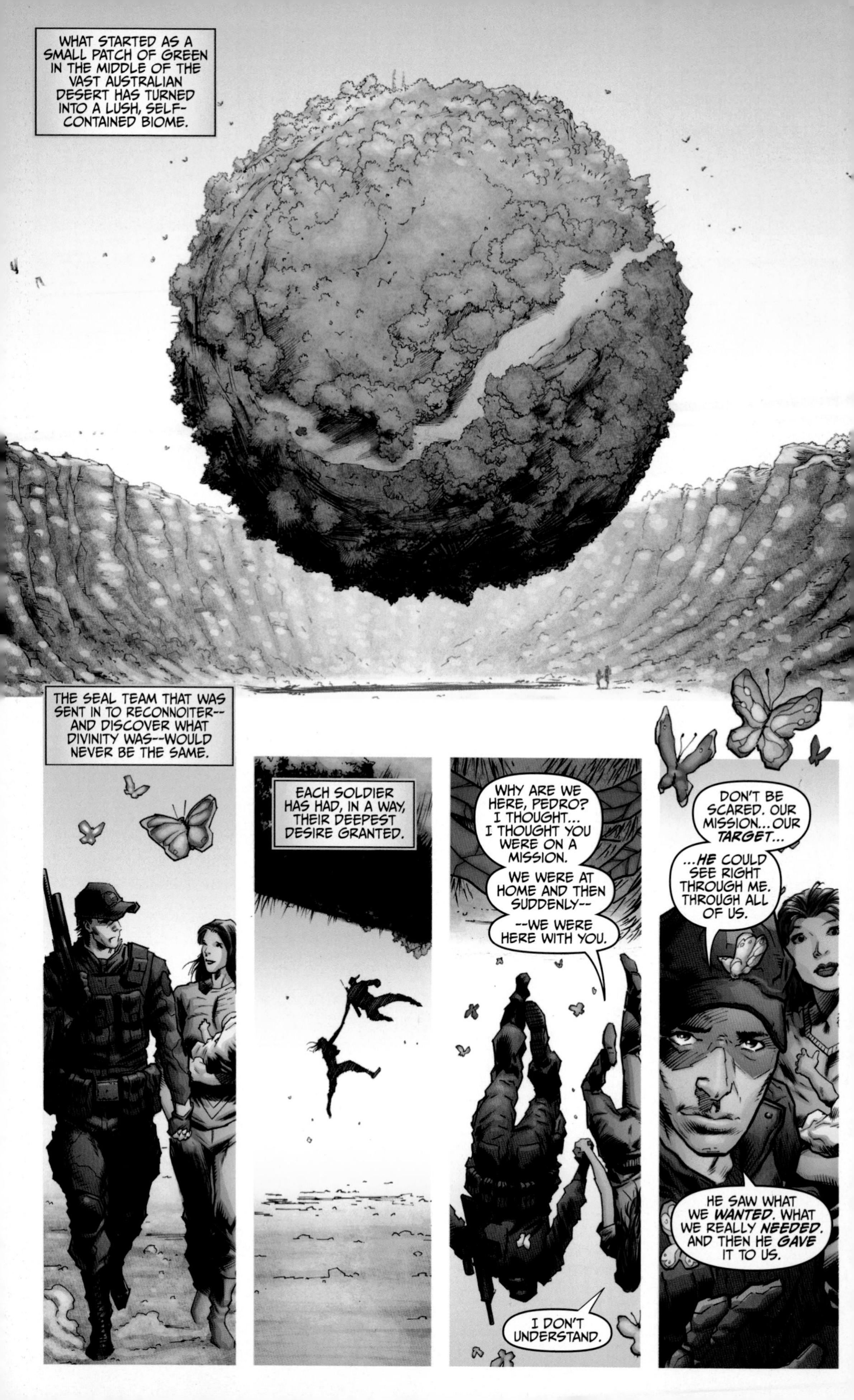
WHAT STARTED AS A SMALL PATCH OF GREEN IN THE MIDDLE OF THE VAST AUSTRALIAN DESERT HAS TURNED INTO A LUSH, SELF-CONTAINED BIOME.
THE SEAL TEAM THAT WAS SENT IN TO RECONNOITER--AND DISCOVER WHAT DIVINITY WAS--WOULD NEVER BE THE SAME.
EACH SOLDIER HAS HAD, IN A WAY, THEIR DEEPEST DESIRE GRANTED.
WHY ARE WE HERE, PEDRO? I THOUGHT... I THOUGHT YOU WERE ON A MISSION.
WE WERE AT HOME AND THEN SUDDENLY--
--WE WERE HERE WITH YOU.
I DON'T UNDERSTAND.
DON'T BE SCARED. OUR MISSION...OUR *TARGET*...
...*HE* COULD SEE RIGHT THROUGH ME. THROUGH ALL OF US.
HE SAW WHAT WE *WANTED*. WHAT WE REALLY *NEEDED*. AND THEN HE *GAVE* IT TO US.

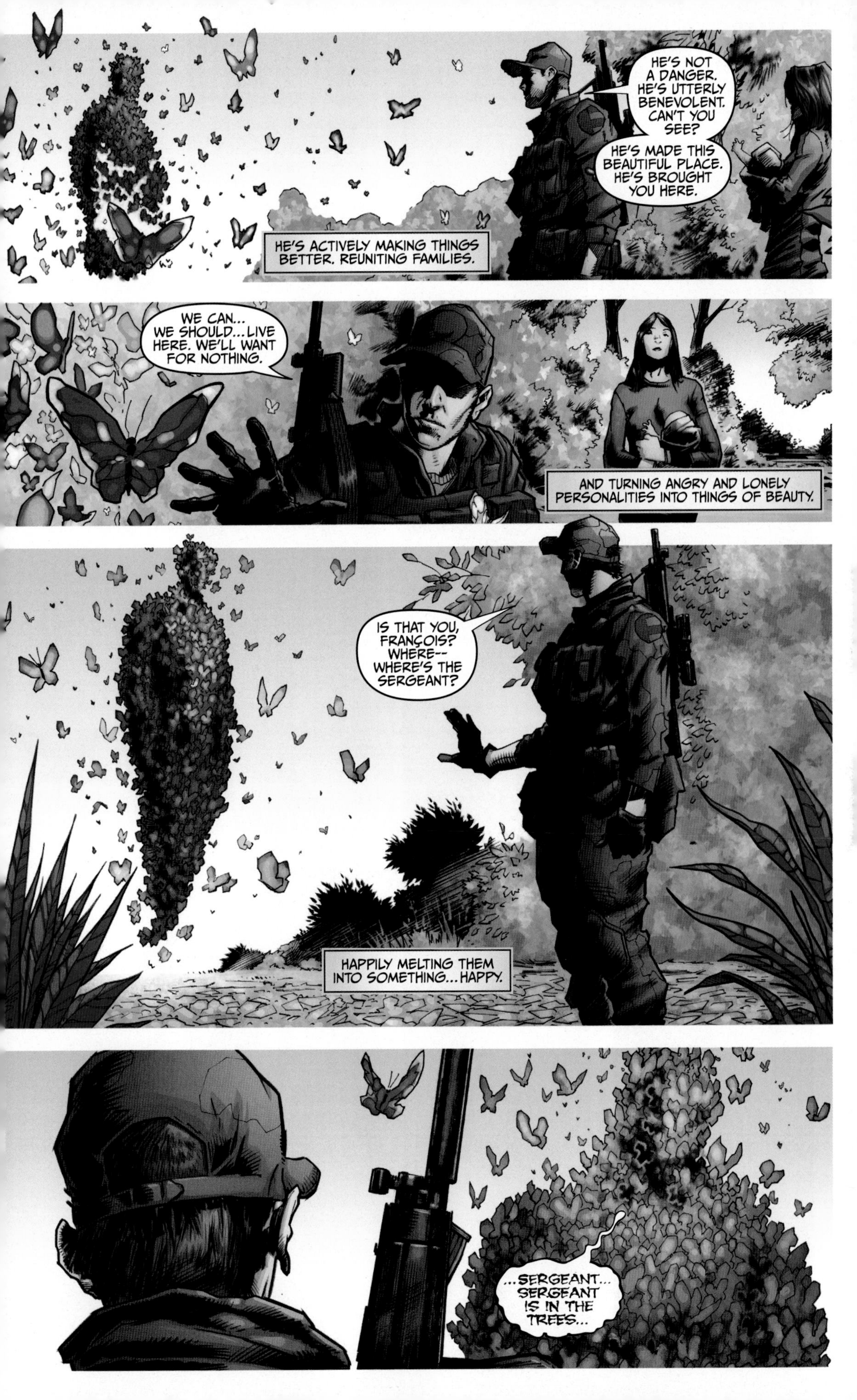
HE'S NOT A DANGER. HE'S UTTERLY BENEVOLENT. CAN'T YOU SEE?
HE'S MADE THIS BEAUTIFUL PLACE. HE'S BROUGHT YOU HERE.
HE'S ACTIVELY MAKING THINGS BETTER. REUNITING FAMILIES.
WE CAN... WE SHOULD... LIVE HERE. WE'LL WANT FOR NOTHING.
AND TURNING ANGRY AND LONELY PERSONALITIES INTO THINGS OF BEAUTY.
IS THAT YOU, FRANÇOIS? WHERE-- WHERE'S THE SERGEANT?
HAPPILY MELTING THEM INTO SOMETHING... HAPPY.
...SERGEANT... SERGEANT IS IN THE TREES...

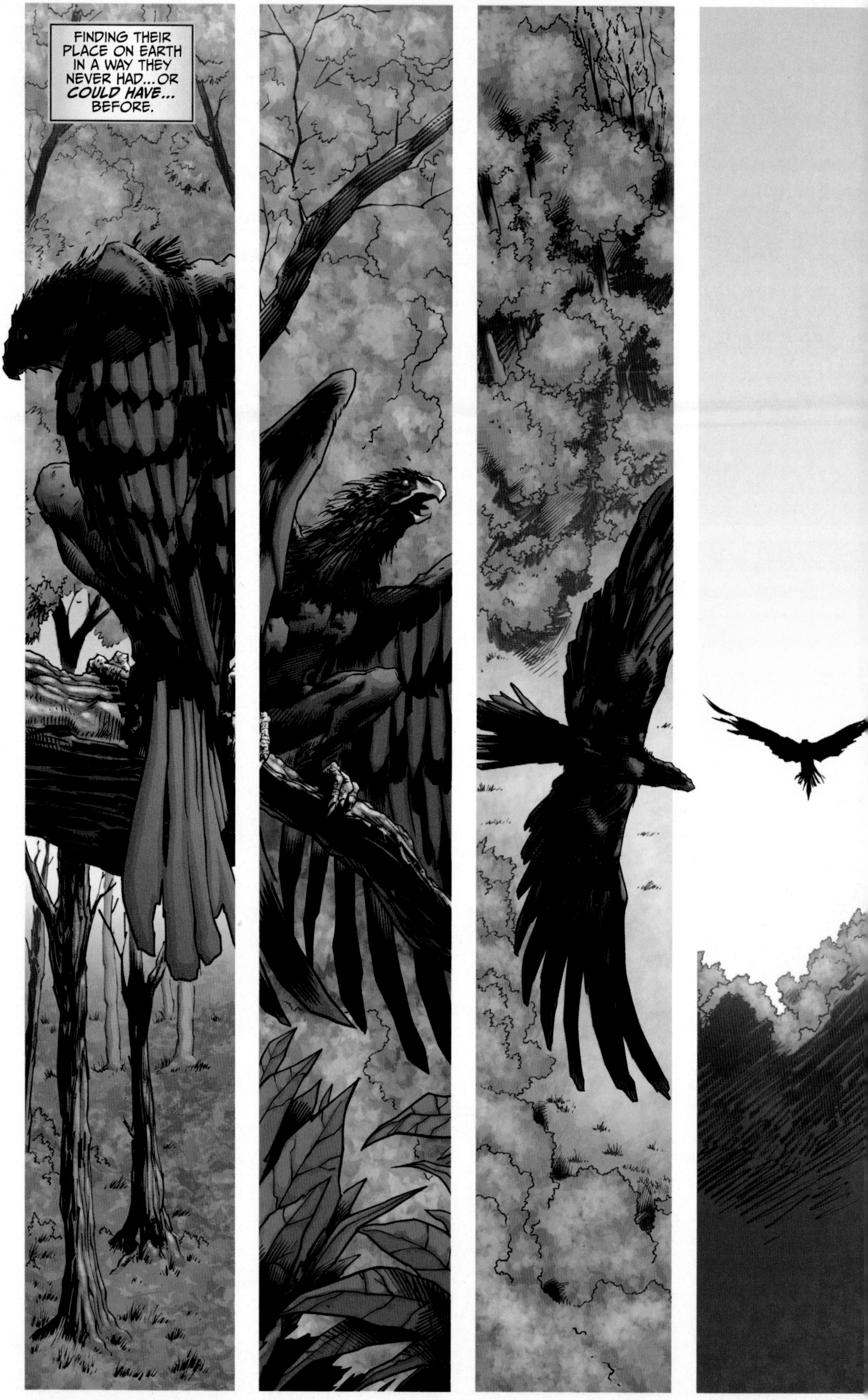
FINDING THEIR PLACE ON EARTH IN A WAY THEY NEVER HAD...OR *COULD HAVE...* BEFORE.

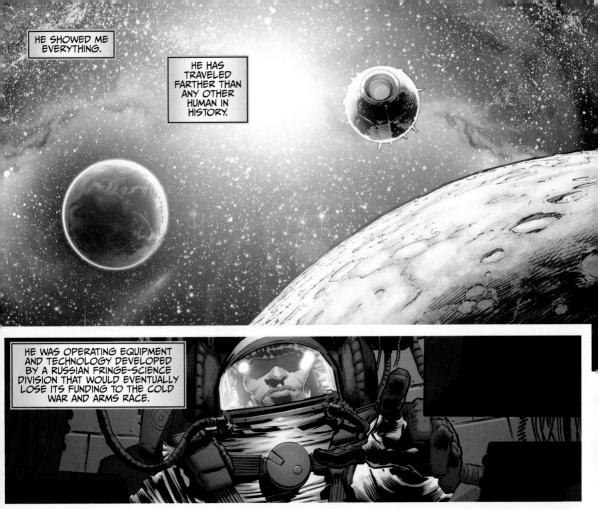

HE SHOWED ME EVERYTHING.

HE HAS TRAVELED FARTHER THAN ANY OTHER HUMAN IN HISTORY.

HE WAS OPERATING EQUIPMENT AND TECHNOLOGY DEVELOPED BY A RUSSIAN FRINGE-SCIENCE DIVISION THAT WOULD EVENTUALLY LOSE ITS FUNDING TO THE COLD WAR AND ARMS RACE.

LEAVING ABRAM ALONE FOR FIFTY YEARS OF LITERAL COLD STORAGE.

DO YOU COPY? ALL SYSTEMS OPERATIONAL. NOT SURE OUR TIME GAUGES ARE WORKING PROPERLY.

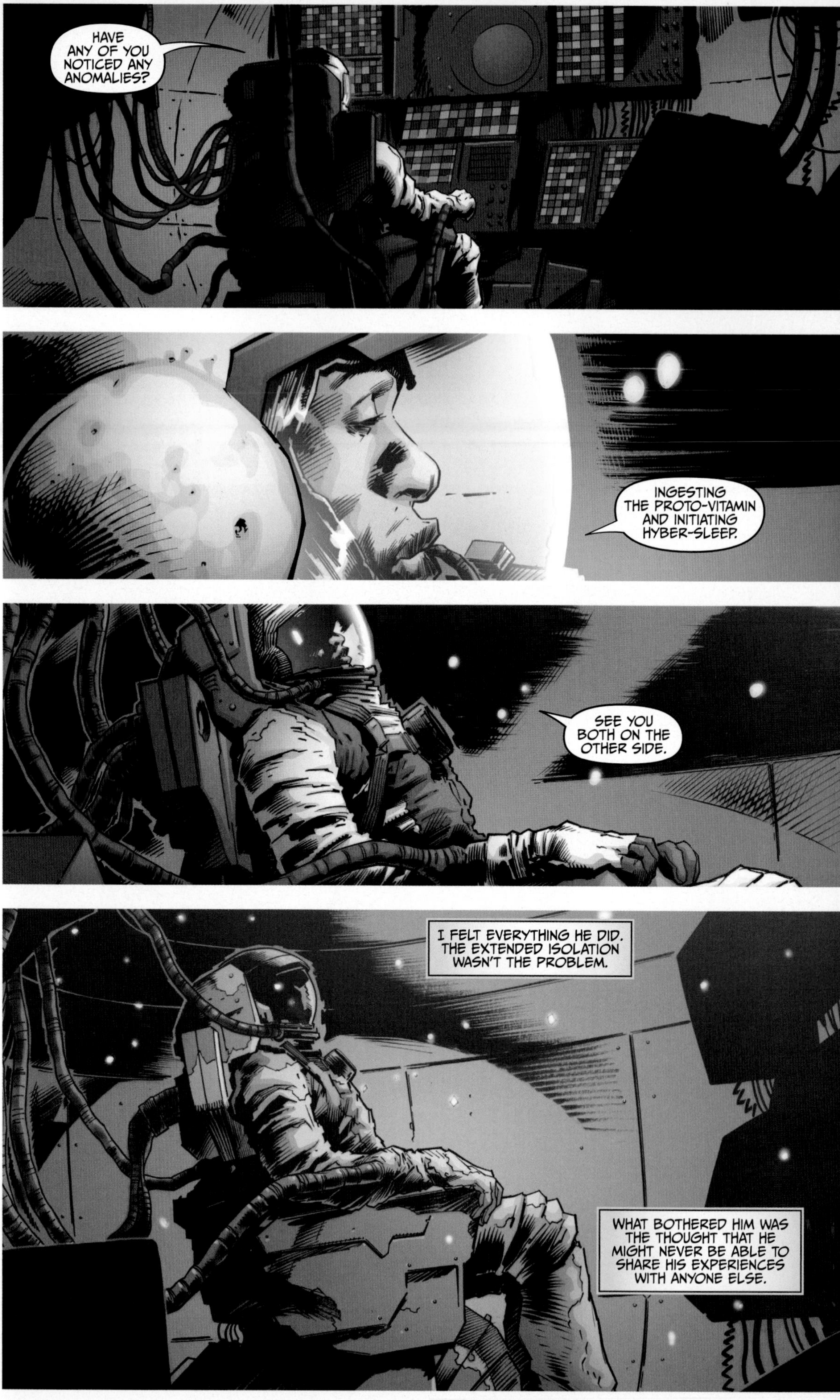
HAVE ANY OF YOU NOTICED ANY ANOMALIES?
INGESTING THE PROTO-VITAMIN AND INITIATING HYBER-SLEEP.
SEE YOU BOTH ON THE OTHER SIDE.
I FELT EVERYTHING HE DID. THE EXTENDED ISOLATION WASN'T THE PROBLEM.
WHAT BOTHERED HIM WAS THE THOUGHT THAT HE MIGHT NEVER BE ABLE TO SHARE HIS EXPERIENCES WITH ANYONE ELSE.

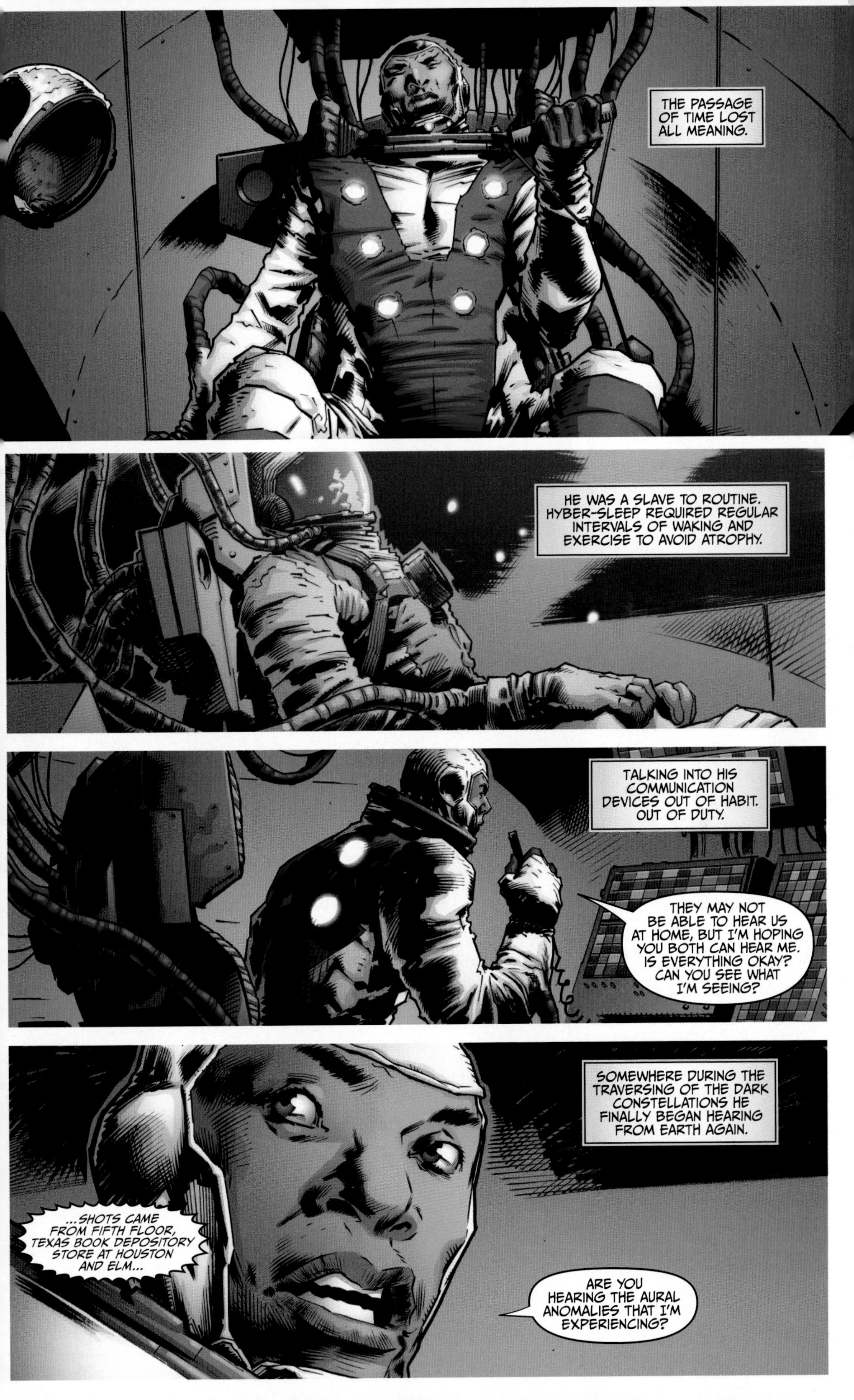
THE PASSAGE OF TIME LOST ALL MEANING.
HE WAS A SLAVE TO ROUTINE. HYBER-SLEEP REQUIRED REGULAR INTERVALS OF WAKING AND EXERCISE TO AVOID ATROPHY.
TALKING INTO HIS COMMUNICATION DEVICES OUT OF HABIT. OUT OF DUTY.
THEY MAY NOT BE ABLE TO HEAR US AT HOME, BUT I'M HOPING YOU BOTH CAN HEAR ME. IS EVERYTHING OKAY? CAN YOU SEE WHAT I'M SEEING?
SOMEWHERE DURING THE TRAVERSING OF THE DARK CONSTELLATIONS HE FINALLY BEGAN HEARING FROM EARTH AGAIN.
...SHOTS CAME FROM FIFTH FLOOR, TEXAS BOOK DEPOSITORY STORE AT HOUSTON AND ELM...
ARE YOU HEARING THE AURAL ANOMALIES THAT I'M EXPERIENCING?

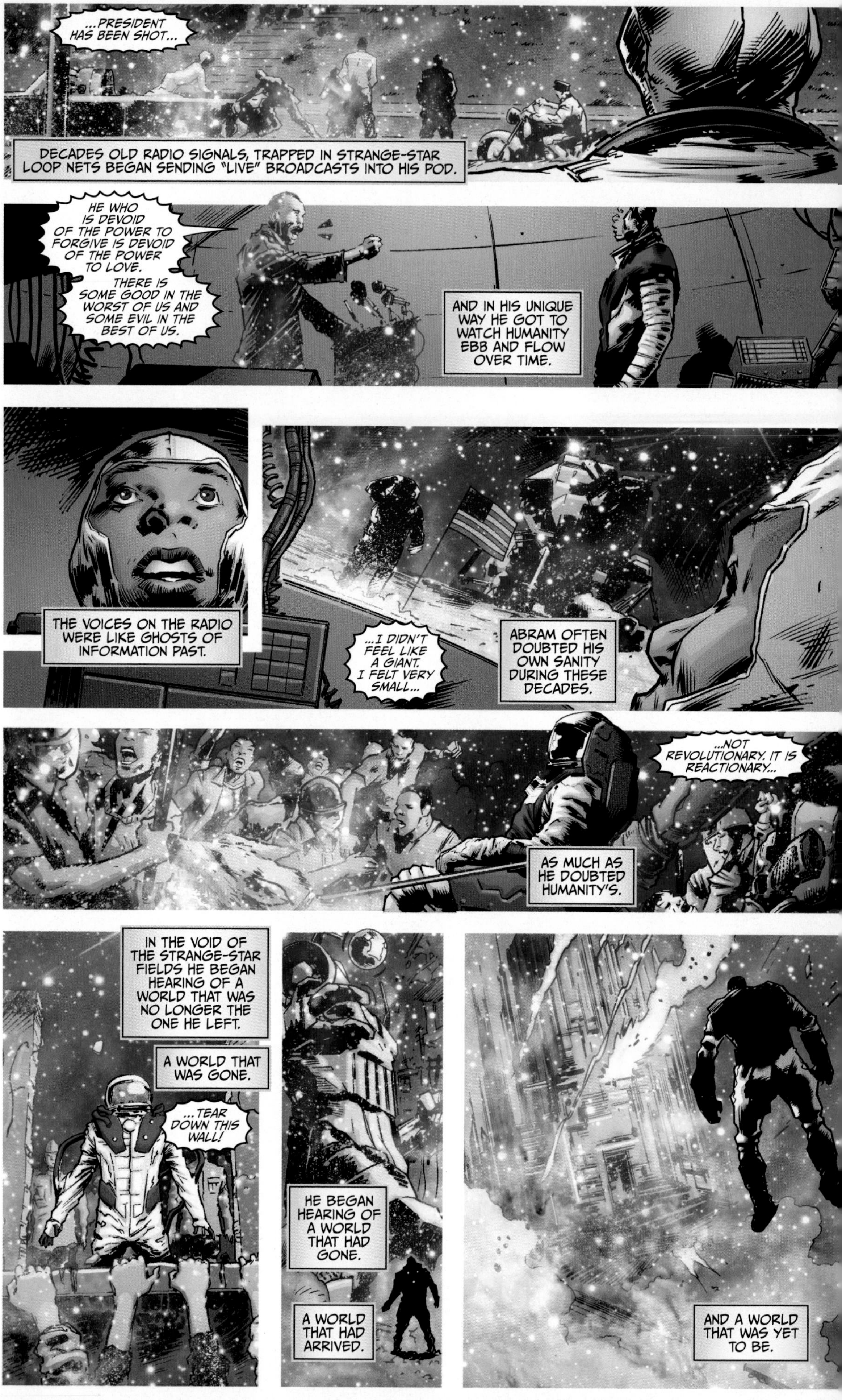
...PRESIDENT HAS BEEN SHOT...
DECADES OLD RADIO SIGNALS, TRAPPED IN STRANGE-STAR LOOP NETS BEGAN SENDING "LIVE" BROADCASTS INTO HIS POD.
HE WHO IS DEVOID OF THE POWER TO FORGIVE IS DEVOID OF THE POWER TO LOVE.
THERE IS SOME GOOD IN THE WORST OF US AND SOME EVIL IN THE BEST OF US.
AND IN HIS UNIQUE WAY HE GOT TO WATCH HUMANITY EBB AND FLOW OVER TIME.
THE VOICES ON THE RADIO WERE LIKE GHOSTS OF INFORMATION PAST.
...I DIDN'T FEEL LIKE A GIANT. I FELT VERY SMALL...
ABRAM OFTEN DOUBTED HIS OWN SANITY DURING THESE DECADES.
...NOT REVOLUTIONARY. IT IS REACTIONARY...
AS MUCH AS HE DOUBTED HUMANITY'S.
IN THE VOID OF THE STRANGE-STAR FIELDS HE BEGAN HEARING OF A WORLD THAT WAS NO LONGER THE ONE HE LEFT.
A WORLD THAT WAS GONE.
...TEAR DOWN THIS WALL!
HE BEGAN HEARING OF A WORLD THAT HAD GONE.
A WORLD THAT HAD ARRIVED.
AND A WORLD THAT WAS YET TO BE.

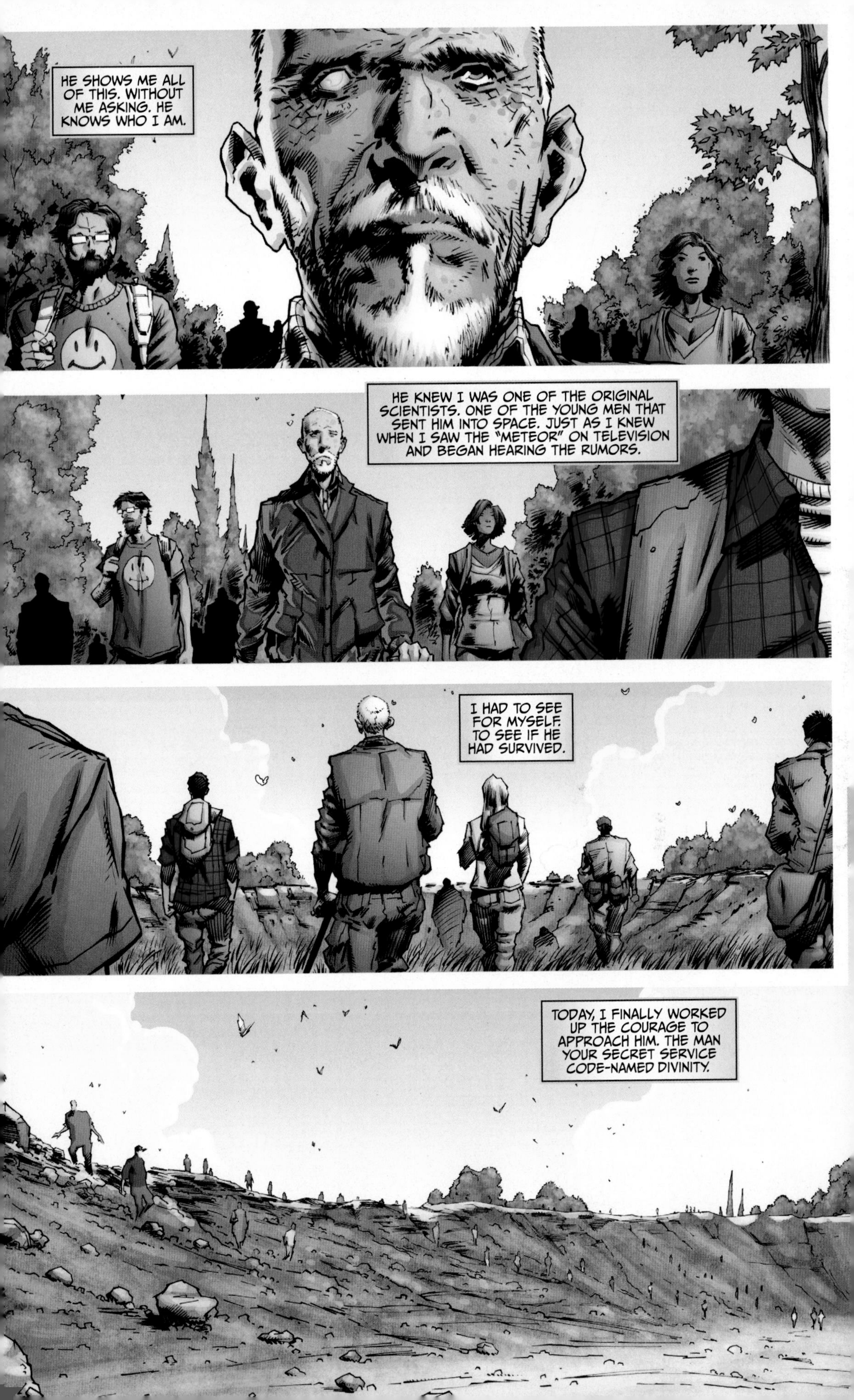
HE SHOWS ME ALL OF THIS. WITHOUT ME ASKING. HE KNOWS WHO I AM.
HE KNEW I WAS ONE OF THE ORIGINAL SCIENTISTS. ONE OF THE YOUNG MEN THAT SENT HIM INTO SPACE. JUST AS I KNEW WHEN I SAW THE "METEOR" ON TELEVISION AND BEGAN HEARING THE RUMORS.
I HAD TO SEE FOR MYSELF. TO SEE IF HE HAD SURVIVED.
TODAY, I FINALLY WORKED UP THE COURAGE TO APPROACH HIM. THE MAN YOUR SECRET SERVICE CODE-NAMED DIVINITY.

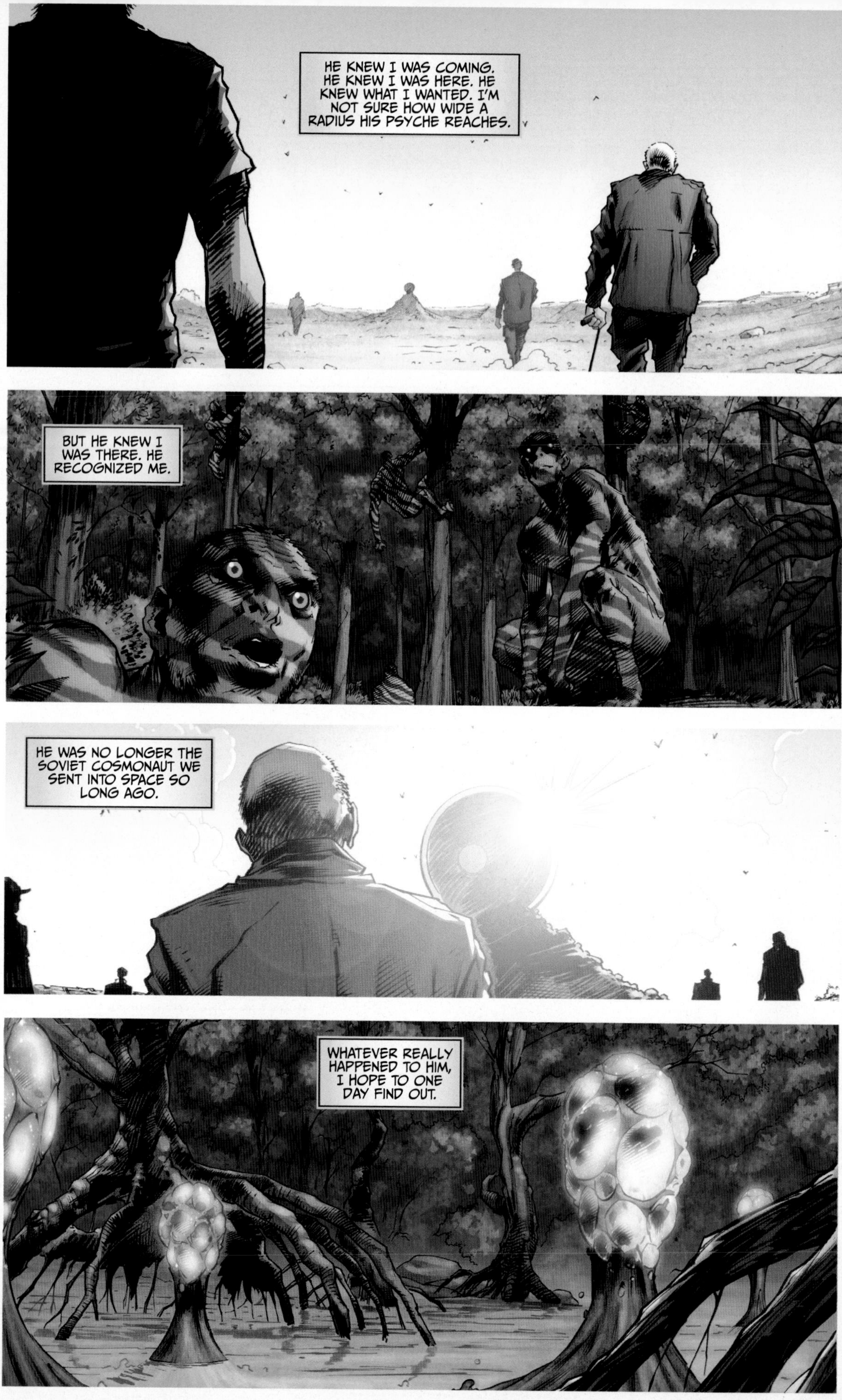
HE KNEW I WAS COMING. HE KNEW I WAS HERE. HE KNEW WHAT I WANTED. I'M NOT SURE HOW WIDE A RADIUS HIS PSYCHE REACHES.
BUT HE KNEW I WAS THERE. HE RECOGNIZED ME.
HE WAS NO LONGER THE SOVIET COSMONAUT WE SENT INTO SPACE SO LONG AGO.
WHATEVER REALLY HAPPENED TO HIM, I HOPE TO ONE DAY FIND OUT.

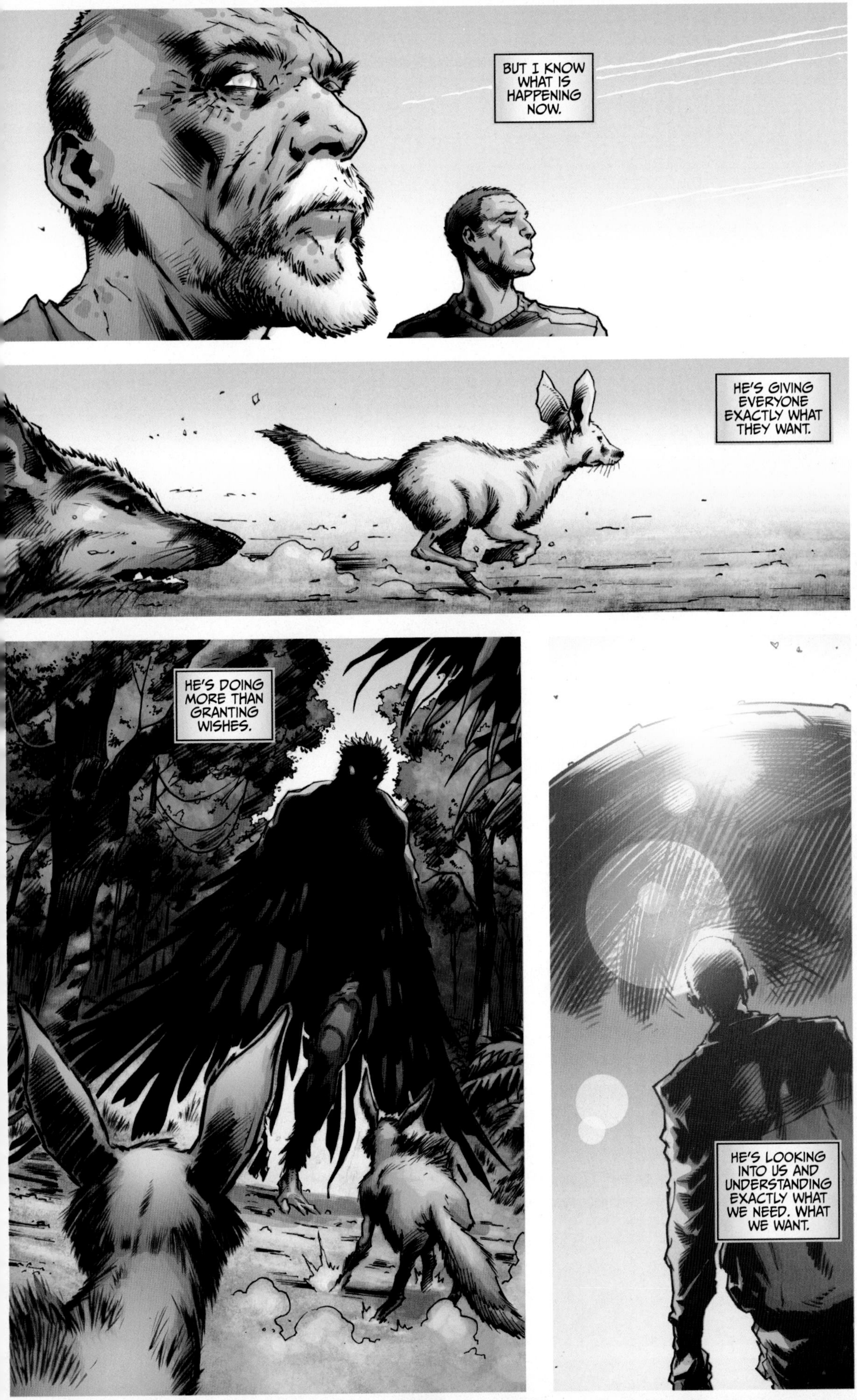
BUT I KNOW WHAT IS HAPPENING NOW.
HE'S GIVING EVERYONE EXACTLY WHAT THEY WANT.
HE'S DOING MORE THAN GRANTING WISHES.
HE'S LOOKING INTO US AND UNDERSTANDING EXACTLY WHAT WE NEED. WHAT WE WANT.

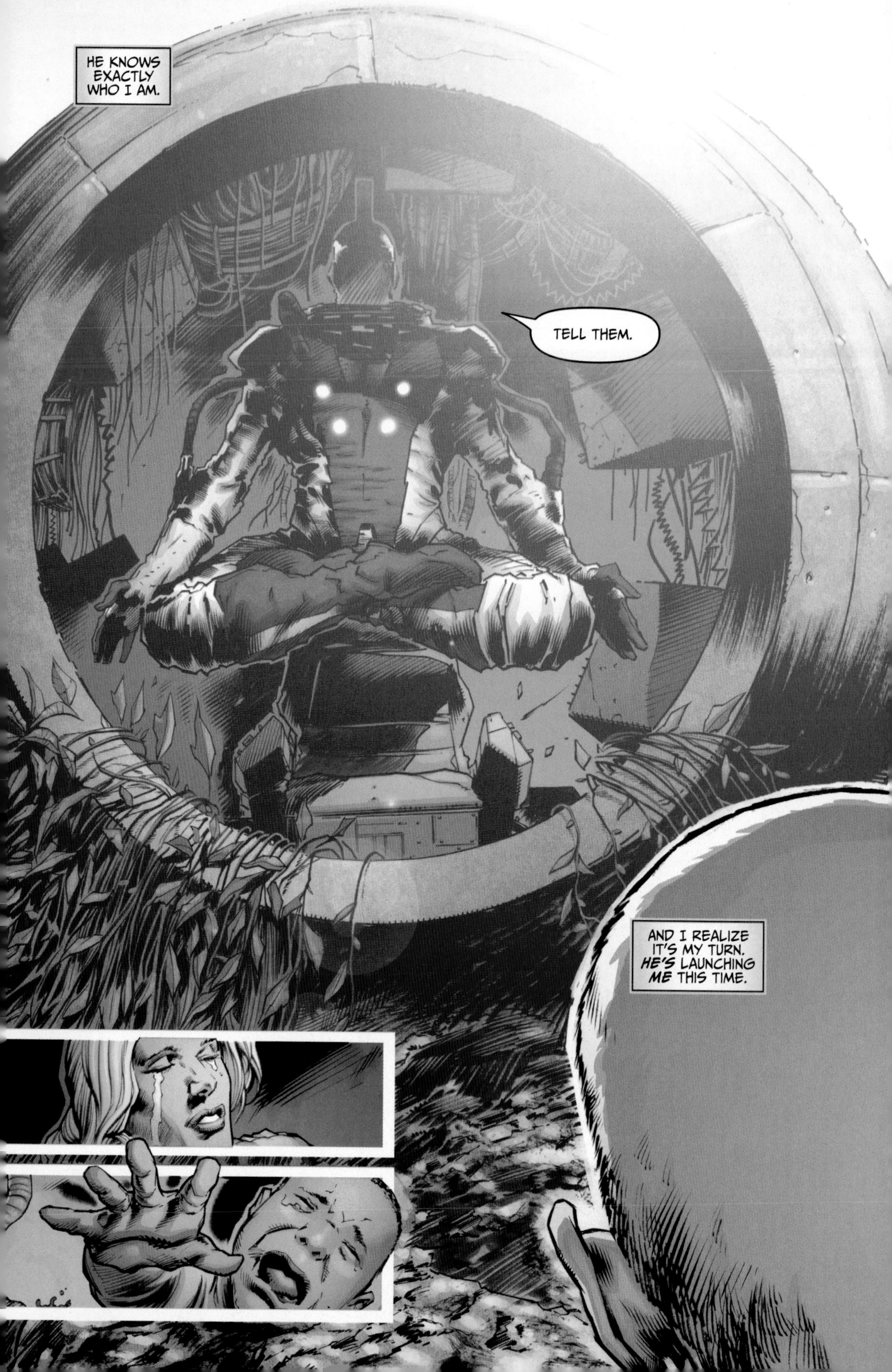
HE KNOWS EXACTLY WHO I AM.
TELL THEM.
AND I REALIZE IT'S MY TURN. *HE'S* LAUNCHING *ME* THIS TIME.

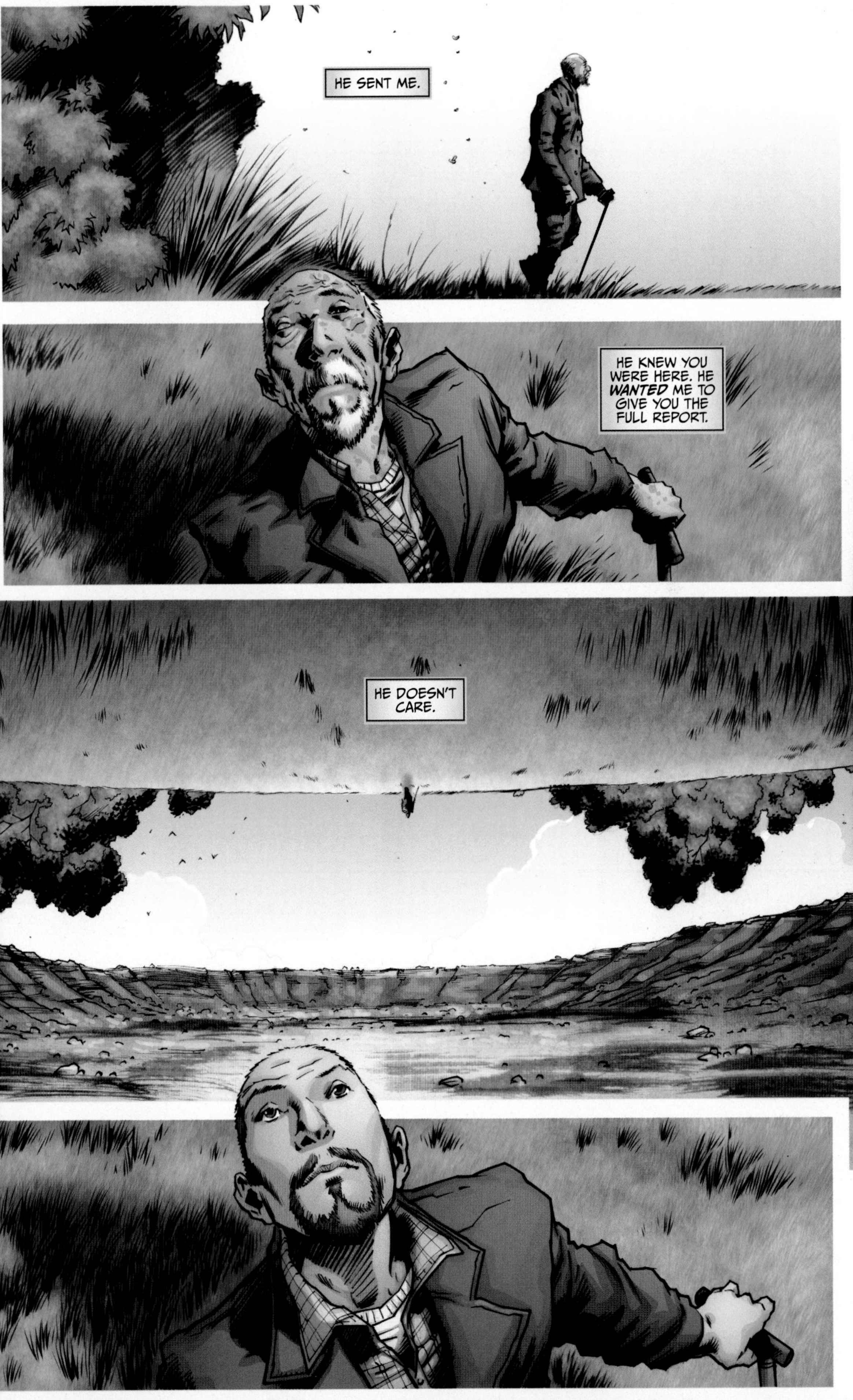
HE SENT ME.
HE KNEW YOU WERE HERE. HE *WANTED* ME TO GIVE YOU THE FULL REPORT.
HE DOESN'T CARE.

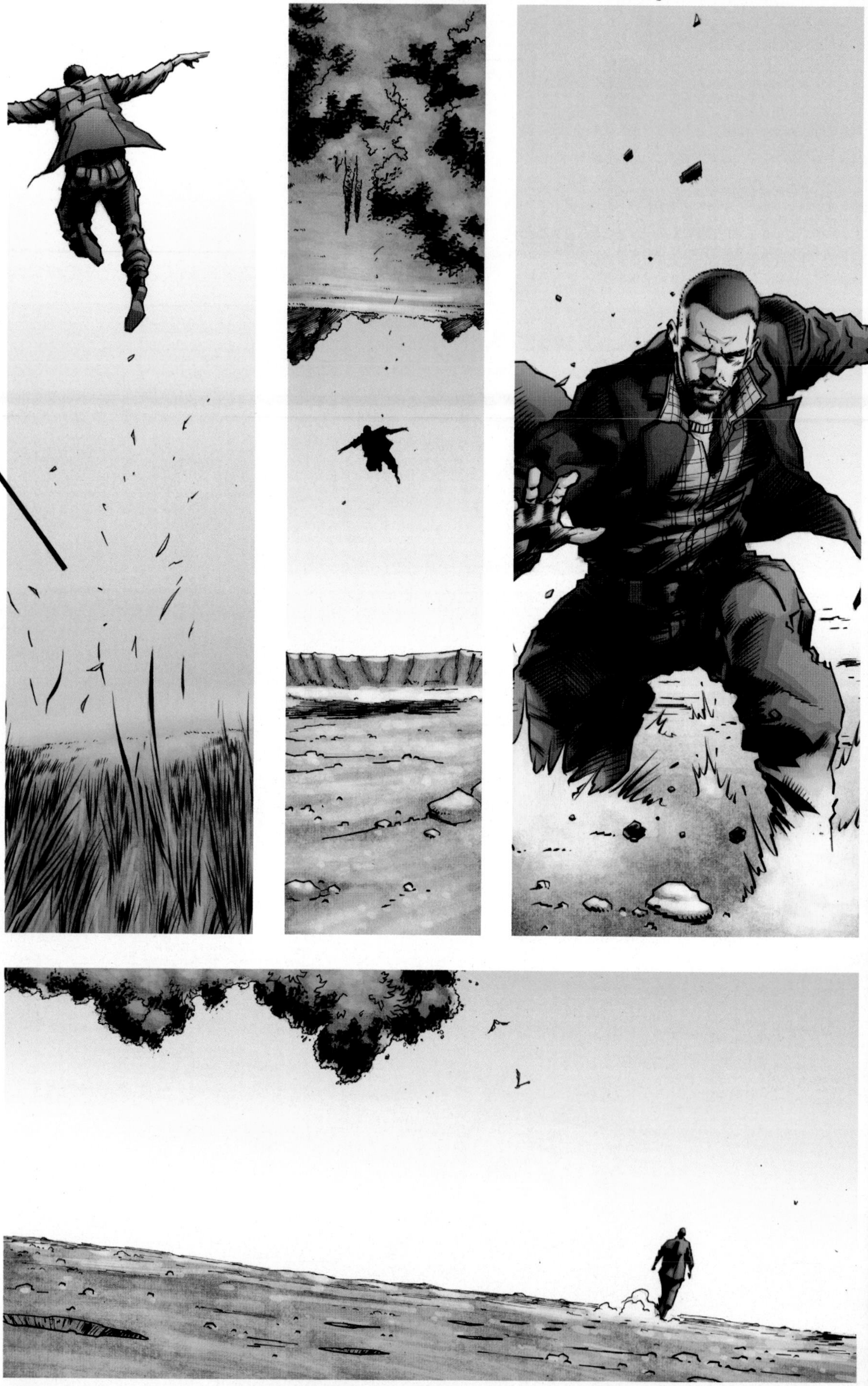

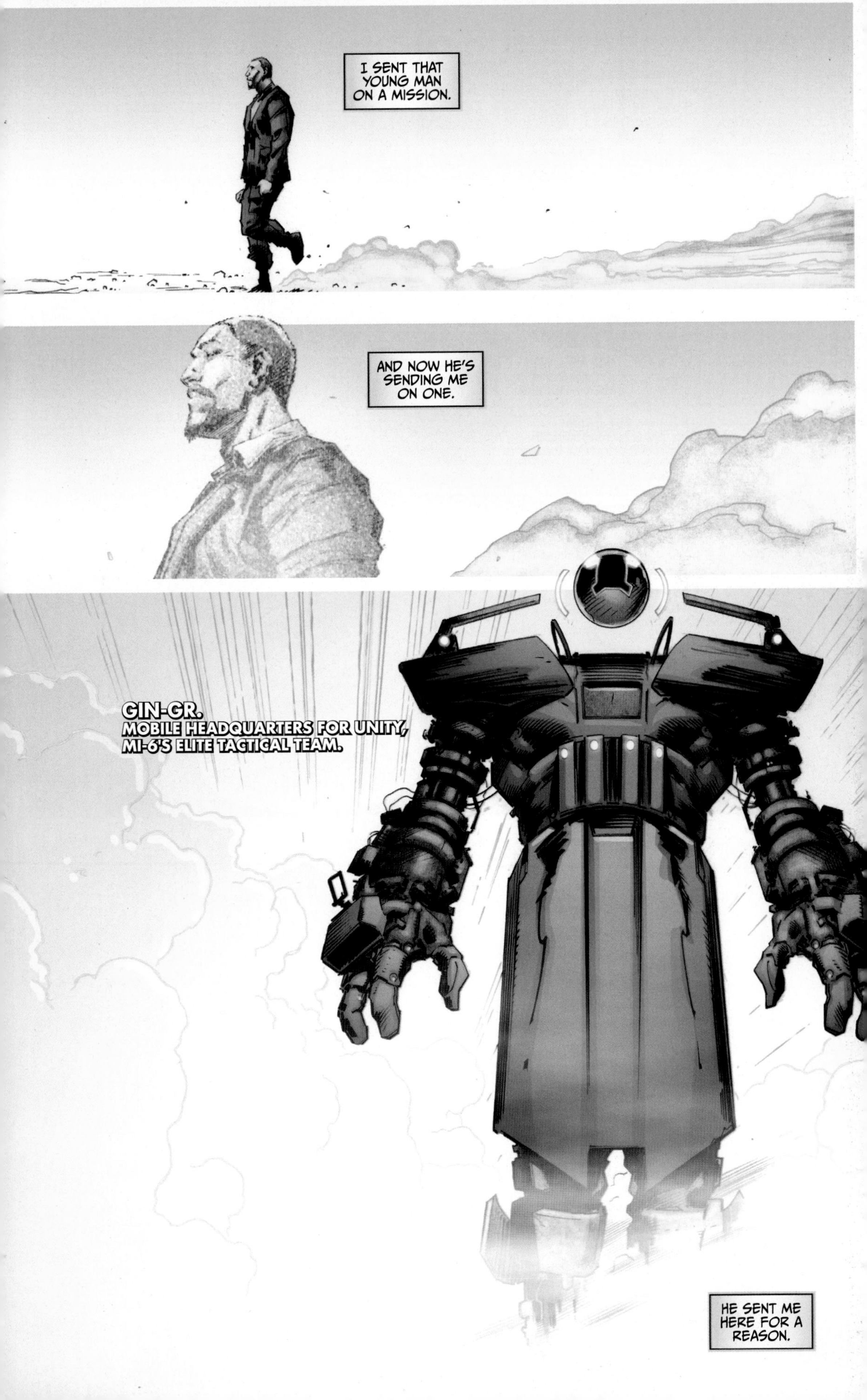
I SENT THAT YOUNG MAN ON A MISSION.
AND NOW HE'S SENDING ME ON ONE.
GIN-GR.
MOBILE HEADQUARTERS FOR UNITY, MI-6'S ELITE TACTICAL TEAM.
HE SENT ME HERE FOR A REASON.

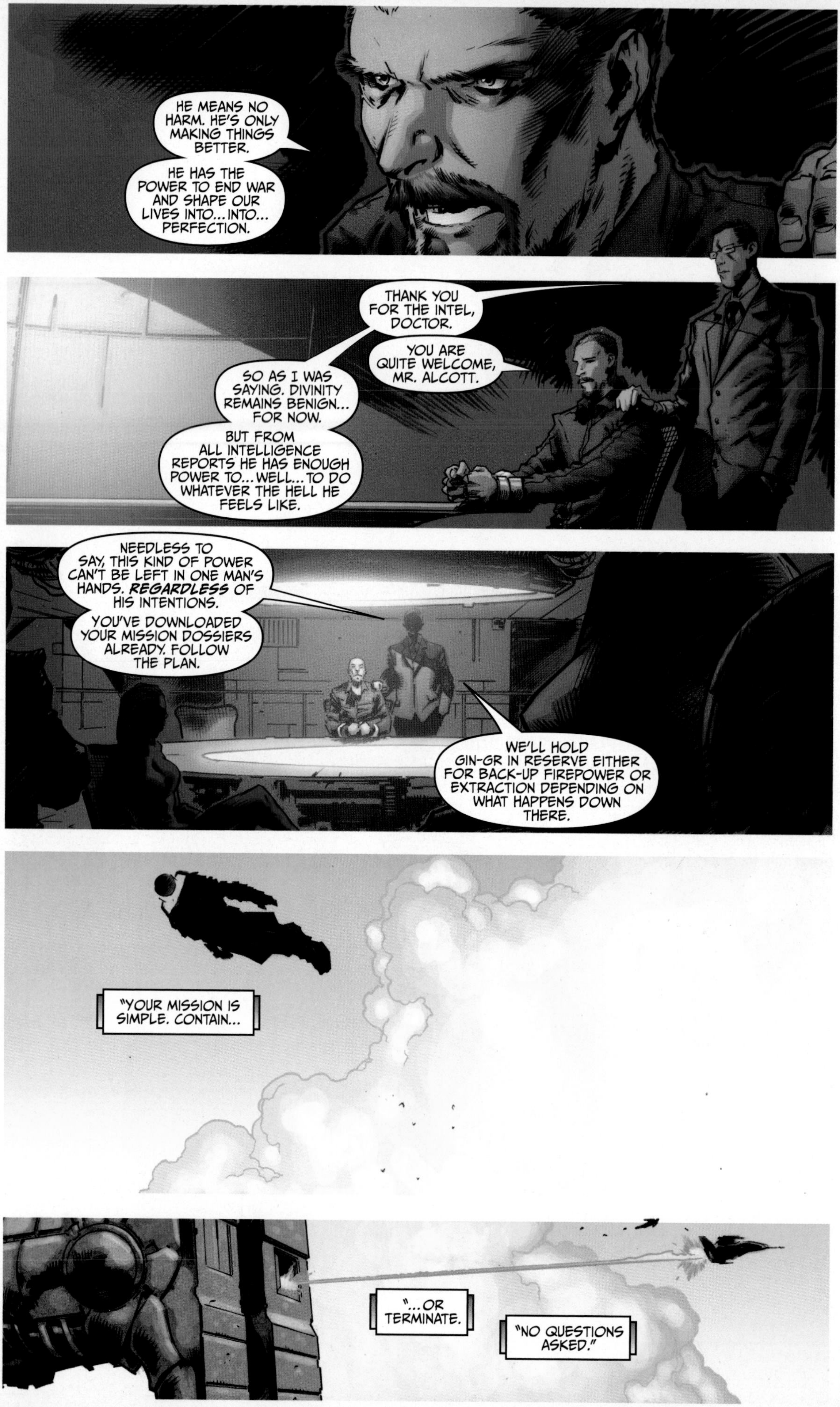
HE MEANS NO HARM. HE'S ONLY MAKING THINGS BETTER.
HE HAS THE POWER TO END WAR AND SHAPE OUR LIVES INTO... INTO... PERFECTION.
THANK YOU FOR THE INTEL, DOCTOR.
YOU ARE QUITE WELCOME, MR. ALCOTT.
SO AS I WAS SAYING. DIVINITY REMAINS BENIGN... FOR NOW.
BUT FROM ALL INTELLIGENCE REPORTS HE HAS ENOUGH POWER TO... WELL... TO DO WHATEVER THE HELL HE FEELS LIKE.
NEEDLESS TO SAY, THIS KIND OF POWER CAN'T BE LEFT IN ONE MAN'S HANDS. REGARDLESS OF HIS INTENTIONS.
YOU'VE DOWNLOADED YOUR MISSION DOSSIERS ALREADY. FOLLOW THE PLAN.
WE'LL HOLD GIN-GR IN RESERVE EITHER FOR BACK-UP FIREPOWER OR EXTRACTION DEPENDING ON WHAT HAPPENS DOWN THERE.
"YOUR MISSION IS SIMPLE. CONTAIN...
"...OR TERMINATE.
"NO QUESTIONS ASKED."

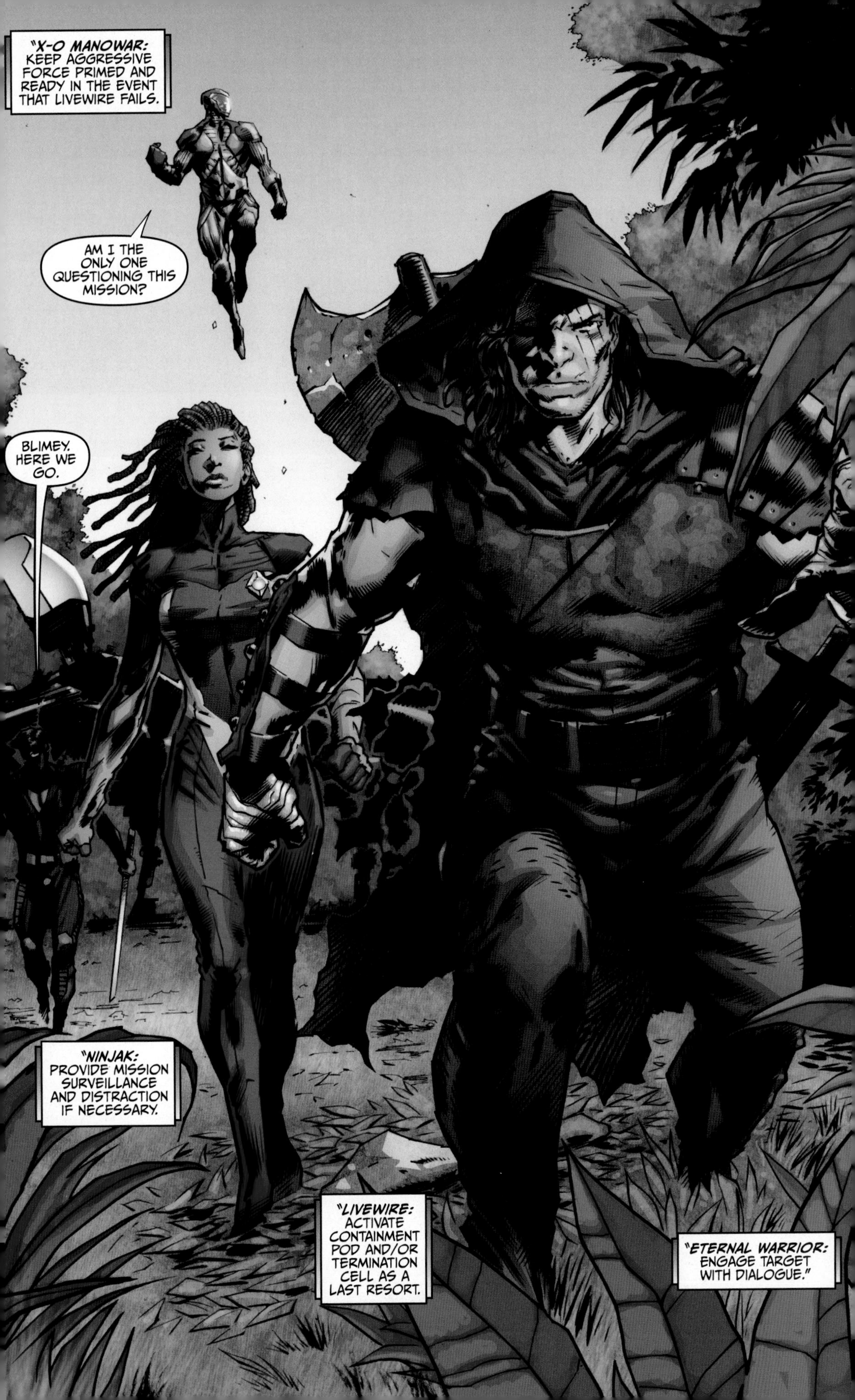
"X-O MANOWAR: KEEP AGGRESSIVE FORCE PRIMED AND READY IN THE EVENT THAT LIVEWIRE FAILS.
AM I THE ONLY ONE QUESTIONING THIS MISSION?
BLIMEY. HERE WE GO.
"NINJAK: PROVIDE MISSION SURVEILLANCE AND DISTRACTION IF NECESSARY.
"LIVEWIRE: ACTIVATE CONTAINMENT POD AND/OR TERMINATION CELL AS A LAST RESORT.
"ETERNAL WARRIOR: ENGAGE TARGET WITH DIALOGUE."

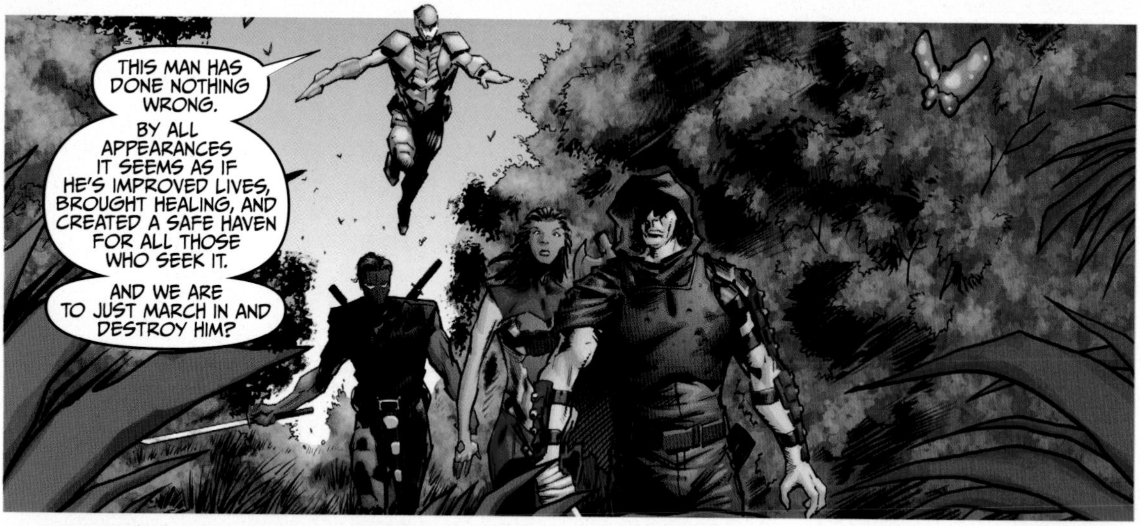
THIS MAN HAS DONE NOTHING WRONG.
BY ALL APPEARANCES IT SEEMS AS IF HE'S IMPROVED LIVES, BROUGHT HEALING, AND CREATED A SAFE HAVEN FOR ALL THOSE WHO SEEK IT.
AND WE ARE TO JUST MARCH IN AND DESTROY HIM?

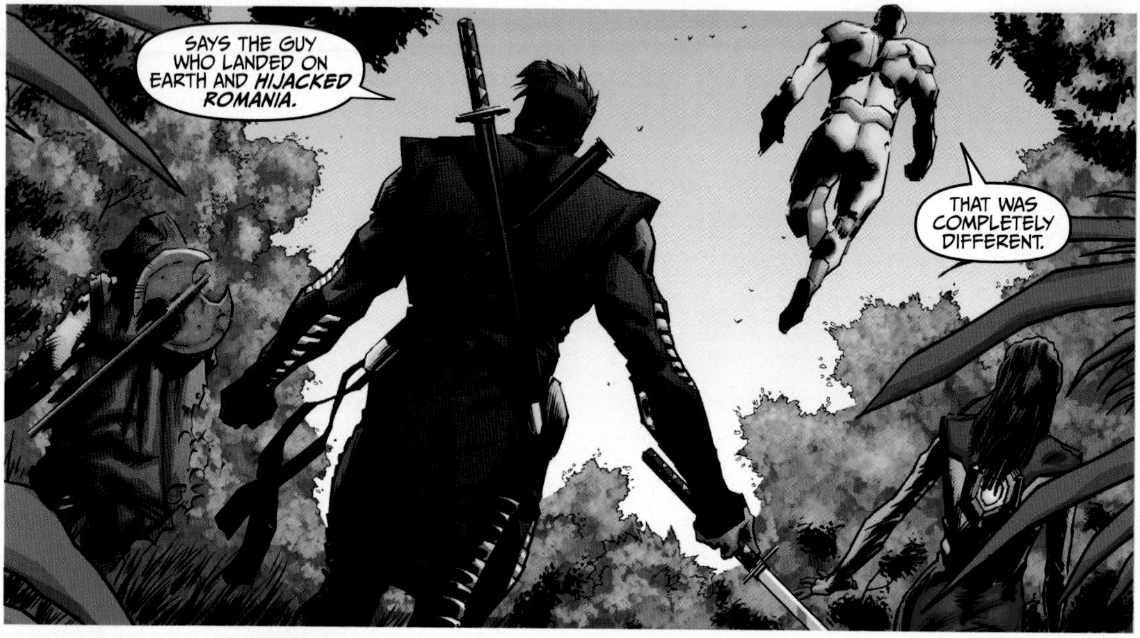
SAYS THE GUY WHO LANDED ON EARTH AND *HIJACKED ROMANIA.*
THAT WAS COMPLETELY DIFFERENT.

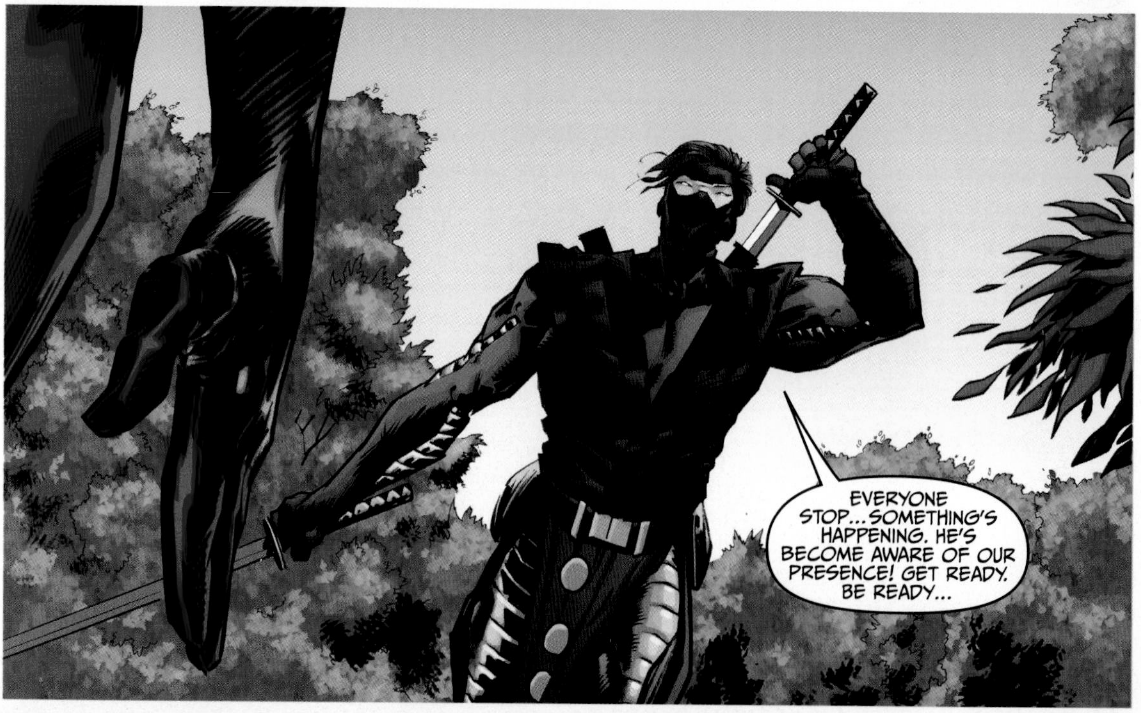
EVERYONE STOP... SOMETHING'S HAPPENING. HE'S BECOME AWARE OF OUR PRESENCE! GET READY. BE READY...

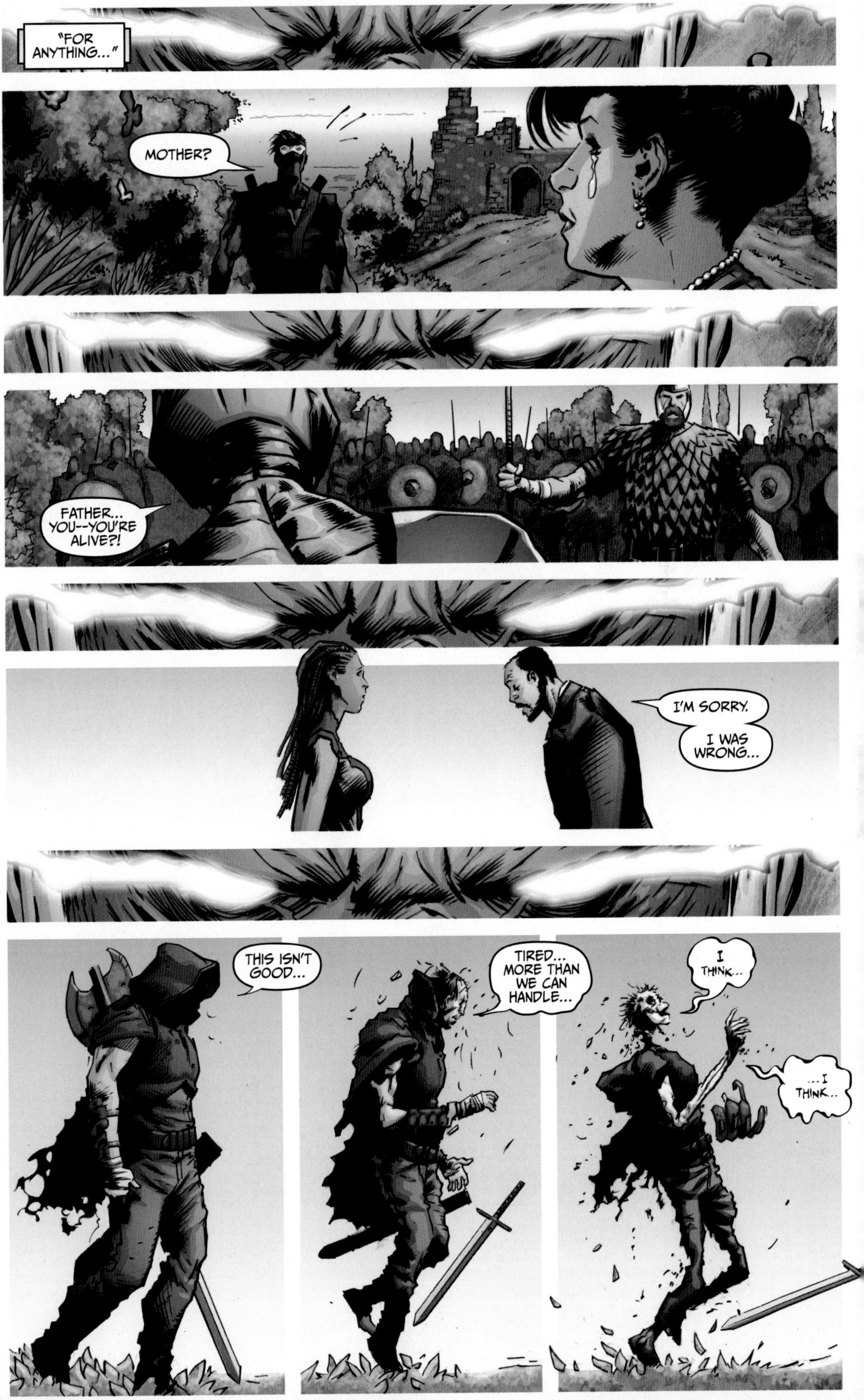
"FOR ANYTHING..."
MOTHER?
FATHER... YOU--YOU'RE ALIVE?!
I'M SORRY.
I WAS WRONG...
THIS ISN'T GOOD...
TIRED... MORE THAN WE CAN HANDLE...
I THINK...
...I THINK...

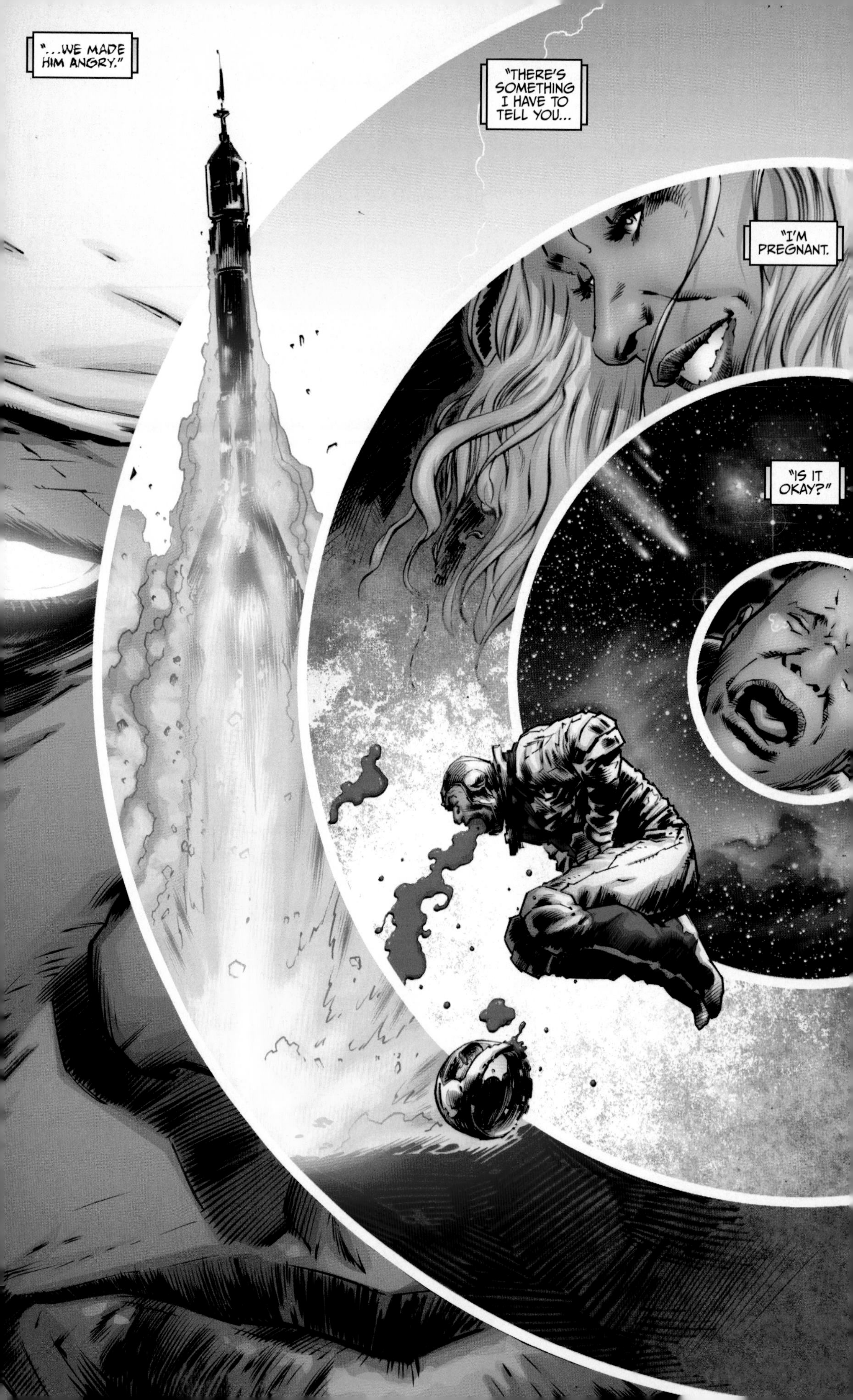
"...WE MADE HIM ANGRY."
"THERE'S SOMETHING I HAVE TO TELL YOU...
"I'M PREGNANT.
"IS IT OKAY?"

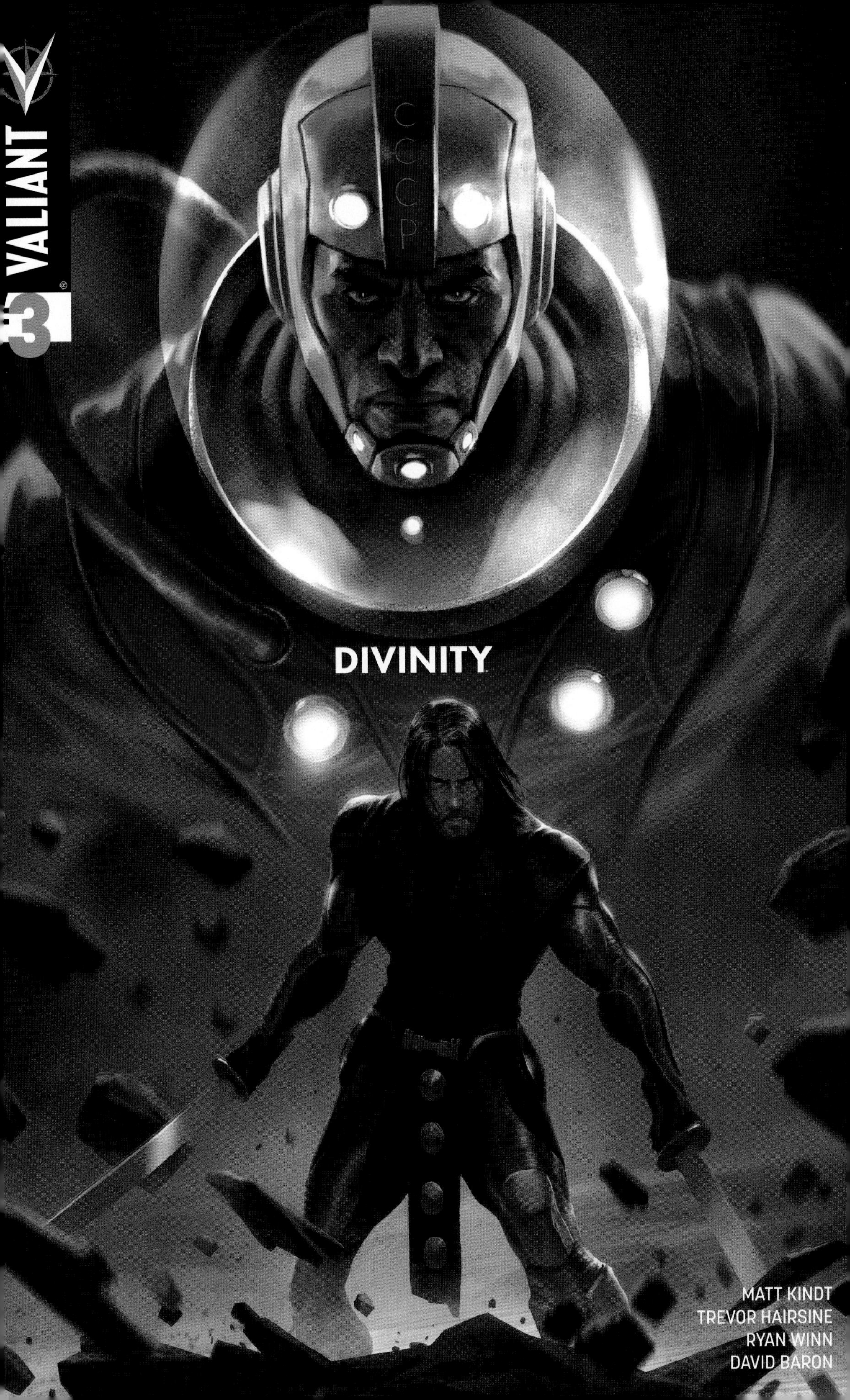
VALIANT
3
CCCP
DIVINITY
MATT KINDT
TREVOR HAIRSINE
RYAN WINN
DAVID BARON

BOOK THREE

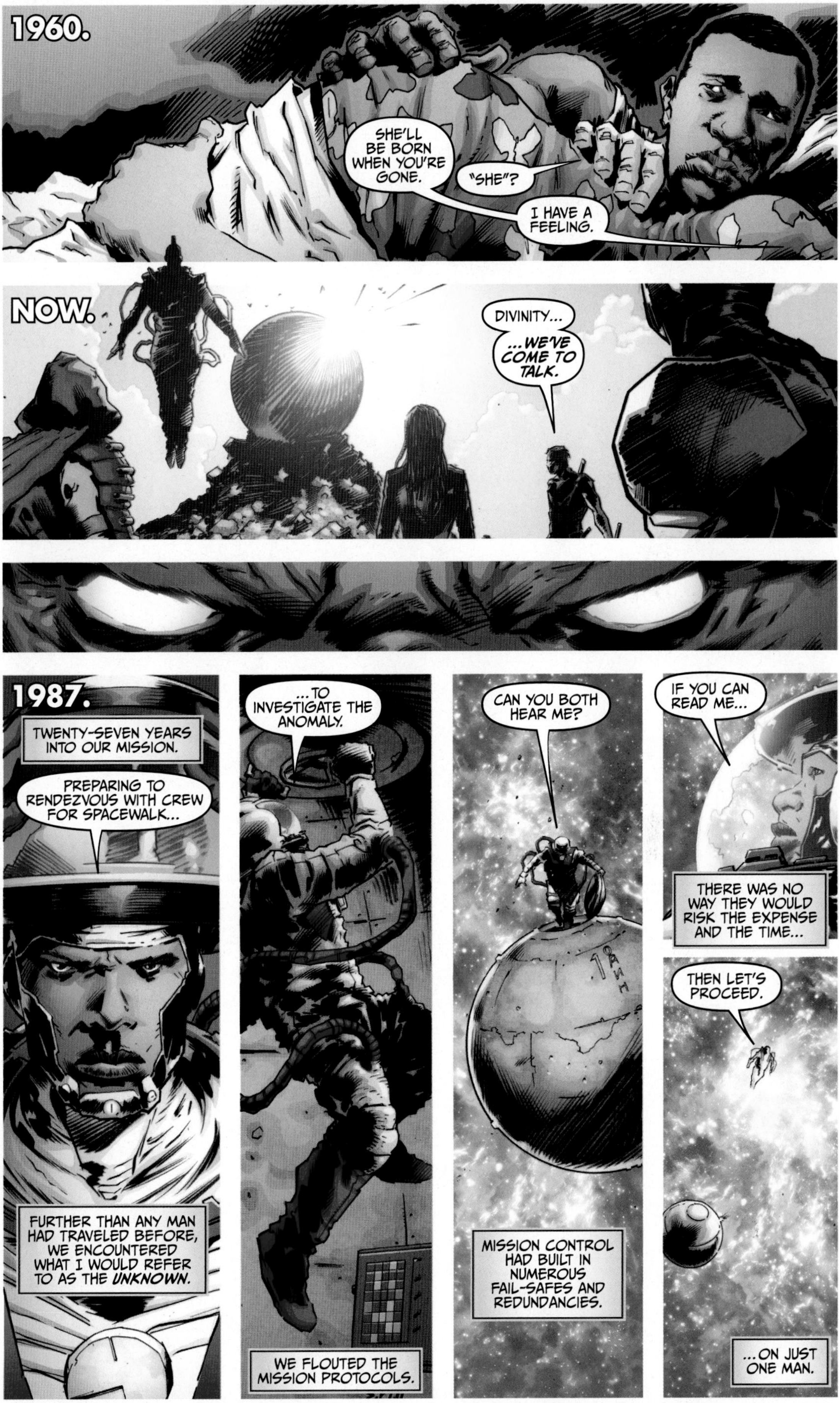
1960.
SHE'LL BE BORN WHEN YOU'RE GONE.
"SHE"?
I HAVE A FEELING.
NOW.
DIVINITY...
...WE'VE COME TO TALK.
1987.
TWENTY-SEVEN YEARS INTO OUR MISSION.
PREPARING TO RENDEZVOUS WITH CREW FOR SPACEWALK...
FURTHER THAN ANY MAN HAD TRAVELED BEFORE, WE ENCOUNTERED WHAT I WOULD REFER TO AS THE *UNKNOWN*.
...TO INVESTIGATE THE ANOMALY.
WE FLOUTED THE MISSION PROTOCOLS.
CAN YOU BOTH HEAR ME?
MISSION CONTROL HAD BUILT IN NUMEROUS FAIL-SAFES AND REDUNDANCIES.
IF YOU CAN READ ME...
THERE WAS NO WAY THEY WOULD RISK THE EXPENSE AND THE TIME...
THEN LET'S PROCEED.
...ON JUST ONE MAN.

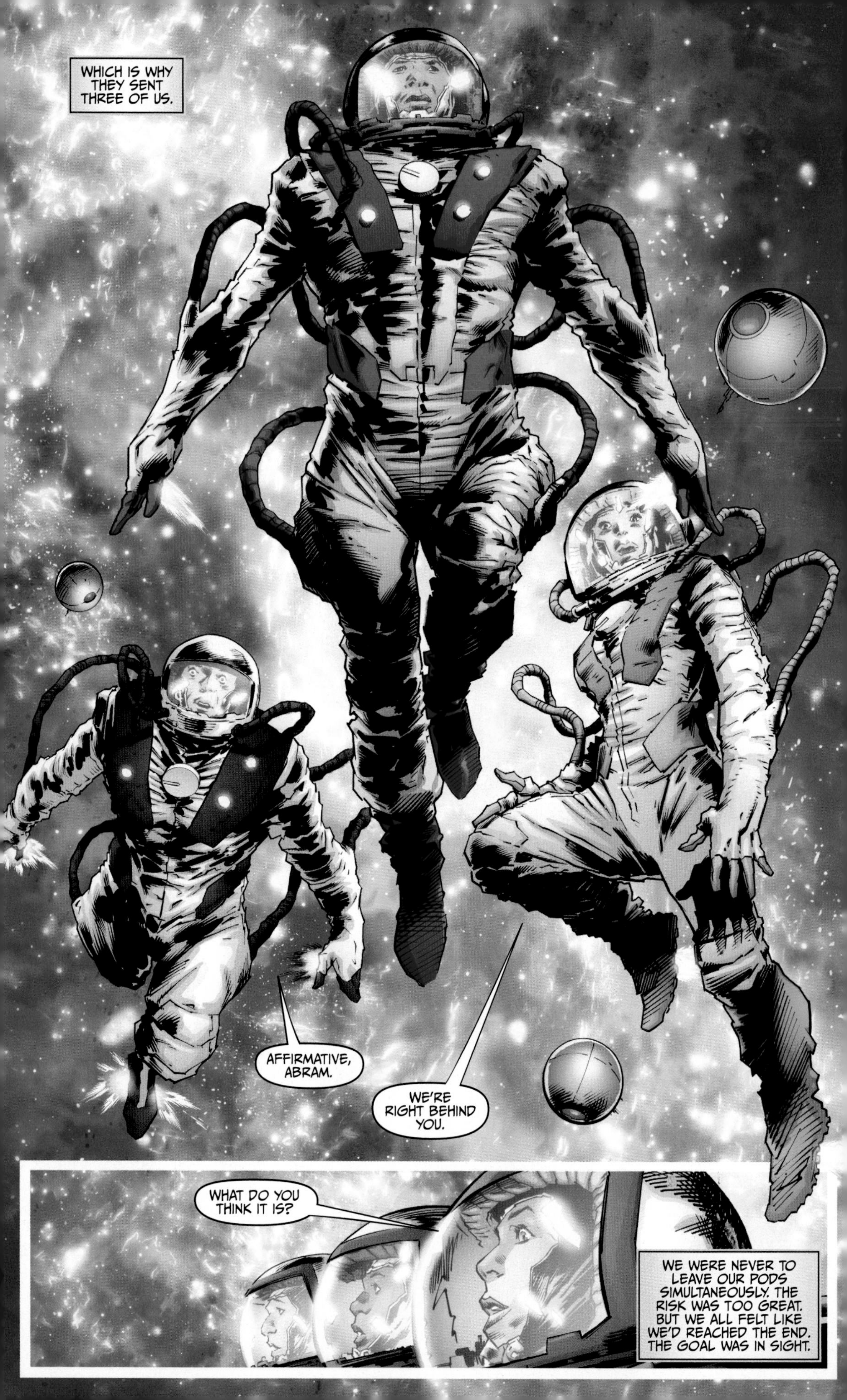
WHICH IS WHY THEY SENT THREE OF US.
AFFIRMATIVE, ABRAM.
WE'RE RIGHT BEHIND YOU.
WHAT DO YOU THINK IT IS?
WE WERE NEVER TO LEAVE OUR PODS SIMULTANEOUSLY. THE RISK WAS TOO GREAT. BUT WE ALL FELT LIKE WE'D REACHED THE END. THE GOAL WAS IN SIGHT.

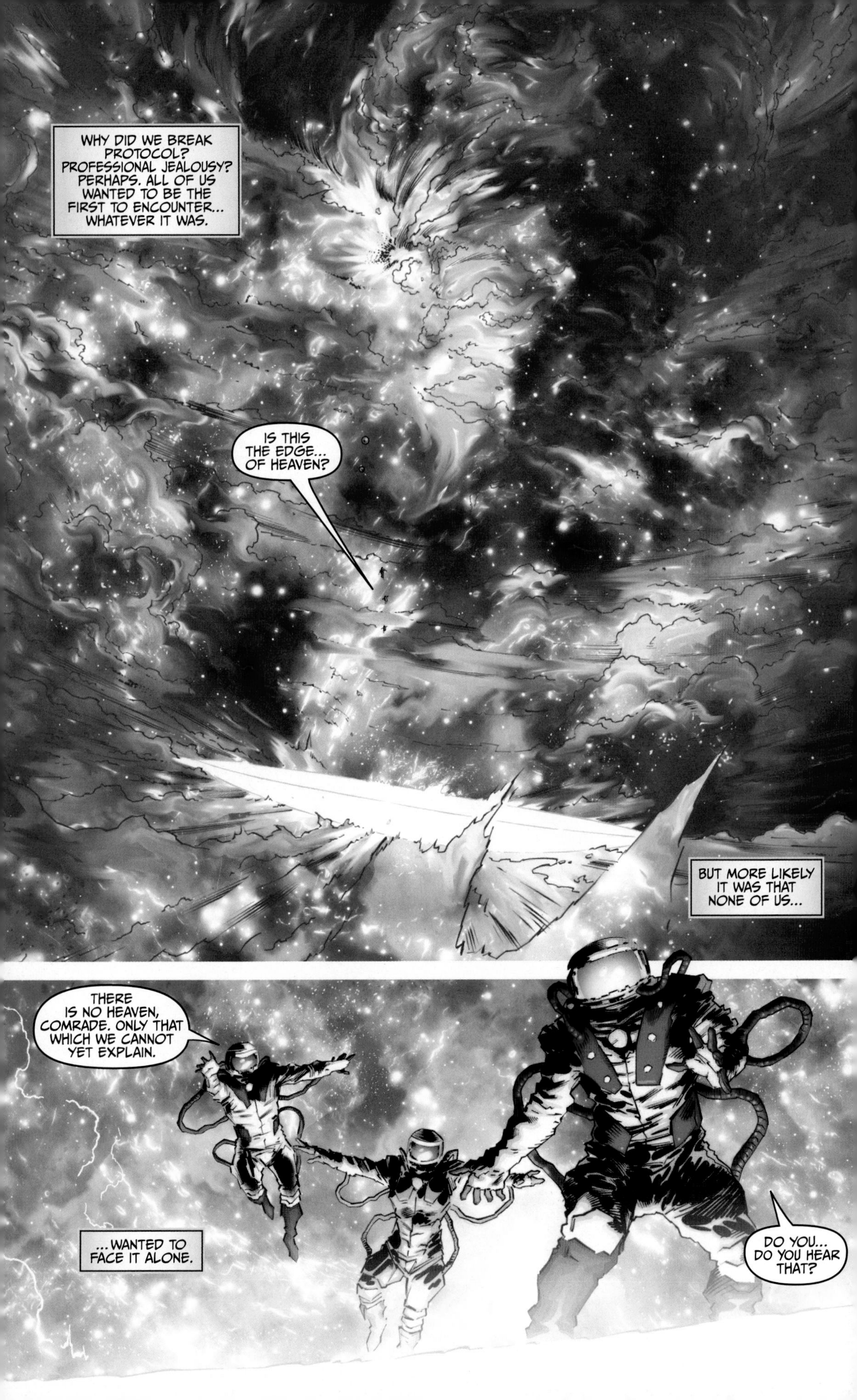
WHY DID WE BREAK PROTOCOL? PROFESSIONAL JEALOUSY? PERHAPS. ALL OF US WANTED TO BE THE FIRST TO ENCOUNTER... WHATEVER IT WAS.
IS THIS THE EDGE... OF HEAVEN?
BUT MORE LIKELY IT WAS THAT NONE OF US...
THERE IS NO HEAVEN, COMRADE. ONLY THAT WHICH WE CANNOT YET EXPLAIN.
...WANTED TO FACE IT ALONE.
DO YOU... DO YOU HEAR THAT?

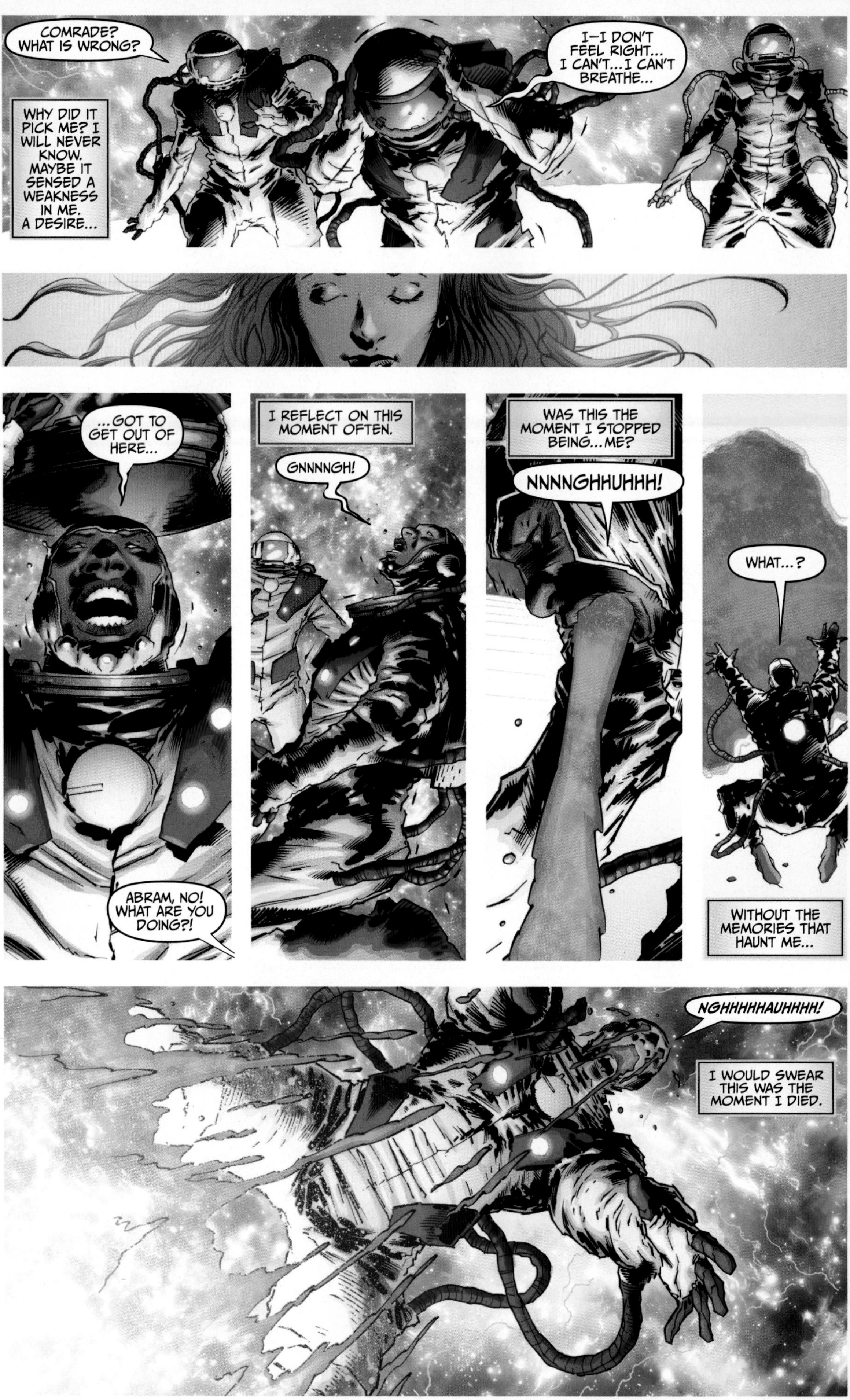
COMRADE? WHAT IS WRONG?
WHY DID IT PICK ME? I WILL NEVER KNOW. MAYBE IT SENSED A WEAKNESS IN ME. A DESIRE...
I—I DON'T FEEL RIGHT... I CAN'T...I CAN'T BREATHE...
...GOT TO GET OUT OF HERE...
ABRAM, NO! WHAT ARE YOU DOING?!
I REFLECT ON THIS MOMENT OFTEN.
GNNNNGH!
WAS THIS THE MOMENT I STOPPED BEING...ME?
NNNNGHHUHHH!
WHAT...?
WITHOUT THE MEMORIES THAT HAUNT ME...
NGHHHHHAUHHHH!
I WOULD SWEAR THIS WAS THE MOMENT I DIED.

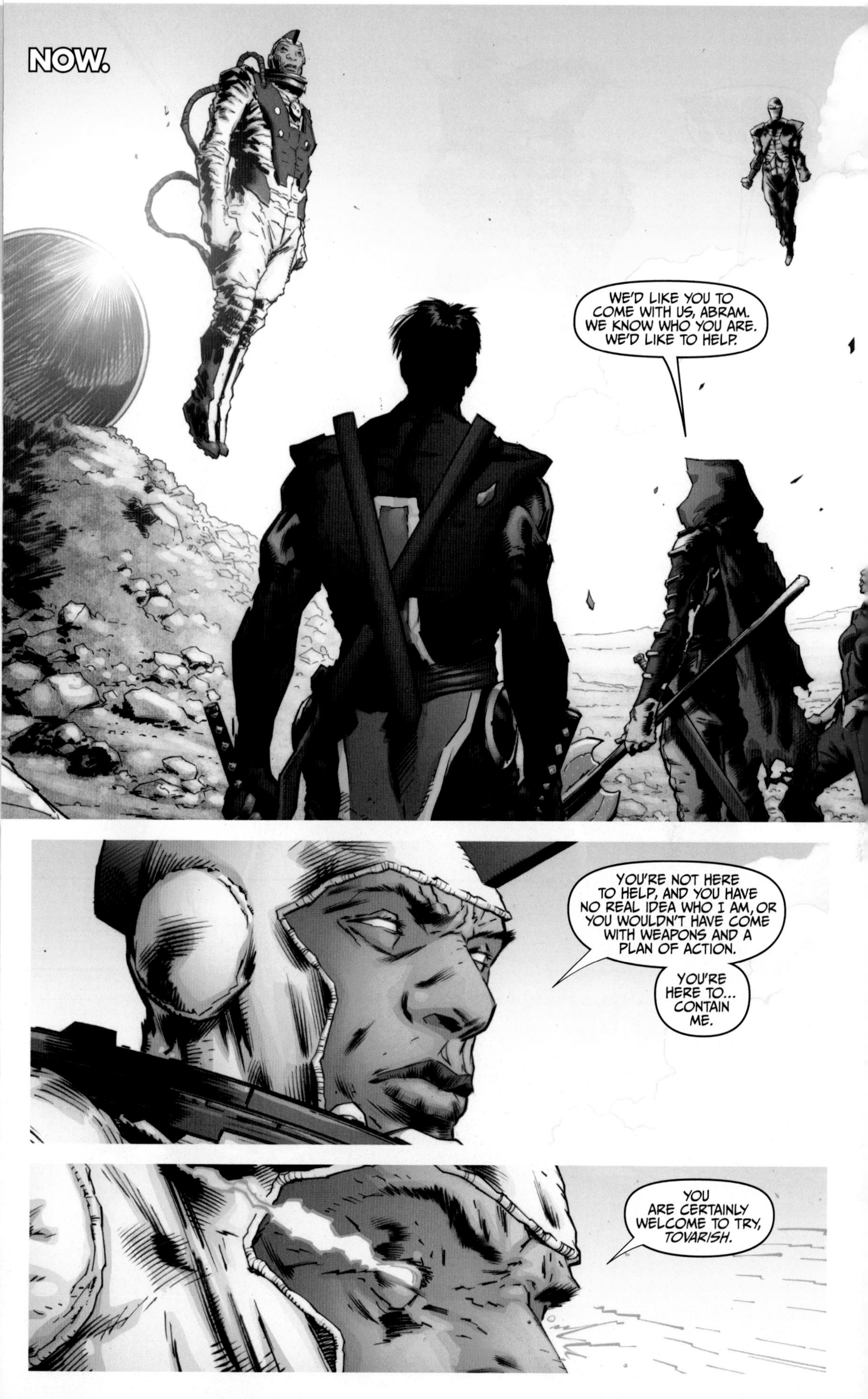
NOW.
WE'D LIKE YOU TO COME WITH US, ABRAM. WE KNOW WHO YOU ARE. WE'D LIKE TO HELP.
YOU'RE NOT HERE TO HELP, AND YOU HAVE NO REAL IDEA WHO I AM, OR YOU WOULDN'T HAVE COME WITH WEAPONS AND A PLAN OF ACTION.
YOU'RE HERE TO... CONTAIN ME.
YOU ARE CERTAINLY WELCOME TO TRY, *TOVARISH.*

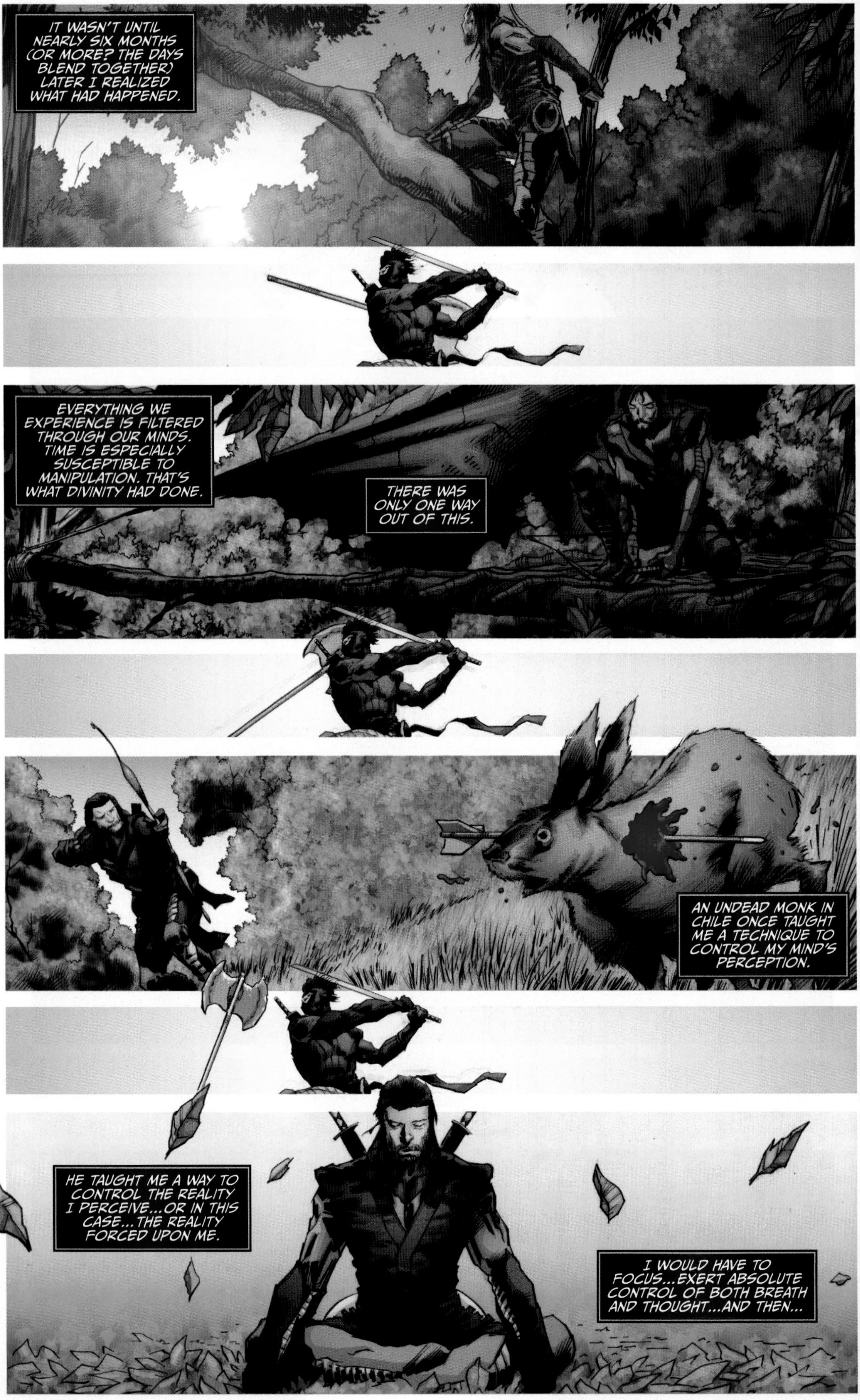
IT WASN'T UNTIL NEARLY SIX MONTHS (OR MORE? THE DAYS BLEND TOGETHER) LATER I REALIZED WHAT HAD HAPPENED.
EVERYTHING WE EXPERIENCE IS FILTERED THROUGH OUR MINDS. TIME IS ESPECIALLY SUSCEPTIBLE TO MANIPULATION. THAT'S WHAT DIVINITY HAD DONE.
THERE WAS ONLY ONE WAY OUT OF THIS.
AN UNDEAD MONK IN CHILE ONCE TAUGHT ME A TECHNIQUE TO CONTROL MY MIND'S PERCEPTION.
HE TAUGHT ME A WAY TO CONTROL THE REALITY I PERCEIVE...OR IN THIS CASE...THE REALITY FORCED UPON ME.
I WOULD HAVE TO FOCUS...EXERT ABSOLUTE CONTROL OF BOTH BREATH AND THOUGHT...AND THEN...

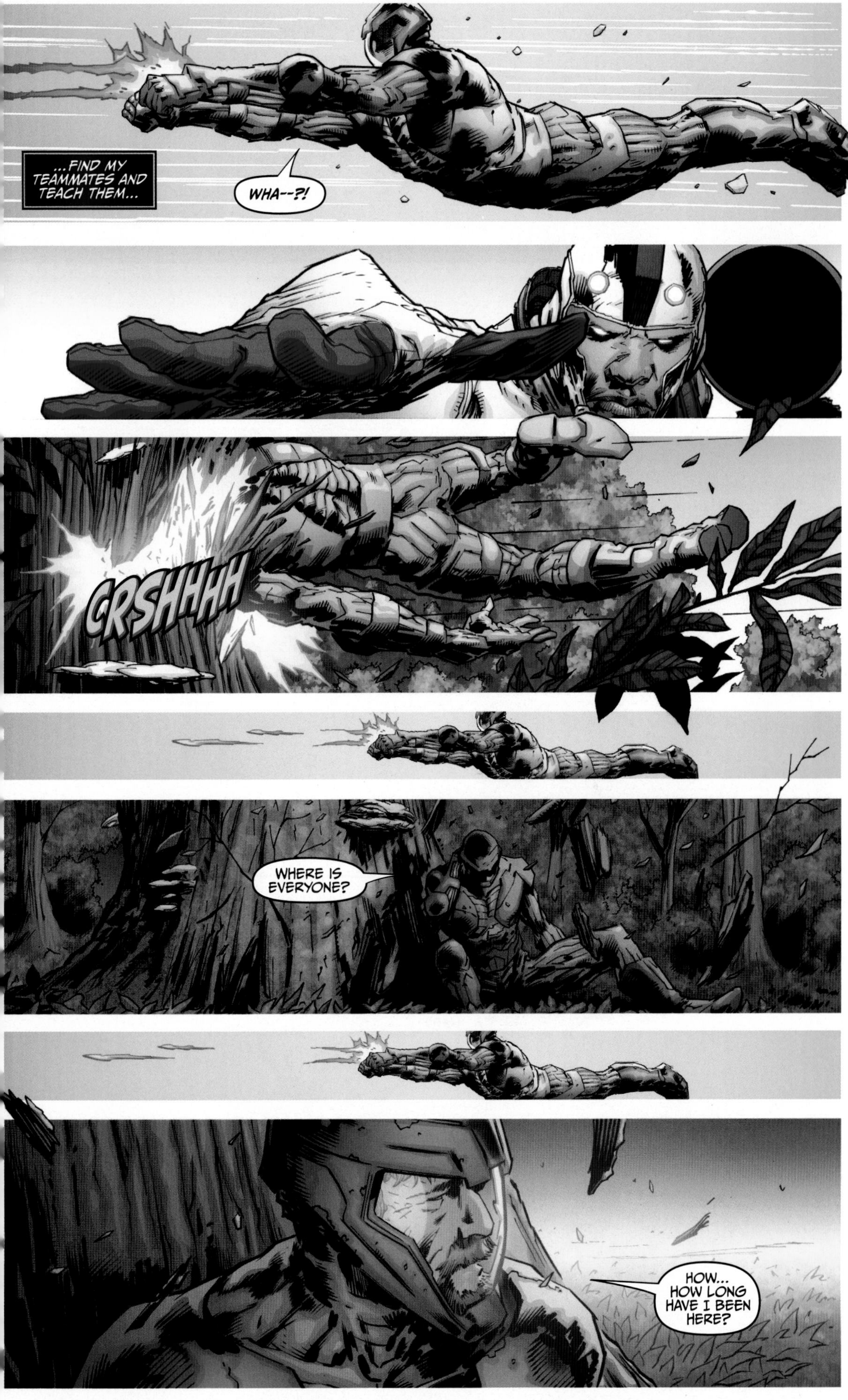
...FIND MY TEAMMATES AND TEACH THEM...
WHA--?!
CRSHHHH
WHERE IS EVERYONE?
HOW... HOW LONG HAVE I BEEN HERE?

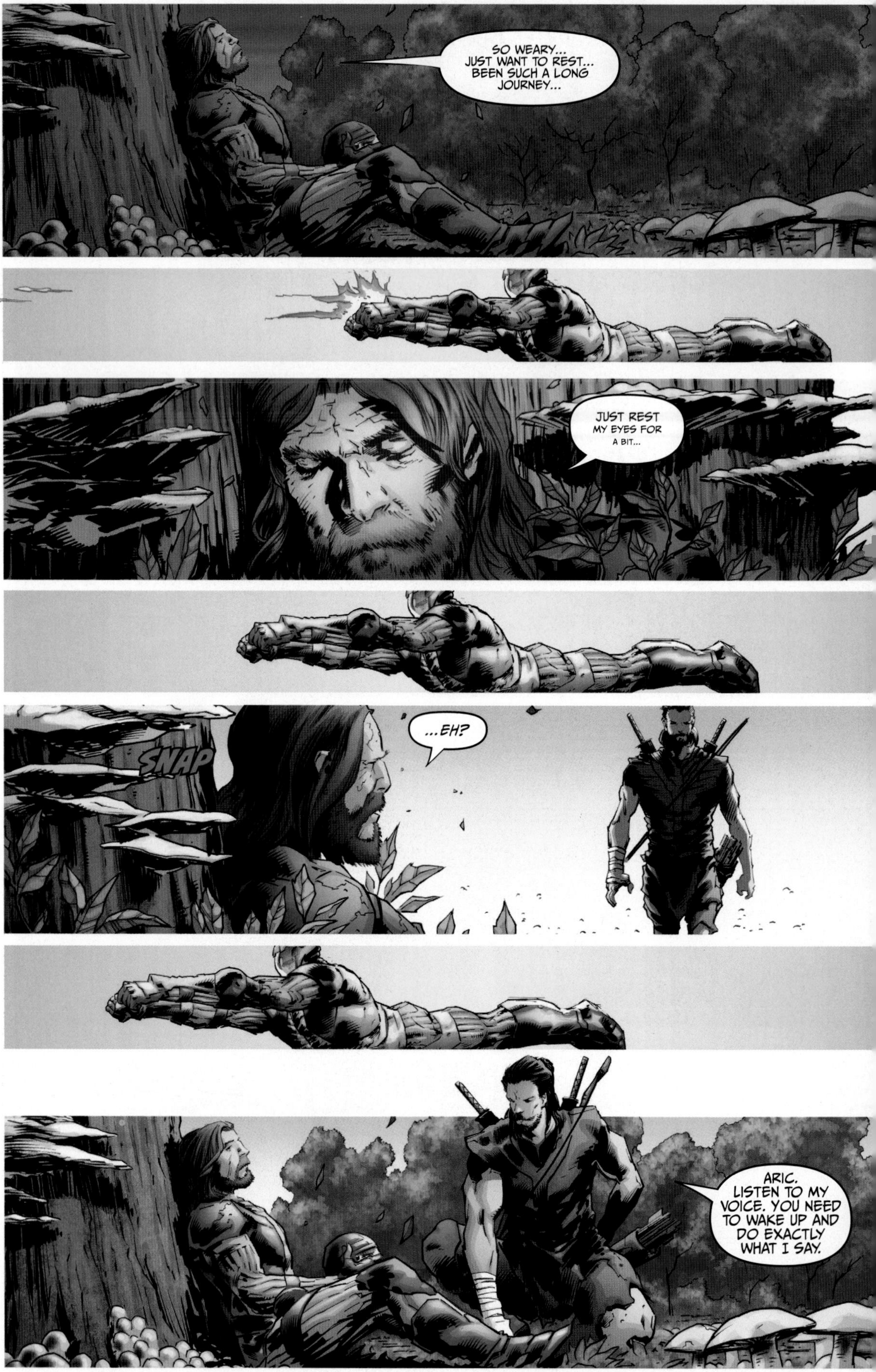
SO WEARY... JUST WANT TO REST... BEEN SUCH A LONG JOURNEY...
JUST REST MY EYES FOR A BIT...
SNAP
...EH?
ARIC. LISTEN TO MY VOICE. YOU NEED TO WAKE UP AND DO EXACTLY WHAT I SAY.

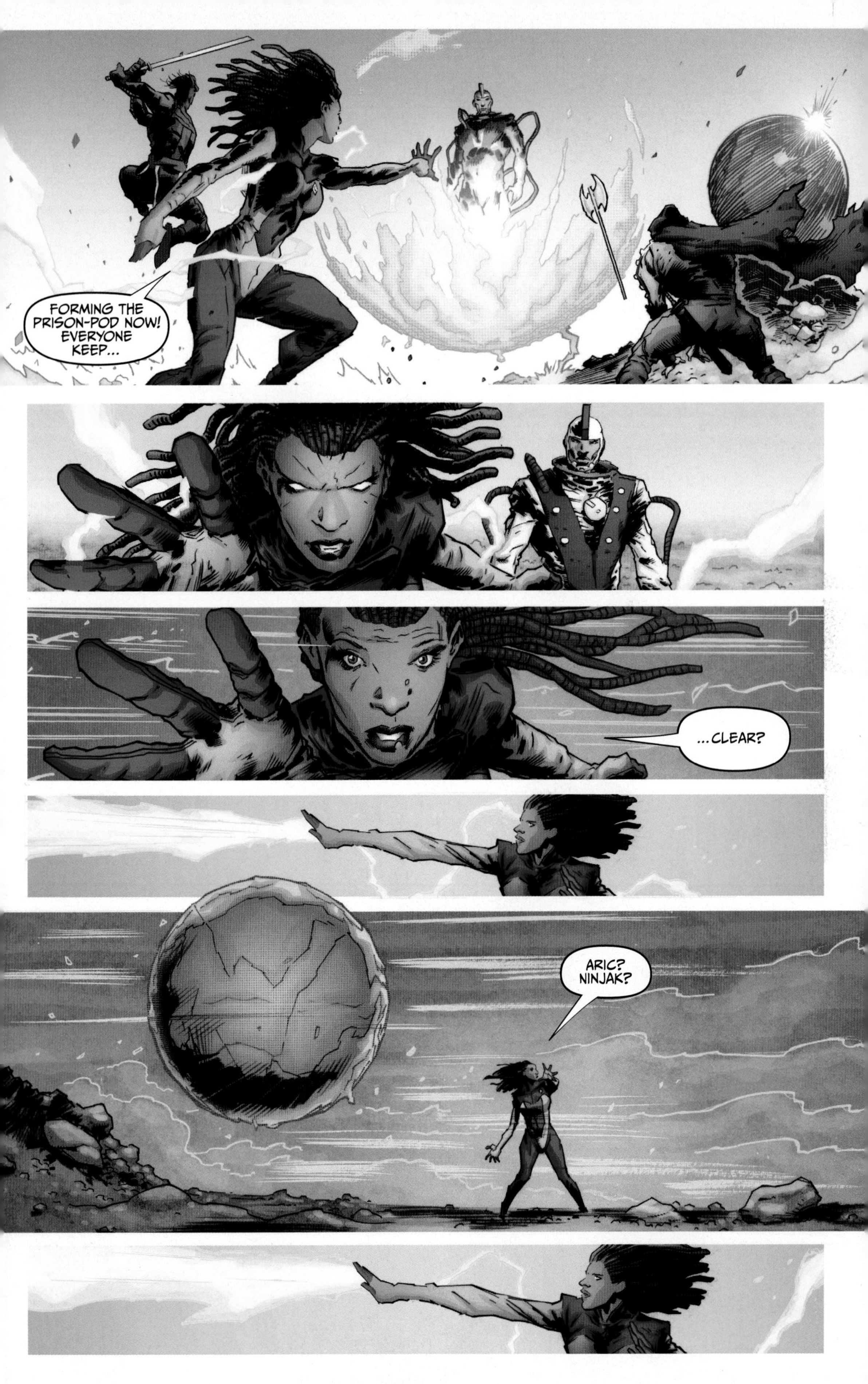
FORMING THE PRISON-POD NOW! EVERYONE KEEP...
...CLEAR?
ARIC? NINJAK?

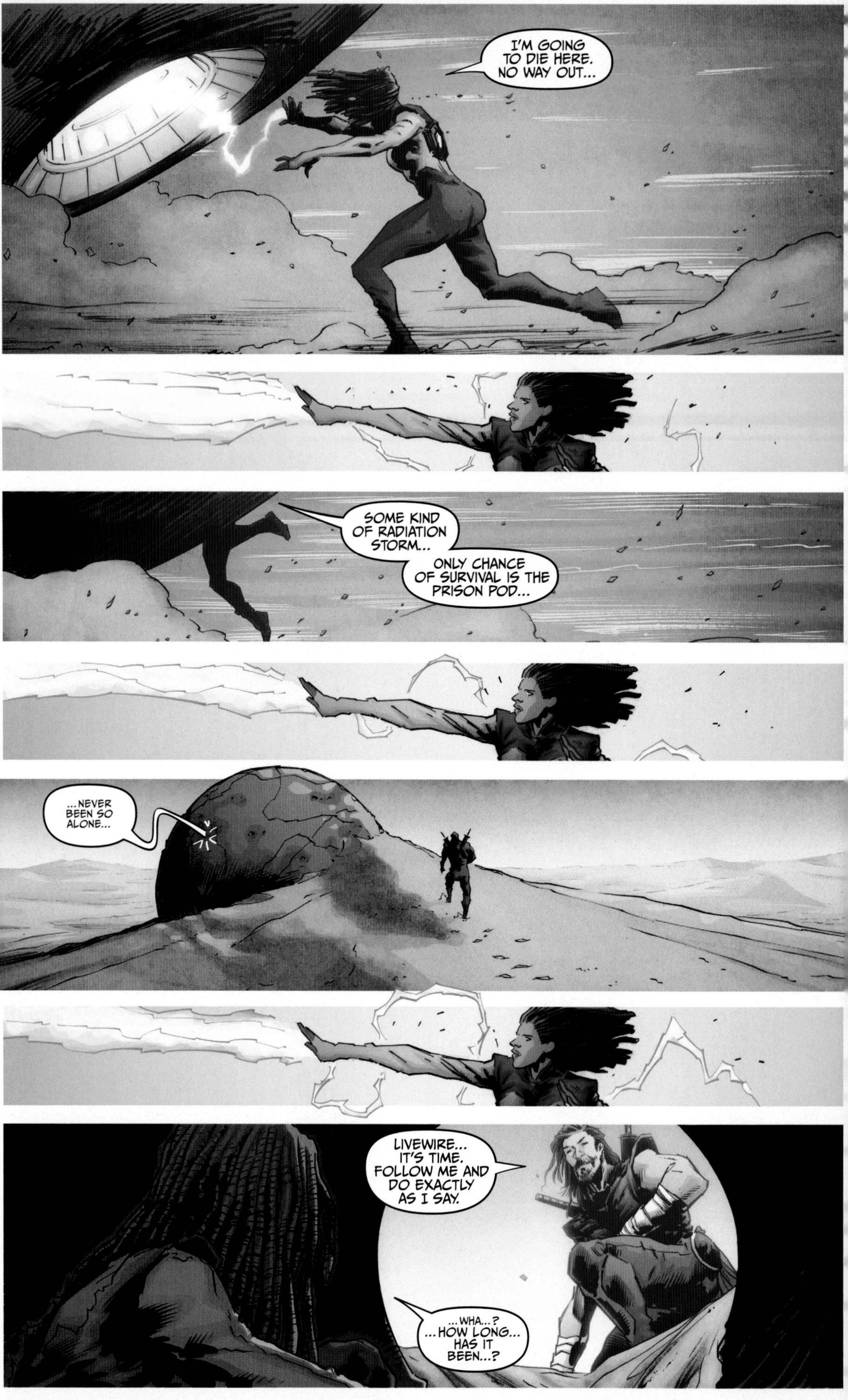
I'M GOING TO DIE HERE. NO WAY OUT...
SOME KIND OF RADIATION STORM...
ONLY CHANCE OF SURVIVAL IS THE PRISON POD...
...NEVER BEEN SO ALONE...
LIVEWIRE... IT'S TIME. FOLLOW ME AND DO EXACTLY AS I SAY.
...WHA...? ...HOW LONG... HAS IT BEEN...?

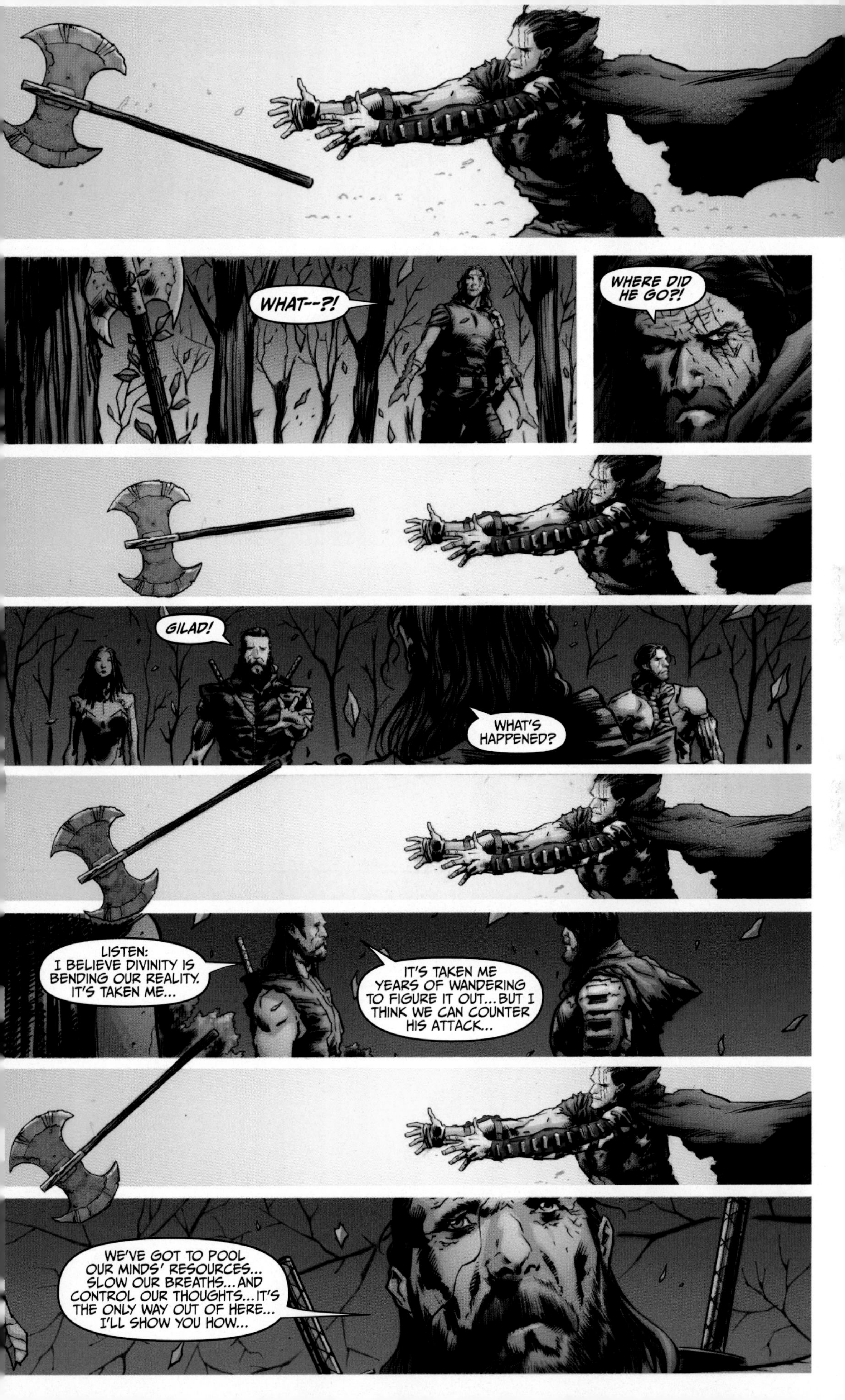
WHAT--?!
WHERE DID HE GO?!
GILAD!
WHAT'S HAPPENED?
LISTEN: I BELIEVE DIVINITY IS BENDING OUR REALITY. IT'S TAKEN ME...
IT'S TAKEN ME YEARS OF WANDERING TO FIGURE IT OUT...BUT I THINK WE CAN COUNTER HIS ATTACK...
WE'VE GOT TO POOL OUR MINDS' RESOURCES... SLOW OUR BREATHS...AND CONTROL OUR THOUGHTS...IT'S THE ONLY WAY OUT OF HERE... I'LL SHOW YOU HOW...

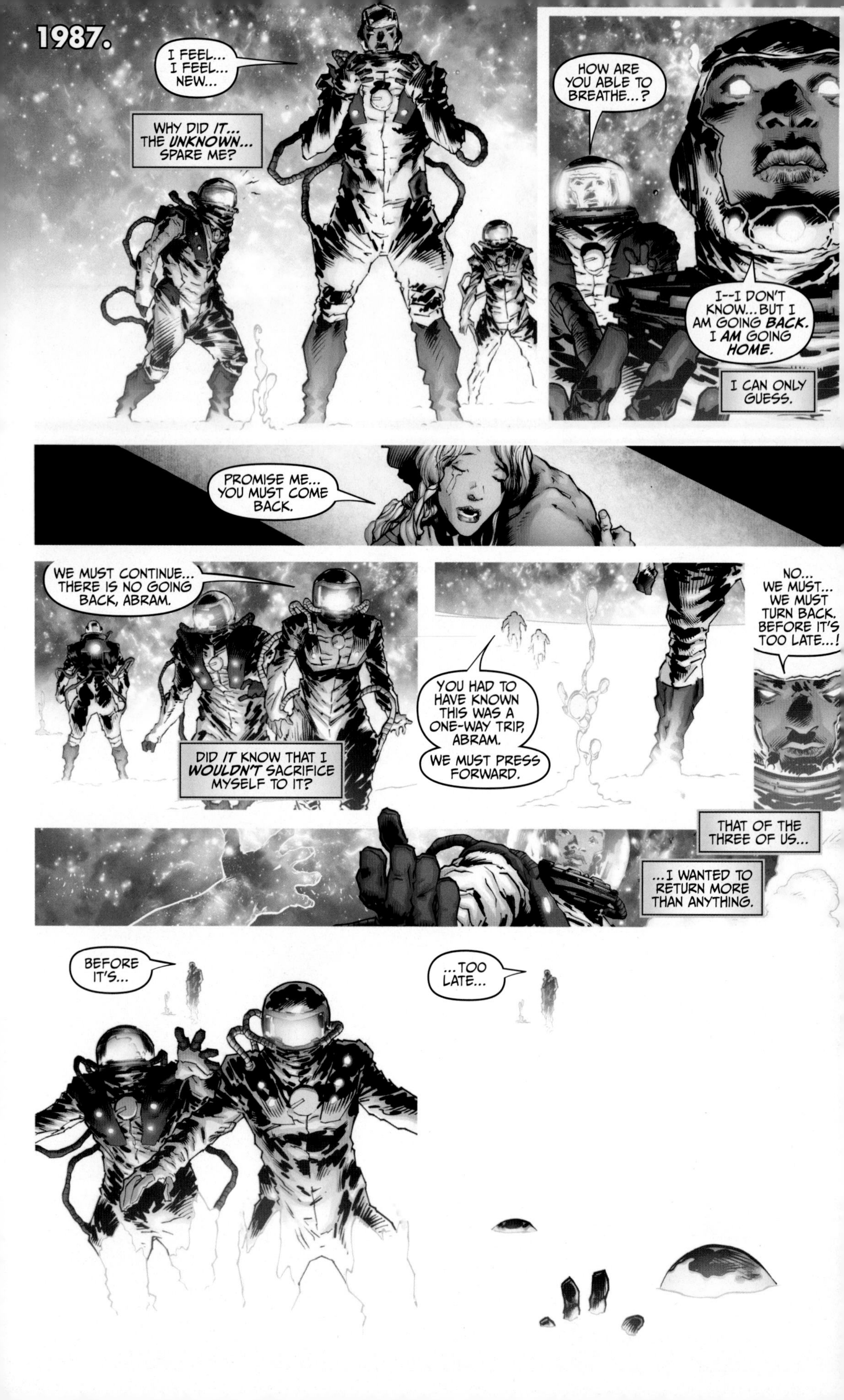
1987.
I FEEL... I FEEL... NEW...
WHY DID IT... THE UNKNOWN... SPARE ME?
HOW ARE YOU ABLE TO BREATHE...?
I--I DON'T KNOW... BUT I AM GOING BACK. I AM GOING HOME.
I CAN ONLY GUESS.
PROMISE ME... YOU MUST COME BACK.
WE MUST CONTINUE... THERE IS NO GOING BACK, ABRAM.
DID IT KNOW THAT I WOULDN'T SACRIFICE MYSELF TO IT?
YOU HAD TO HAVE KNOWN THIS WAS A ONE-WAY TRIP, ABRAM.
WE MUST PRESS FORWARD.
NO... WE MUST... WE MUST TURN BACK. BEFORE IT'S TOO LATE...!
THAT OF THE THREE OF US...
...I WANTED TO RETURN MORE THAN ANYTHING.
BEFORE IT'S...
...TOO LATE...

WAS I SIMPLY A VESSEL? A HOST FOR THE UNKNOWN? DID IT KNOW I WOULD BE THE ONE TO RETURN HOME?

WAS I ITS VEHICLE?

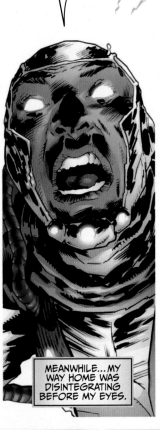

NO...!

MEANWHILE... MY WAY HOME WAS DISINTEGRATING BEFORE MY EYES.

I USED EVERY TOOL AND SCRAP TO REPAIR THE SHIP...

I WORKED WITH THE FERVOR OF A DESPERATE MAN.

BUT EVENTUALLY I REALIZED... I WAS A CHANGED MAN.

AND TO REPAIR THE SHIP...

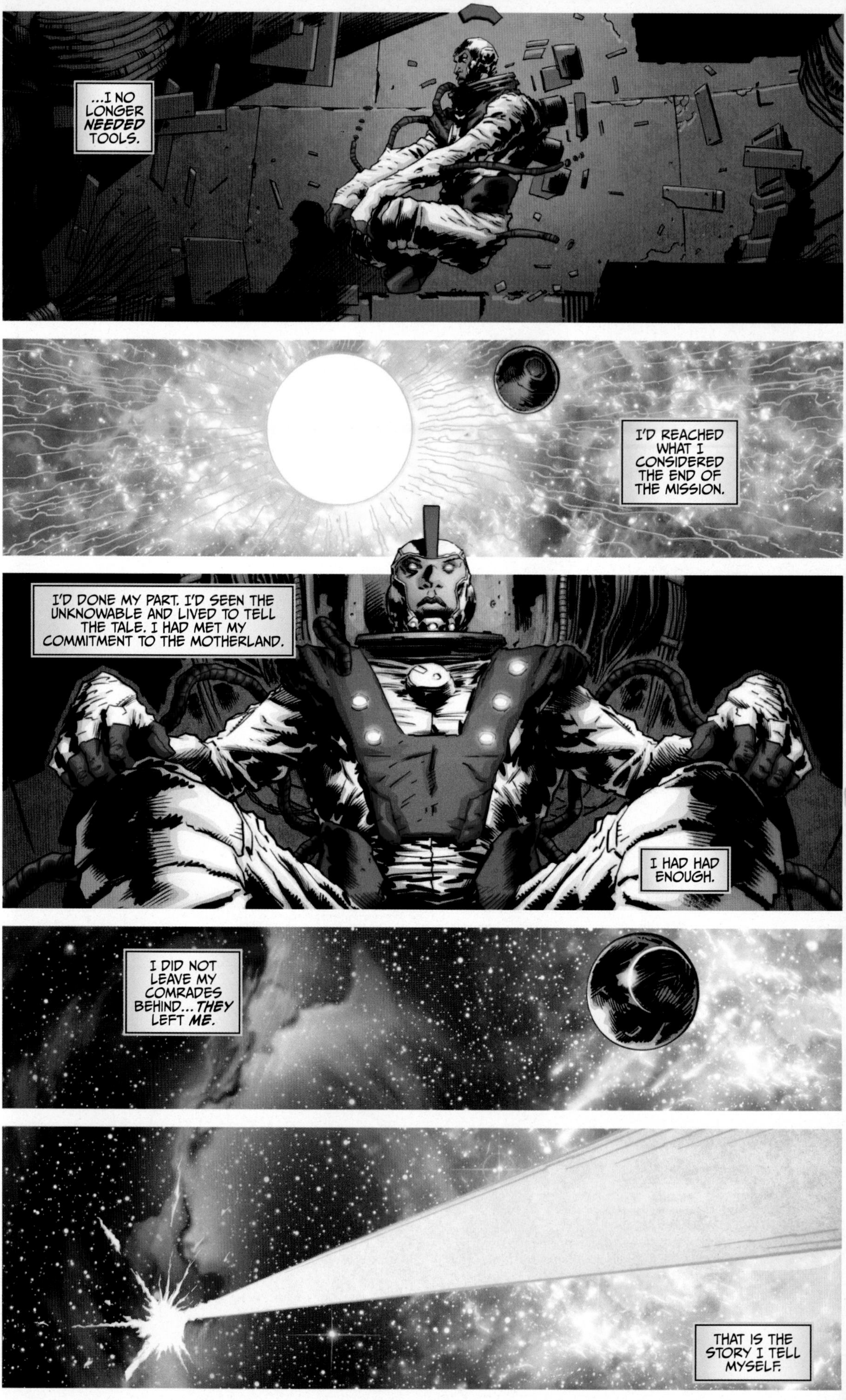
...I NO LONGER NEEDED TOOLS.
I'D REACHED WHAT I CONSIDERED THE END OF THE MISSION.
I'D DONE MY PART. I'D SEEN THE UNKNOWABLE AND LIVED TO TELL THE TALE. I HAD MET MY COMMITMENT TO THE MOTHERLAND.
I HAD HAD ENOUGH.
I DID NOT LEAVE MY COMRADES BEHIND... THEY LEFT ME.
THAT IS THE STORY I TELL MYSELF.

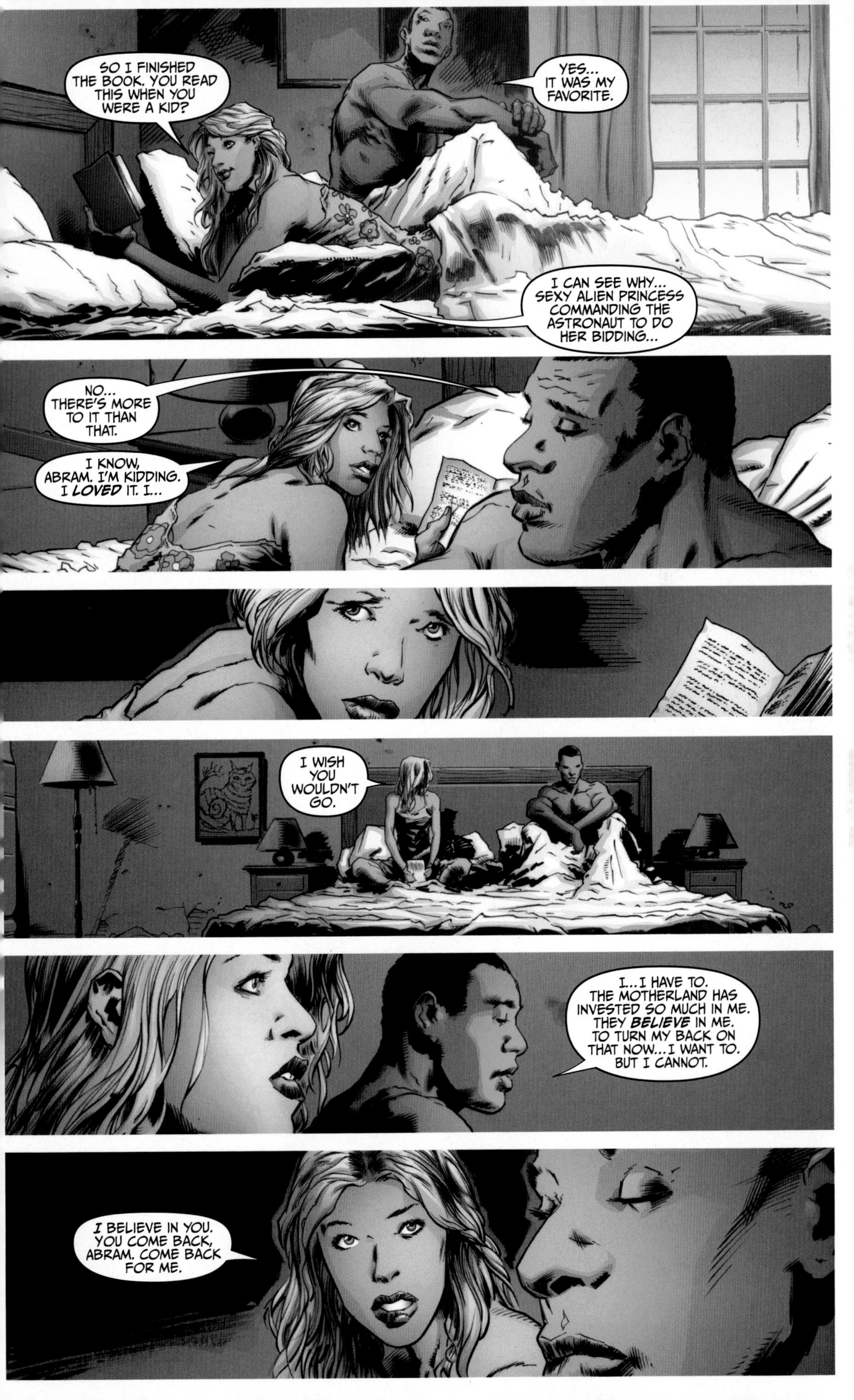

SO I FINISHED THE BOOK. YOU READ THIS WHEN YOU WERE A KID?
YES... IT WAS MY FAVORITE.
I CAN SEE WHY... SEXY ALIEN PRINCESS COMMANDING THE ASTRONAUT TO DO HER BIDDING...
NO... THERE'S MORE TO IT THAN THAT.
I KNOW, ABRAM. I'M KIDDING. I *LOVED* IT. I...
I WISH YOU WOULDN'T GO.
I...I HAVE TO. THE MOTHERLAND HAS INVESTED SO MUCH IN ME. THEY *BELIEVE* IN ME. TO TURN MY BACK ON THAT NOW...I WANT TO. BUT I CANNOT.
I BELIEVE IN YOU. YOU COME BACK, ABRAM. COME BACK FOR ME.

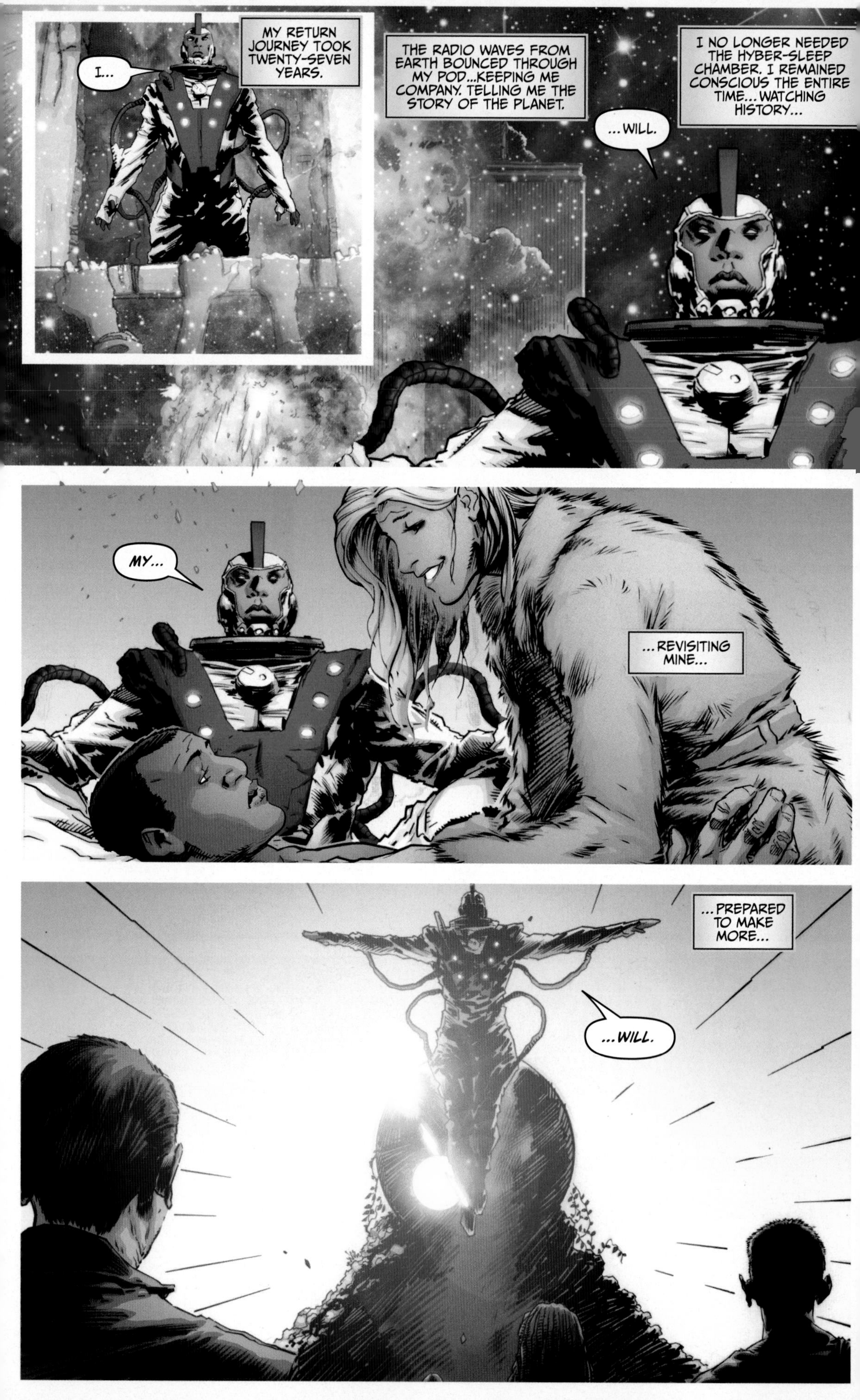
MY RETURN JOURNEY TOOK TWENTY-SEVEN YEARS.
I...
THE RADIO WAVES FROM EARTH BOUNCED THROUGH MY POD...KEEPING ME COMPANY. TELLING ME THE STORY OF THE PLANET.
I NO LONGER NEEDED THE HYBER-SLEEP CHAMBER. I REMAINED CONSCIOUS THE ENTIRE TIME...WATCHING HISTORY...
...WILL.
MY...
...REVISITING MINE...
...PREPARED TO MAKE MORE...
...WILL.

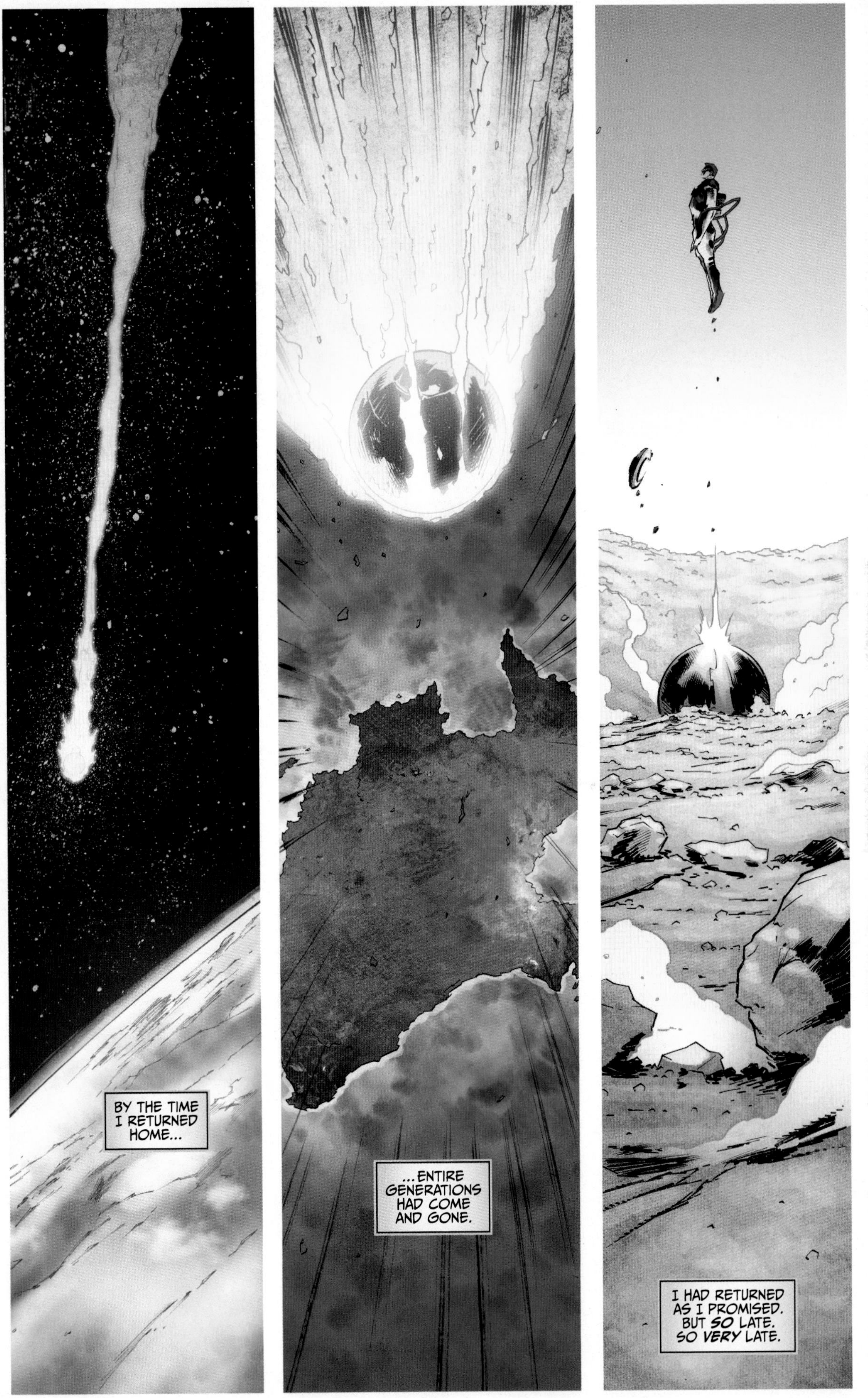
BY THE TIME I RETURNED HOME...
...ENTIRE GENERATIONS HAD COME AND GONE.
I HAD RETURNED AS I PROMISED. BUT SO LATE. SO VERY LATE.

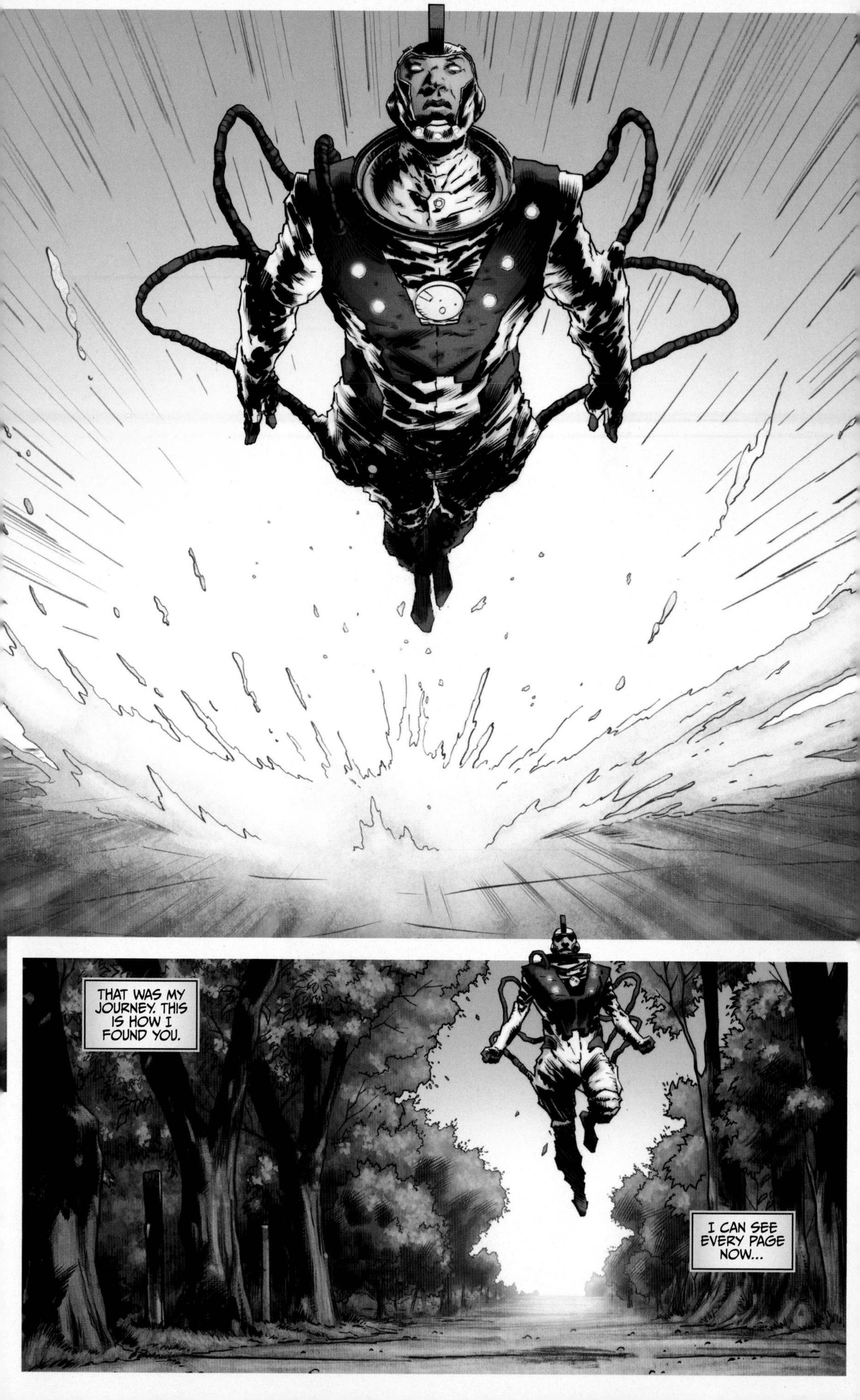
THAT WAS MY JOURNEY. THIS IS HOW I FOUND YOU.
I CAN SEE EVERY PAGE NOW...

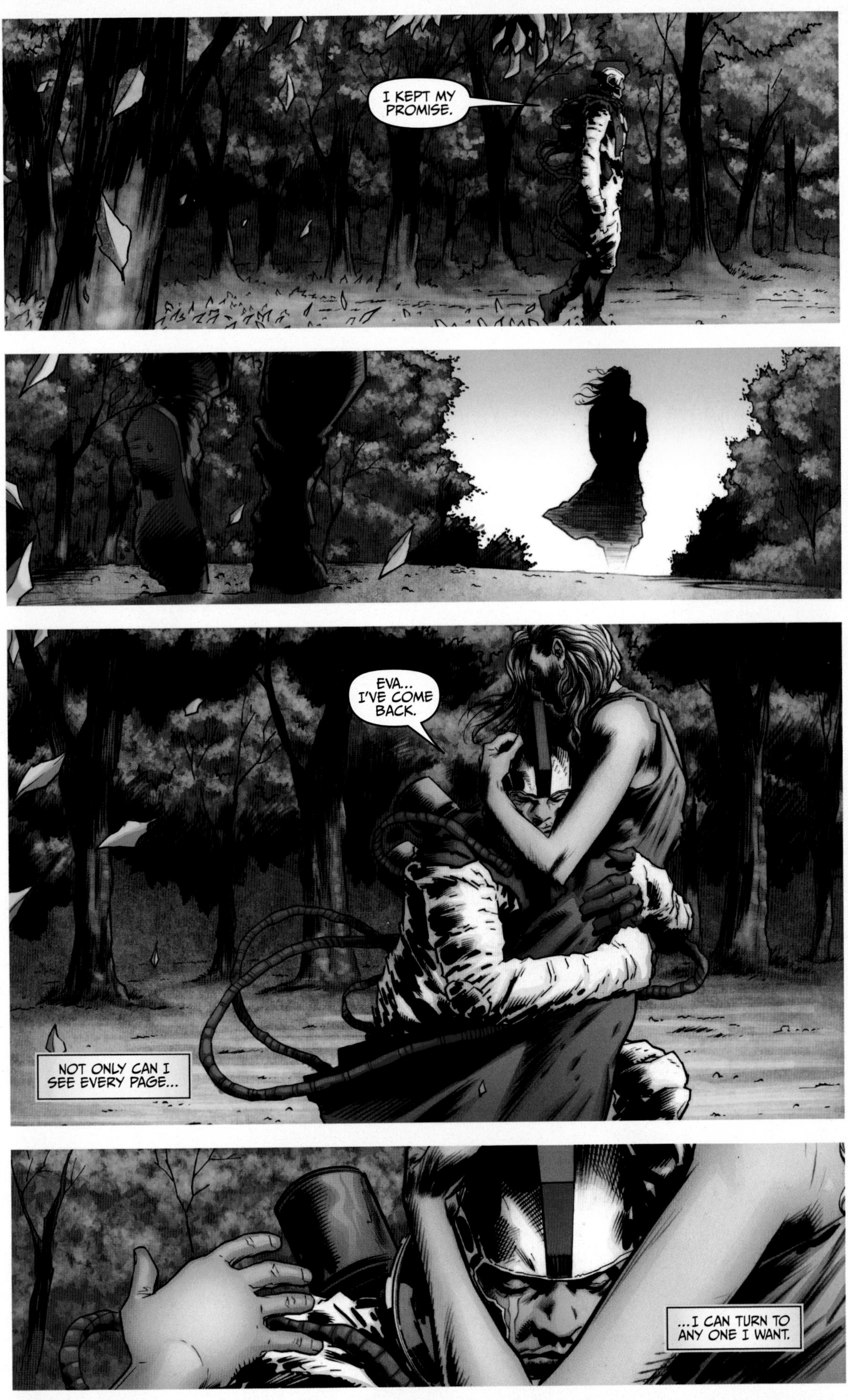
I KEPT MY PROMISE.
EVA... I'VE COME BACK.
NOT ONLY CAN I SEE EVERY PAGE...
...I CAN TURN TO ANY ONE I WANT.

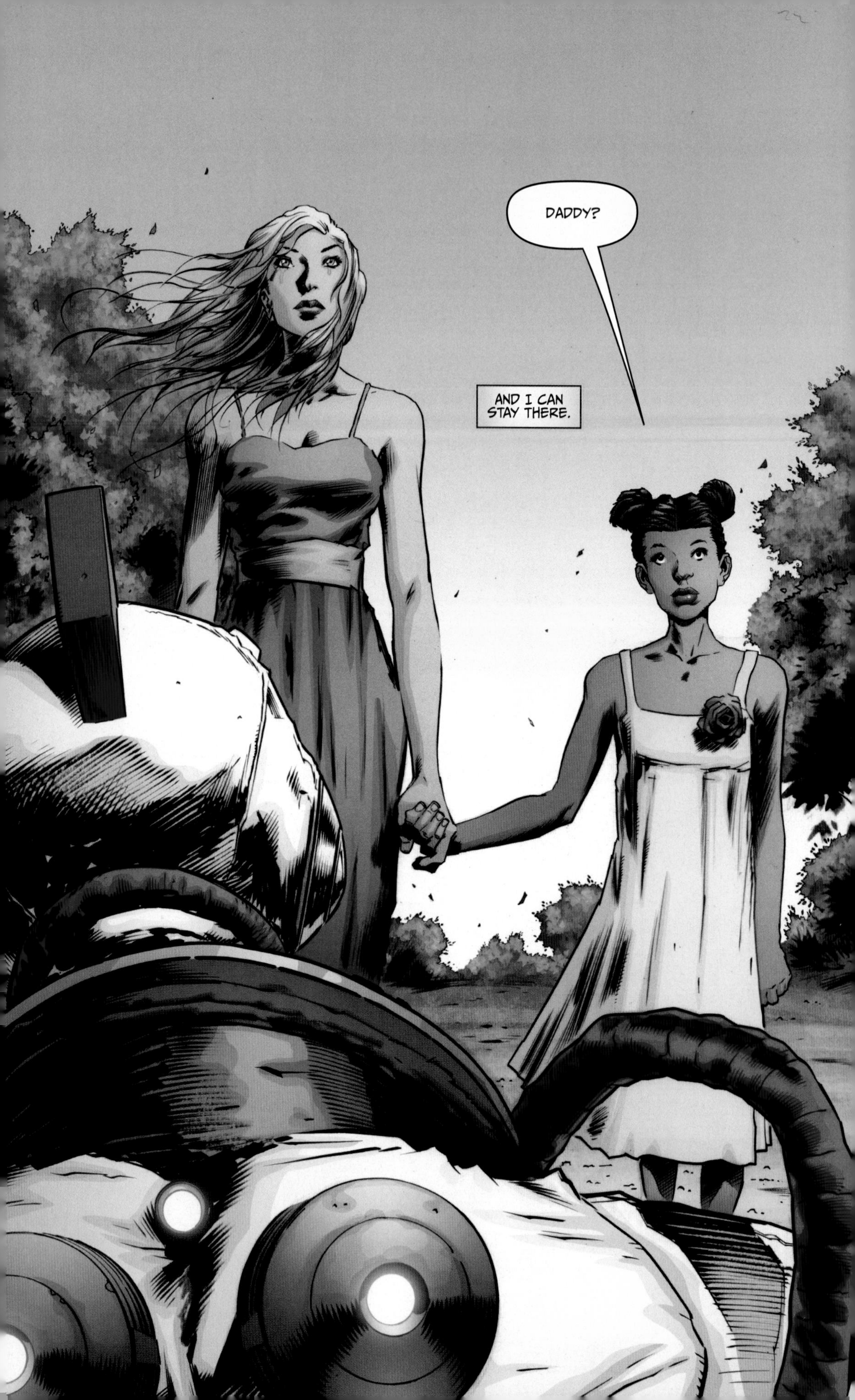
DADDY?
AND I CAN STAY THERE.

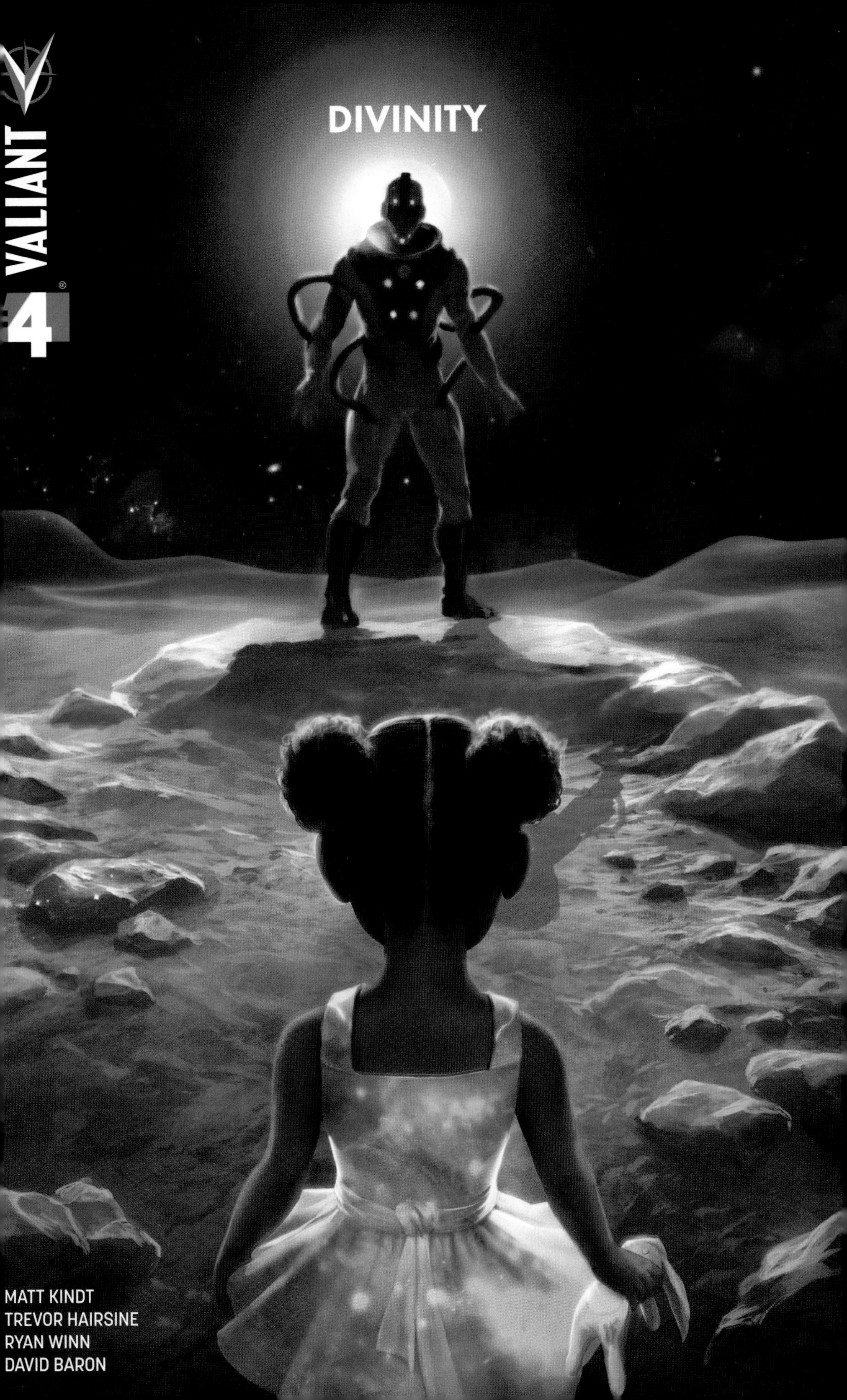
VALIANT
#4
DIVINITY
MATT KINDT
TREVOR HAIRSINE
RYAN WINN
DAVID BARON

BOOK FOUR

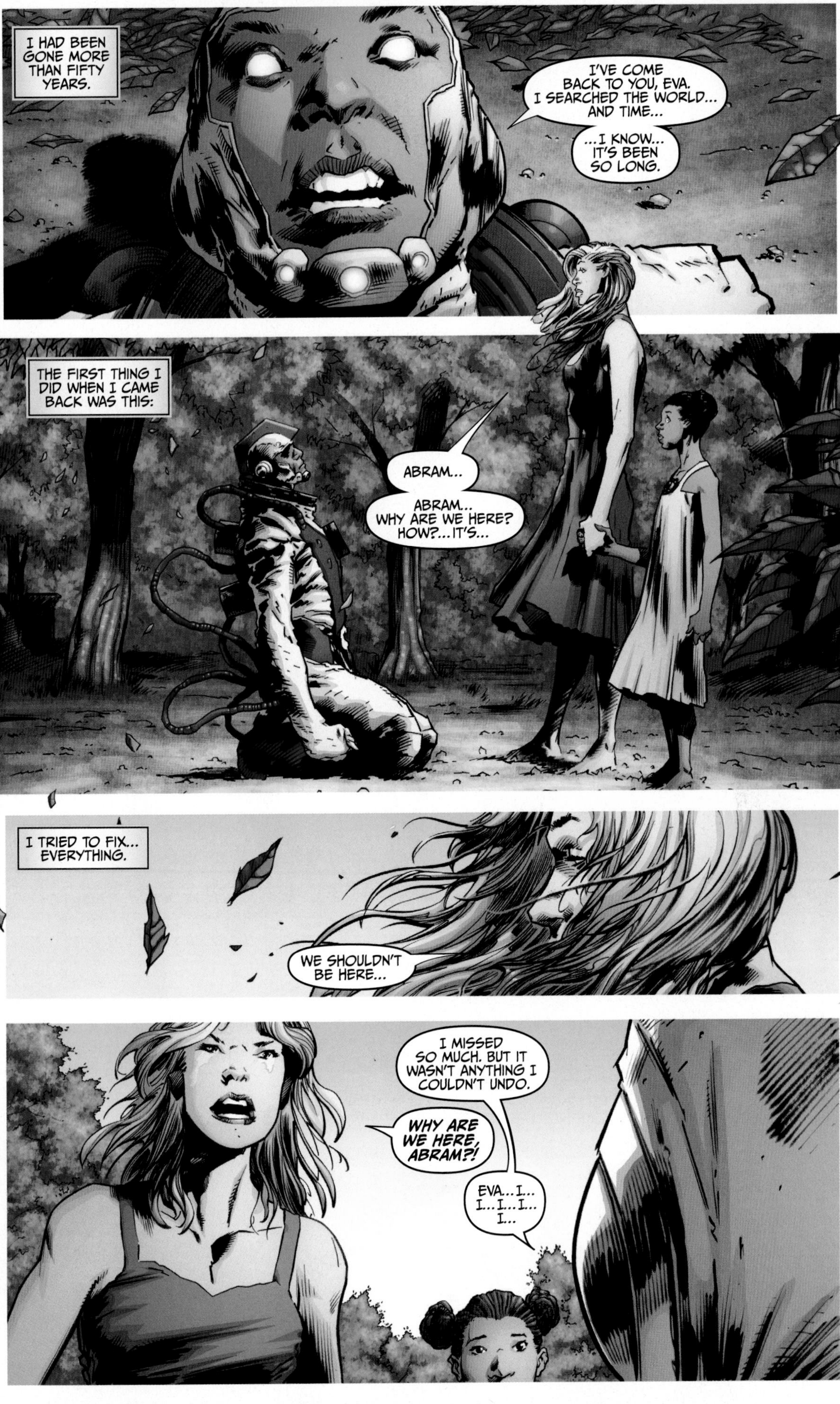
I HAD BEEN GONE MORE THAN FIFTY YEARS.
I'VE COME BACK TO YOU, EVA. I SEARCHED THE WORLD... AND TIME...
...I KNOW... IT'S BEEN SO LONG.
THE FIRST THING I DID WHEN I CAME BACK WAS THIS:
ABRAM...
ABRAM... WHY ARE WE HERE? HOW?... IT'S...
I TRIED TO FIX... EVERYTHING.
WE SHOULDN'T BE HERE...
I MISSED SO MUCH. BUT IT WASN'T ANYTHING I COULDN'T UNDO.
WHY ARE WE HERE, ABRAM?!
EVA... I... I... I... I... I...

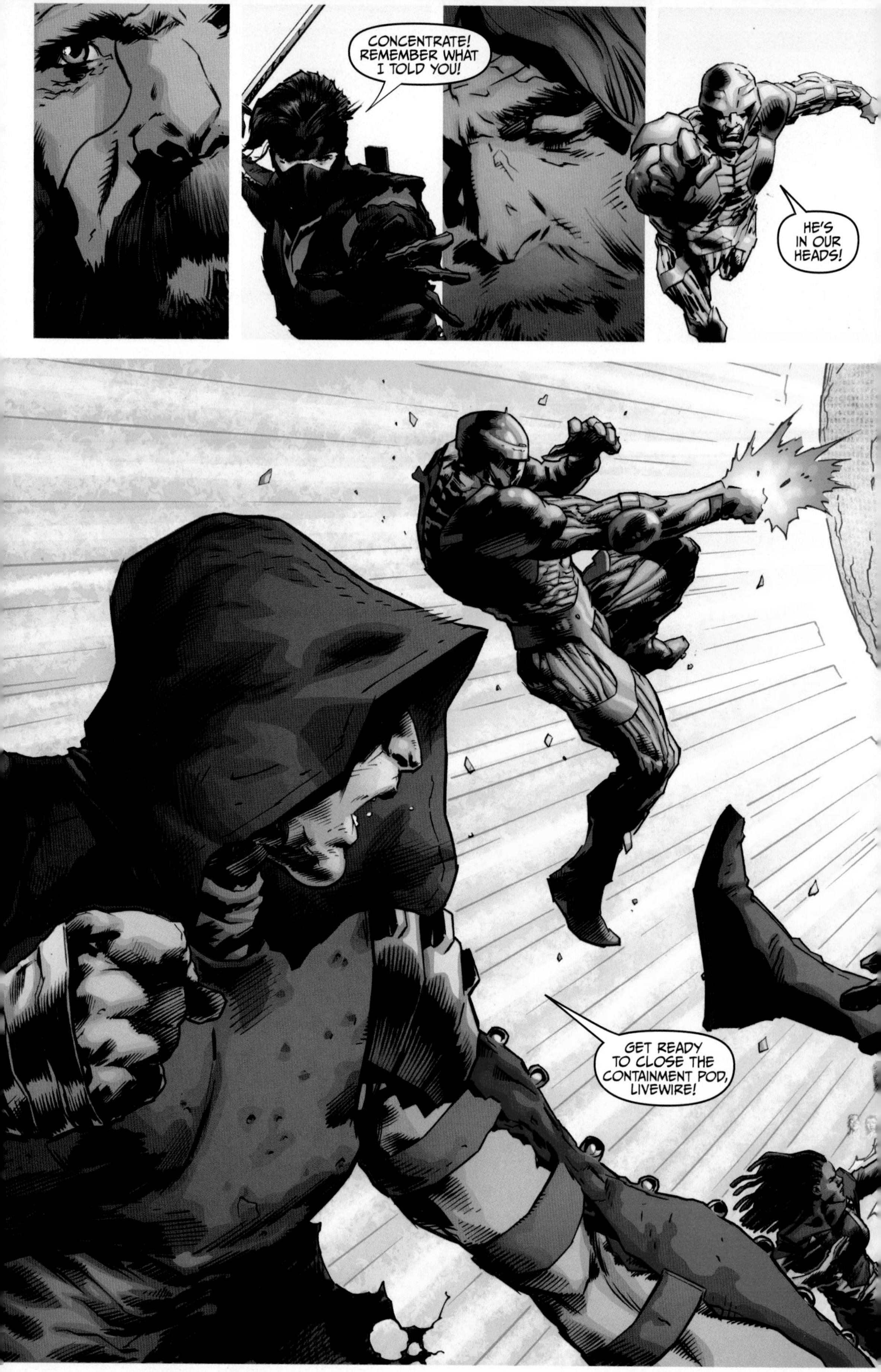
CONCENTRATE! REMEMBER WHAT I TOLD YOU!
HE'S IN OUR HEADS!
GET READY TO CLOSE THE CONTAINMENT POD, LIVEWIRE!

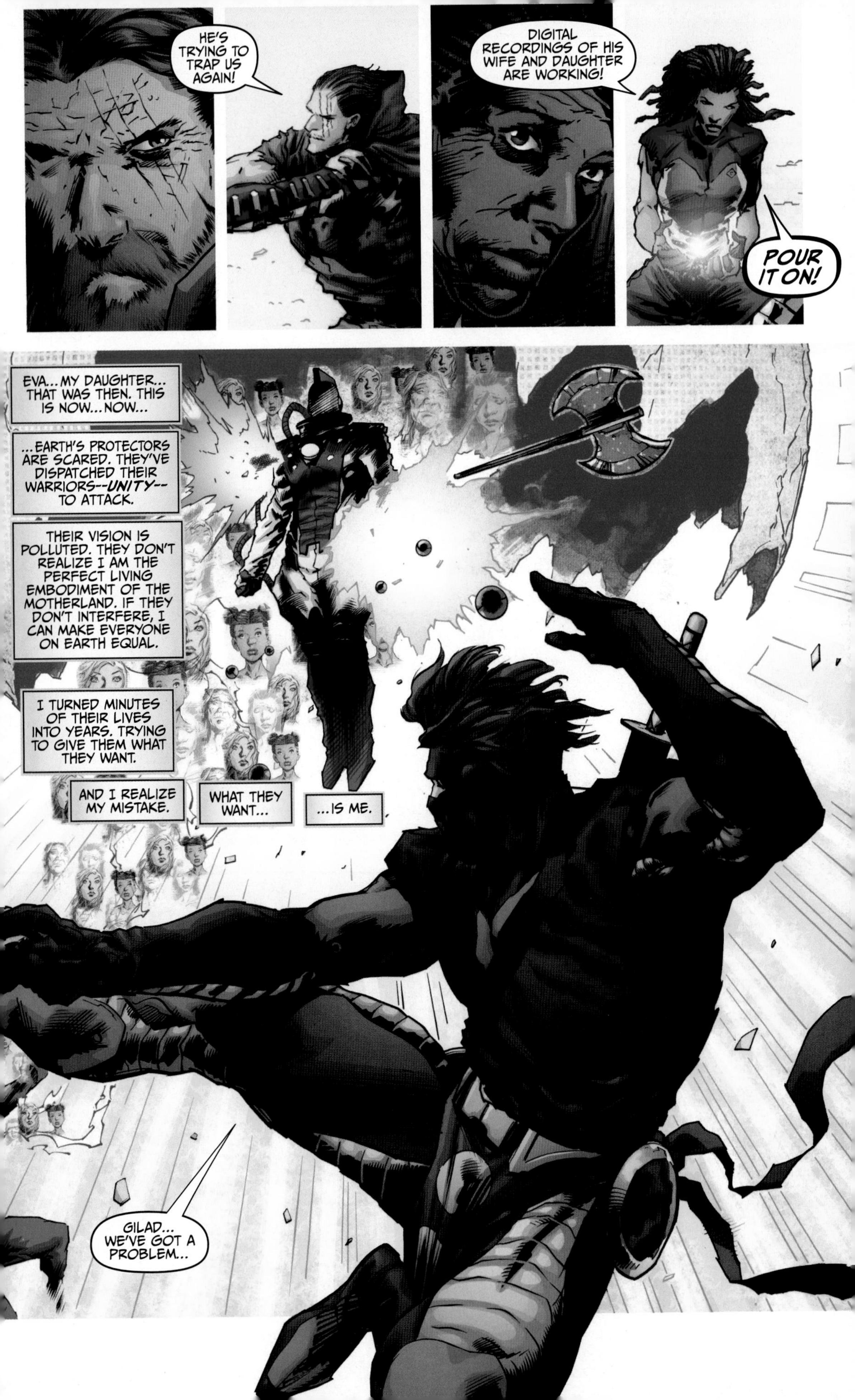
HE'S TRYING TO TRAP US AGAIN!
DIGITAL RECORDINGS OF HIS WIFE AND DAUGHTER ARE WORKING!
POUR IT ON!
EVA... MY DAUGHTER... THAT WAS THEN. THIS IS NOW... NOW...
...EARTH'S PROTECTORS ARE SCARED. THEY'VE DISPATCHED THEIR WARRIORS--UNITY--TO ATTACK.
THEIR VISION IS POLLUTED. THEY DON'T REALIZE I AM THE PERFECT LIVING EMBODIMENT OF THE MOTHERLAND. IF THEY DON'T INTERFERE, I CAN MAKE EVERYONE ON EARTH EQUAL.
I TURNED MINUTES OF THEIR LIVES INTO YEARS. TRYING TO GIVE THEM WHAT THEY WANT.
AND I REALIZE MY MISTAKE.
WHAT THEY WANT...
...IS ME.
GILAD... WE'VE GOT A PROBLEM...

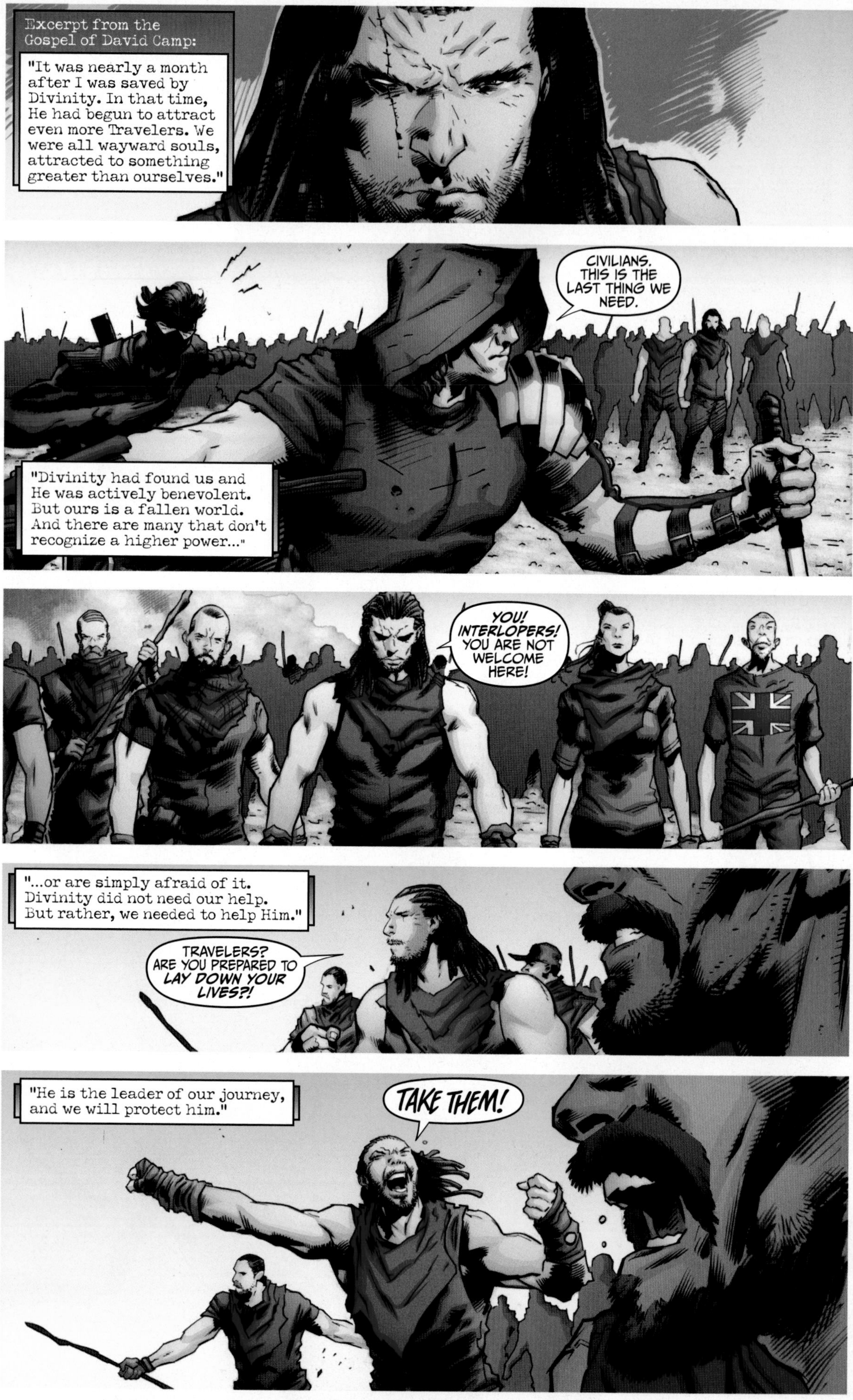
Excerpt from the Gospel of David Camp:
"It was nearly a month after I was saved by Divinity. In that time, He had begun to attract even more Travelers. We were all wayward souls, attracted to something greater than ourselves."
CIVILIANS. THIS IS THE LAST THING WE NEED.
"Divinity had found us and He was actively benevolent. But ours is a fallen world. And there are many that don't recognize a higher power..."
YOU! INTERLOPERS! YOU ARE NOT WELCOME HERE!
"...or are simply afraid of it. Divinity did not need our help. But rather, we needed to help Him."
TRAVELERS? ARE YOU PREPARED TO LAY DOWN YOUR LIVES?!
"He is the leader of our journey, and we will protect him."
TAKE THEM!

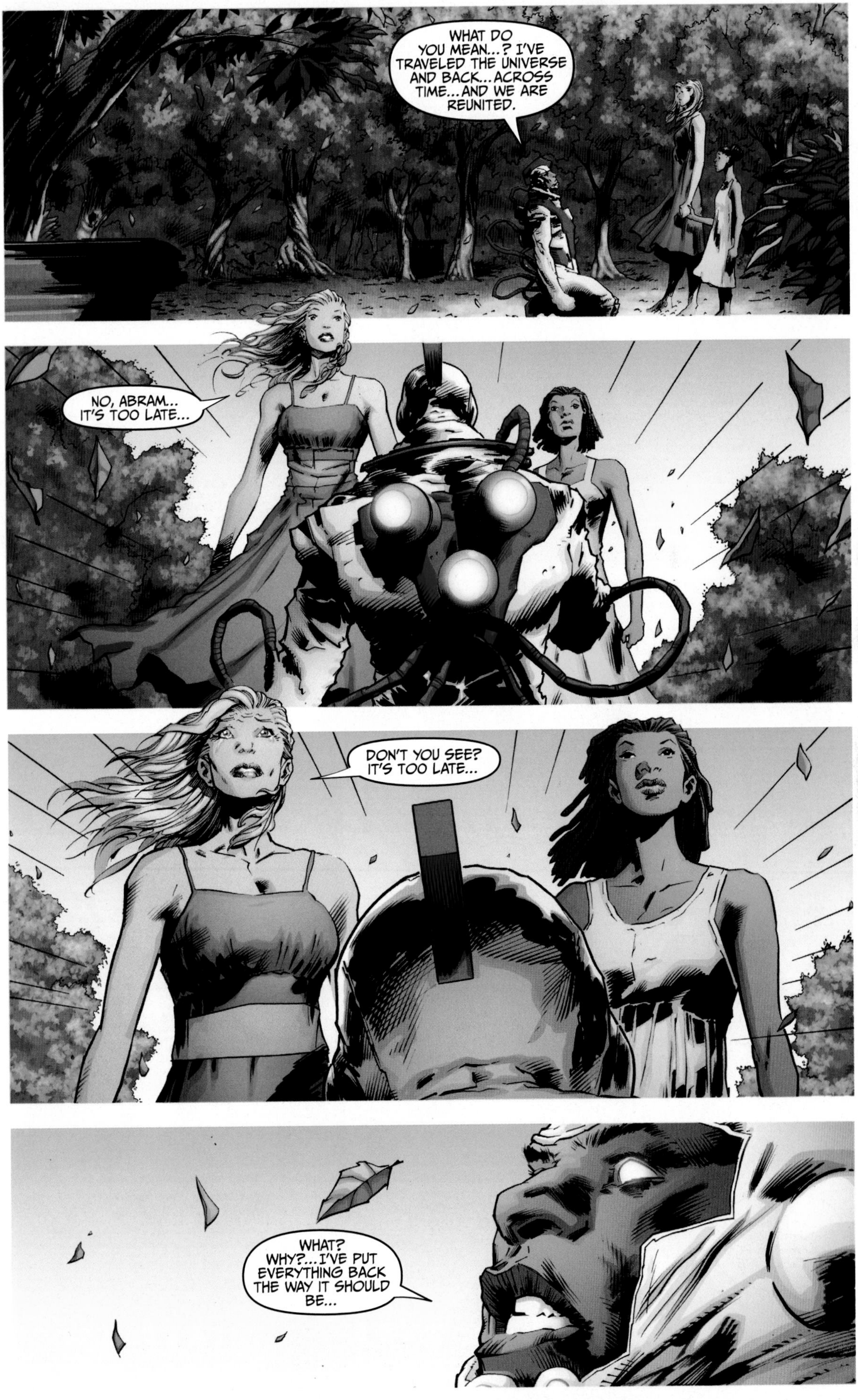
WHAT DO YOU MEAN...? I'VE TRAVELED THE UNIVERSE AND BACK...ACROSS TIME...AND WE ARE REUNITED.
NO, ABRAM... IT'S TOO LATE...
DON'T YOU SEE? IT'S TOO LATE...
WHAT? WHY?...I'VE PUT EVERYTHING BACK THE WAY IT SHOULD BE...

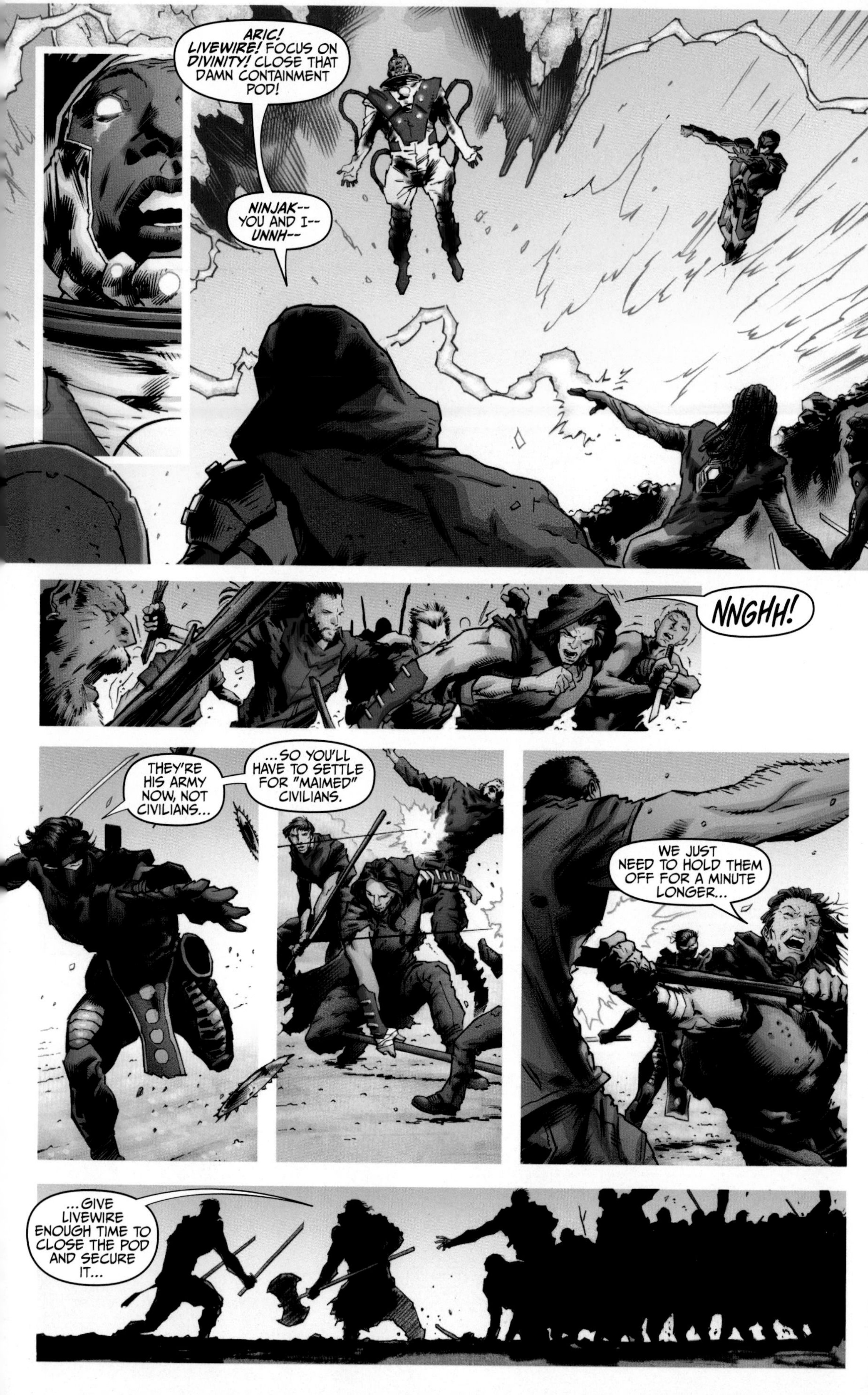
ARIC! LIVEWIRE! FOCUS ON DIVINITY! CLOSE THAT DAMN CONTAINMENT POD!
NINJAK-- YOU AND I-- UNNH--
NNGHH!
THEY'RE HIS ARMY NOW, NOT CIVILIANS...
...SO YOU'LL HAVE TO SETTLE FOR "MAIMED" CIVILIANS.
WE JUST NEED TO HOLD THEM OFF FOR A MINUTE LONGER...
...GIVE LIVEWIRE ENOUGH TIME TO CLOSE THE POD AND SECURE IT...

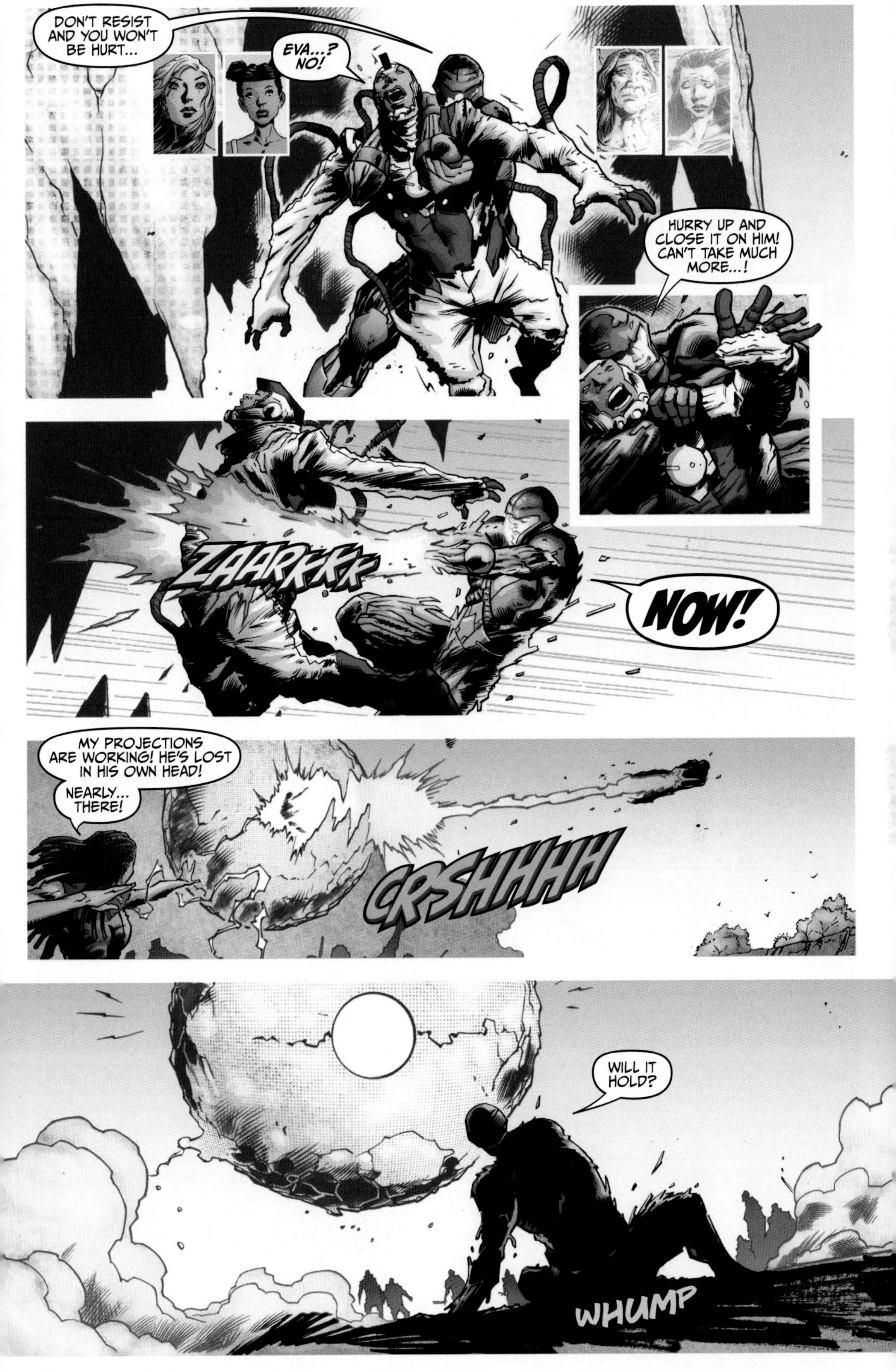
DON'T RESIST AND YOU WON'T BE HURT...
EVA...? NO!
HURRY UP AND CLOSE IT ON HIM! CAN'T TAKE MUCH MORE...!
ZAARKKR
NOW!
MY PROJECTIONS ARE WORKING! HE'S LOST IN HIS OWN HEAD!
NEARLY... THERE!
CRSHHHH
WILL IT HOLD?
WHUMP

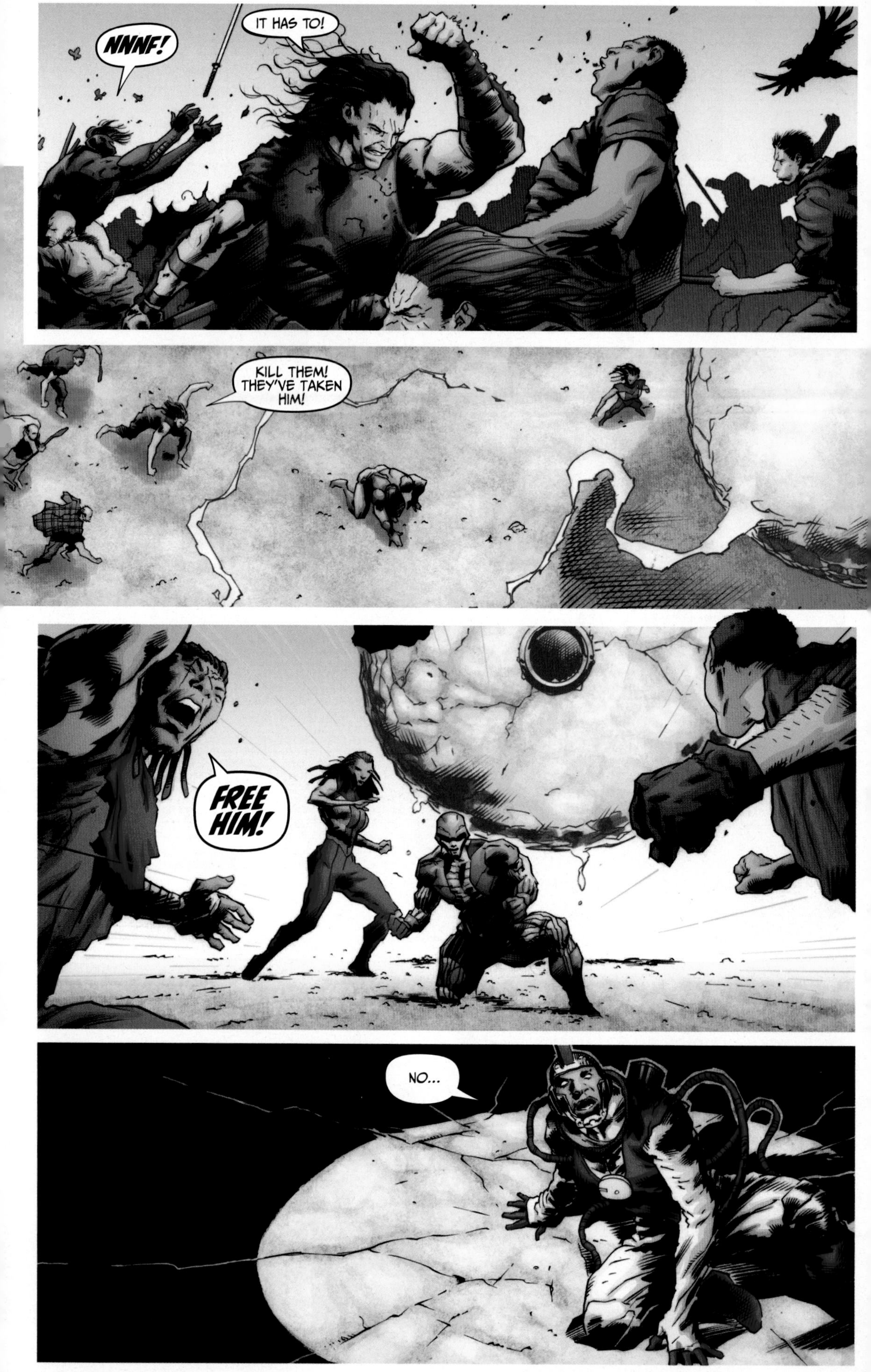
NNNF!
IT HAS TO!
KILL THEM! THEY'VE TAKEN HIM!
FREE HIM!
NO...

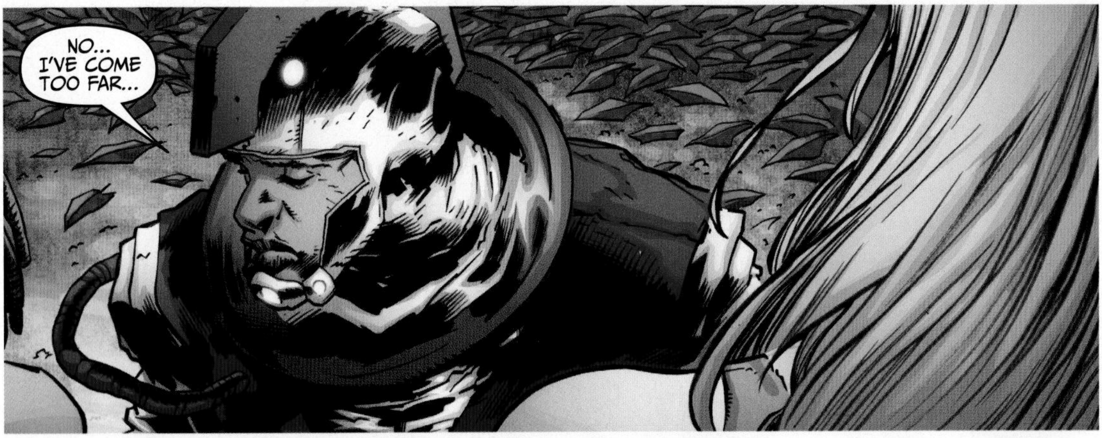
NO... I'VE COME TOO FAR...

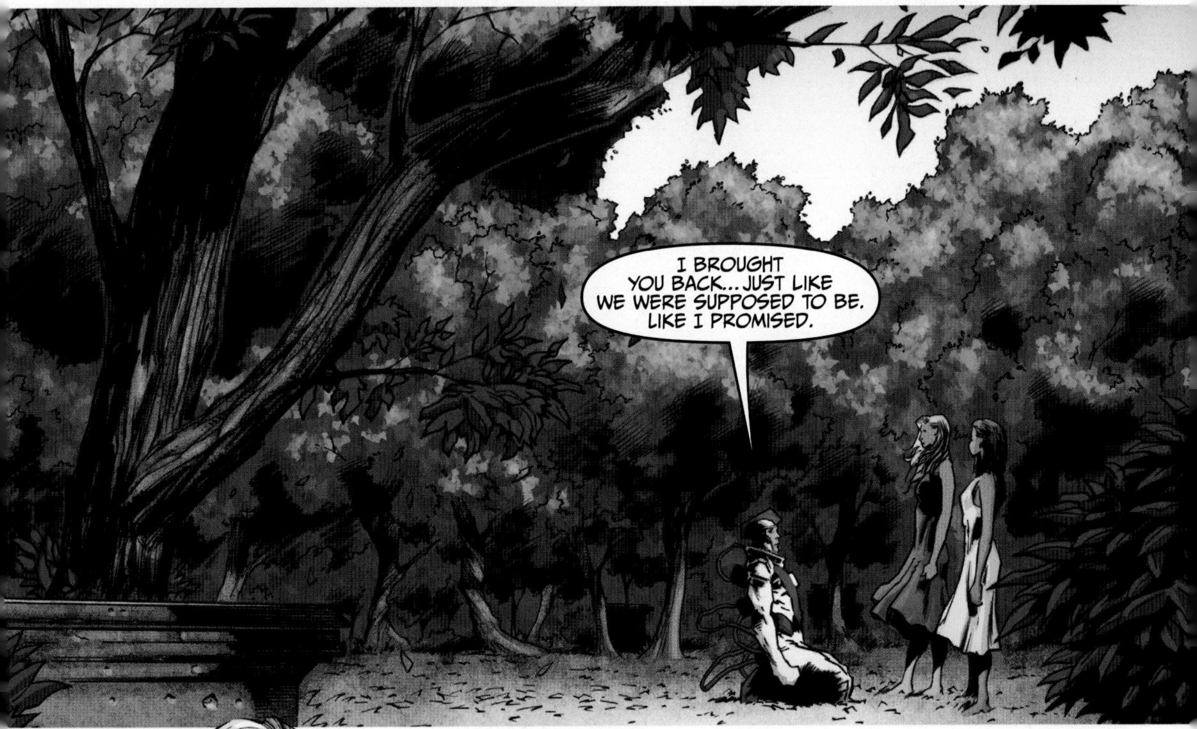
I BROUGHT YOU BACK... JUST LIKE WE WERE SUPPOSED TO BE. LIKE I PROMISED.

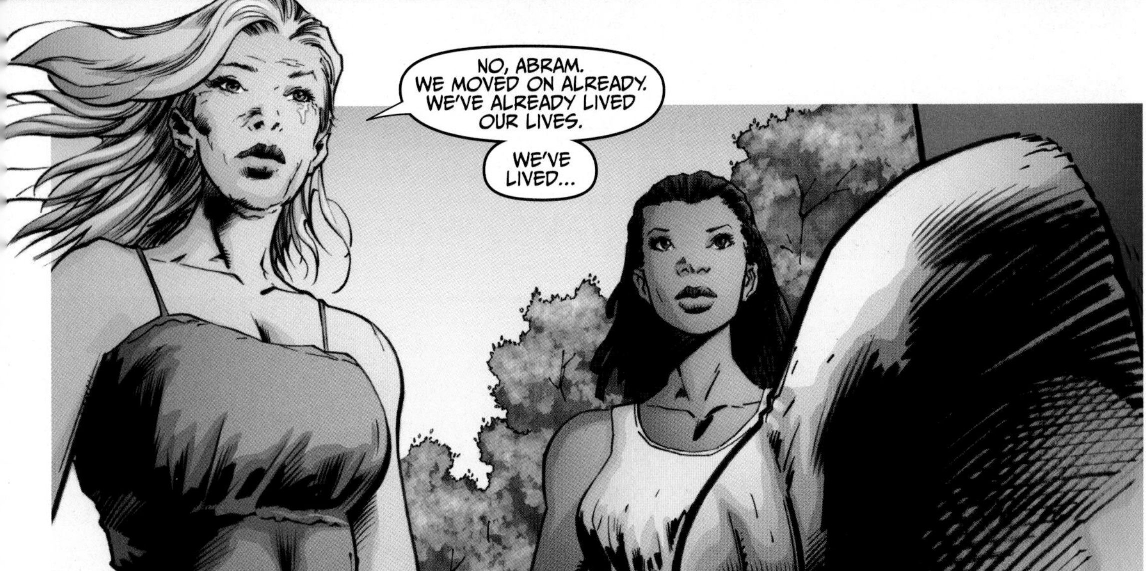
NO, ABRAM. WE MOVED ON ALREADY. WE'VE ALREADY LIVED OUR LIVES.
WE'VE LIVED...

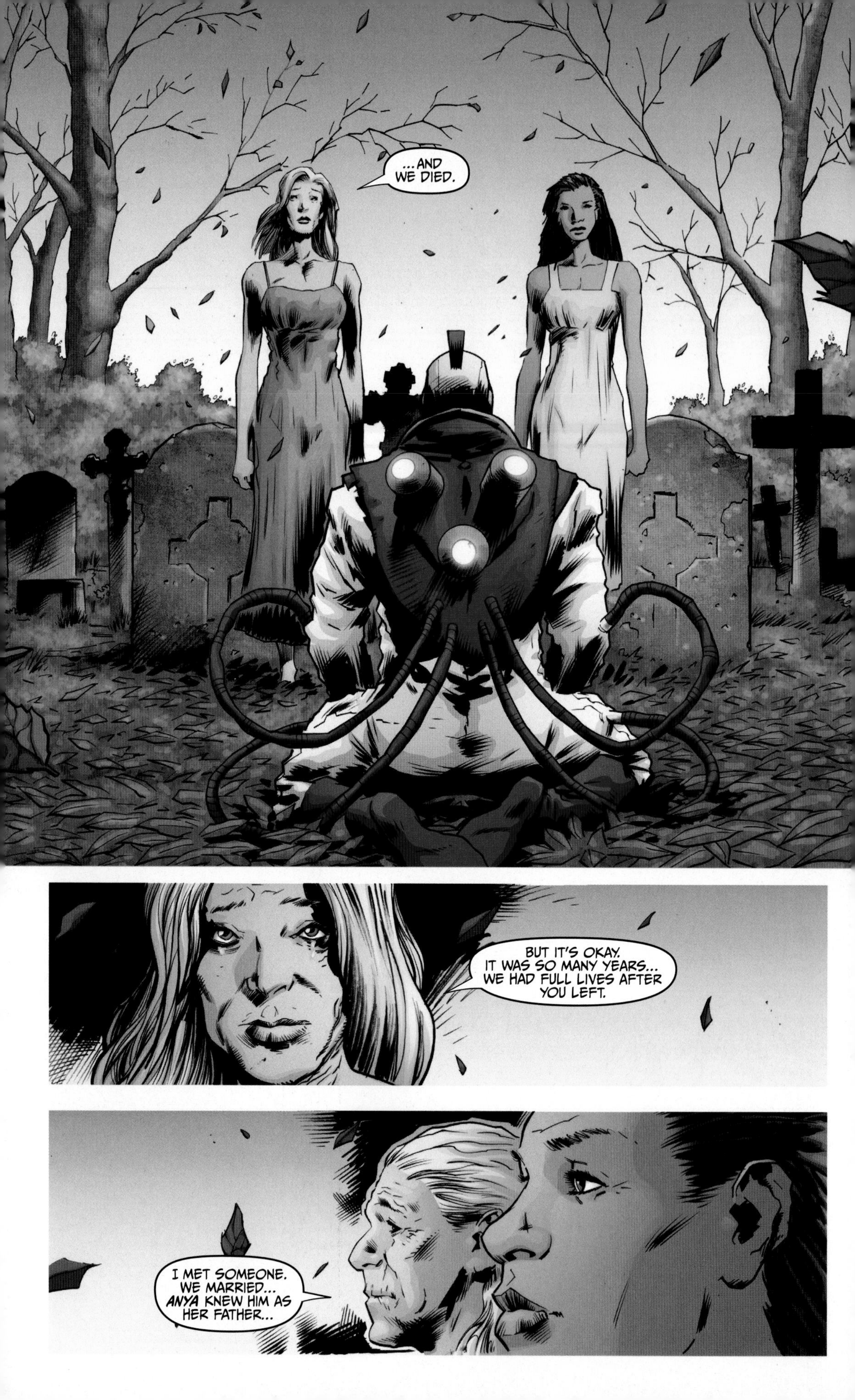
...AND WE DIED.
BUT IT'S OKAY. IT WAS SO MANY YEARS... WE HAD FULL LIVES AFTER YOU LEFT.
I MET SOMEONE. WE MARRIED... ANYA KNEW HIM AS HER FATHER...

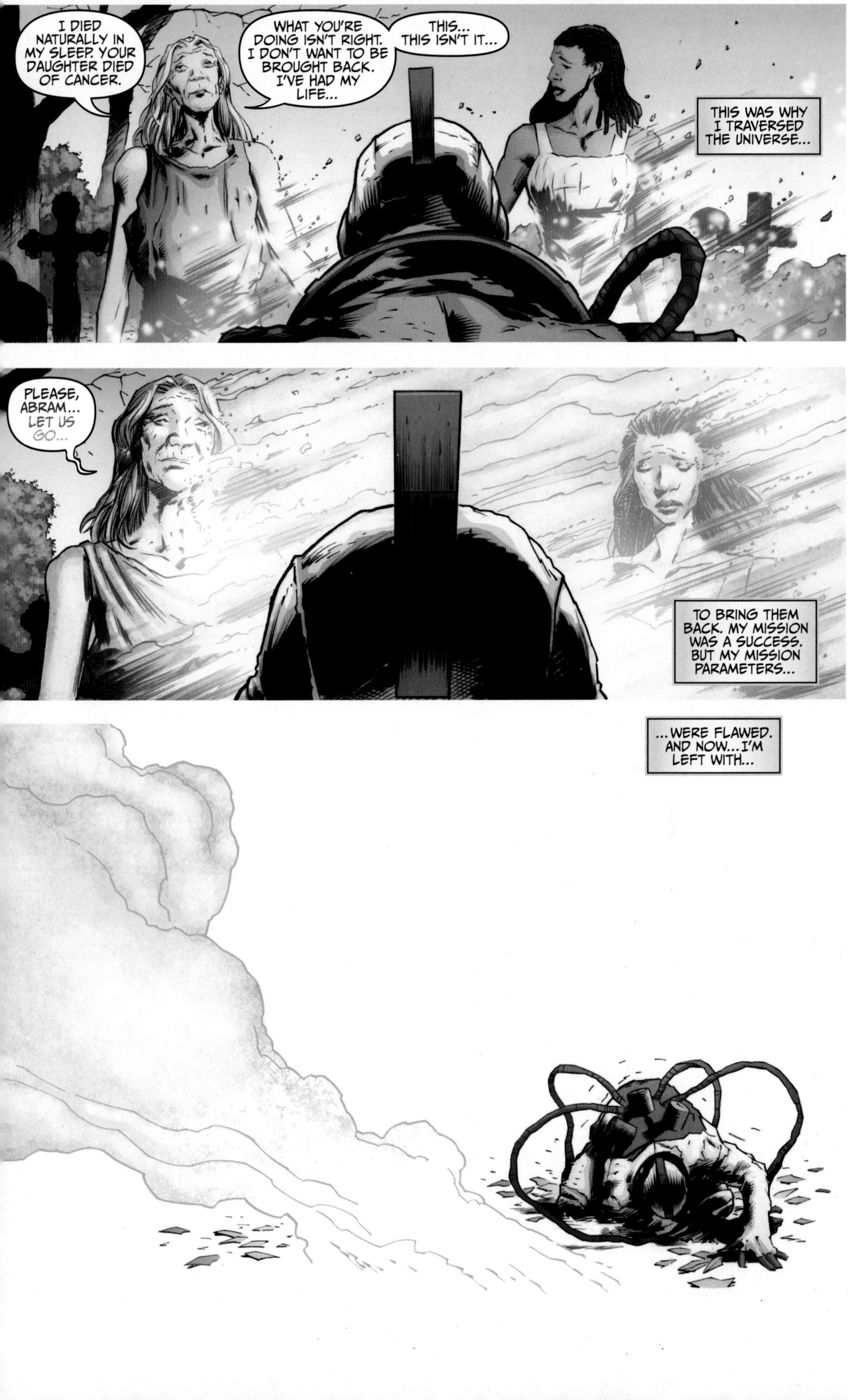
I DIED NATURALLY IN MY SLEEP. YOUR DAUGHTER DIED OF CANCER.
WHAT YOU'RE DOING ISN'T RIGHT. I DON'T WANT TO BE BROUGHT BACK. I'VE HAD MY LIFE...
THIS... THIS ISN'T IT...
THIS WAS WHY I TRAVERSED THE UNIVERSE...
PLEASE, ABRAM... LET US GO...
TO BRING THEM BACK. MY MISSION WAS A SUCCESS. BUT MY MISSION PARAMETERS...
...WERE FLAWED. AND NOW...I'M LEFT WITH...

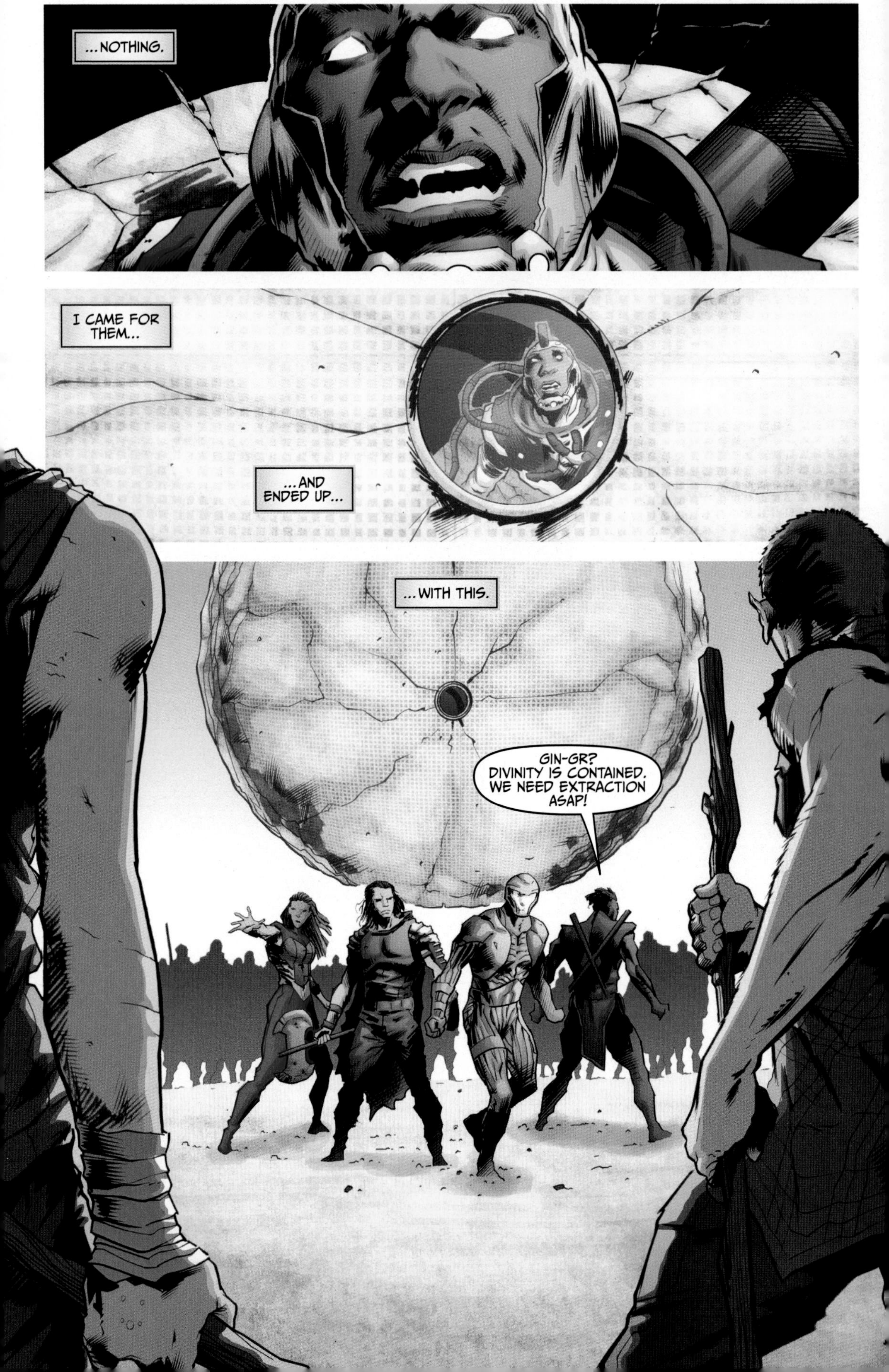
...NOTHING.
I CAME FOR THEM...
...AND ENDED UP...
...WITH THIS.
GIN-GR? DIVINITY IS CONTAINED. WE NEED EXTRACTION ASAP!

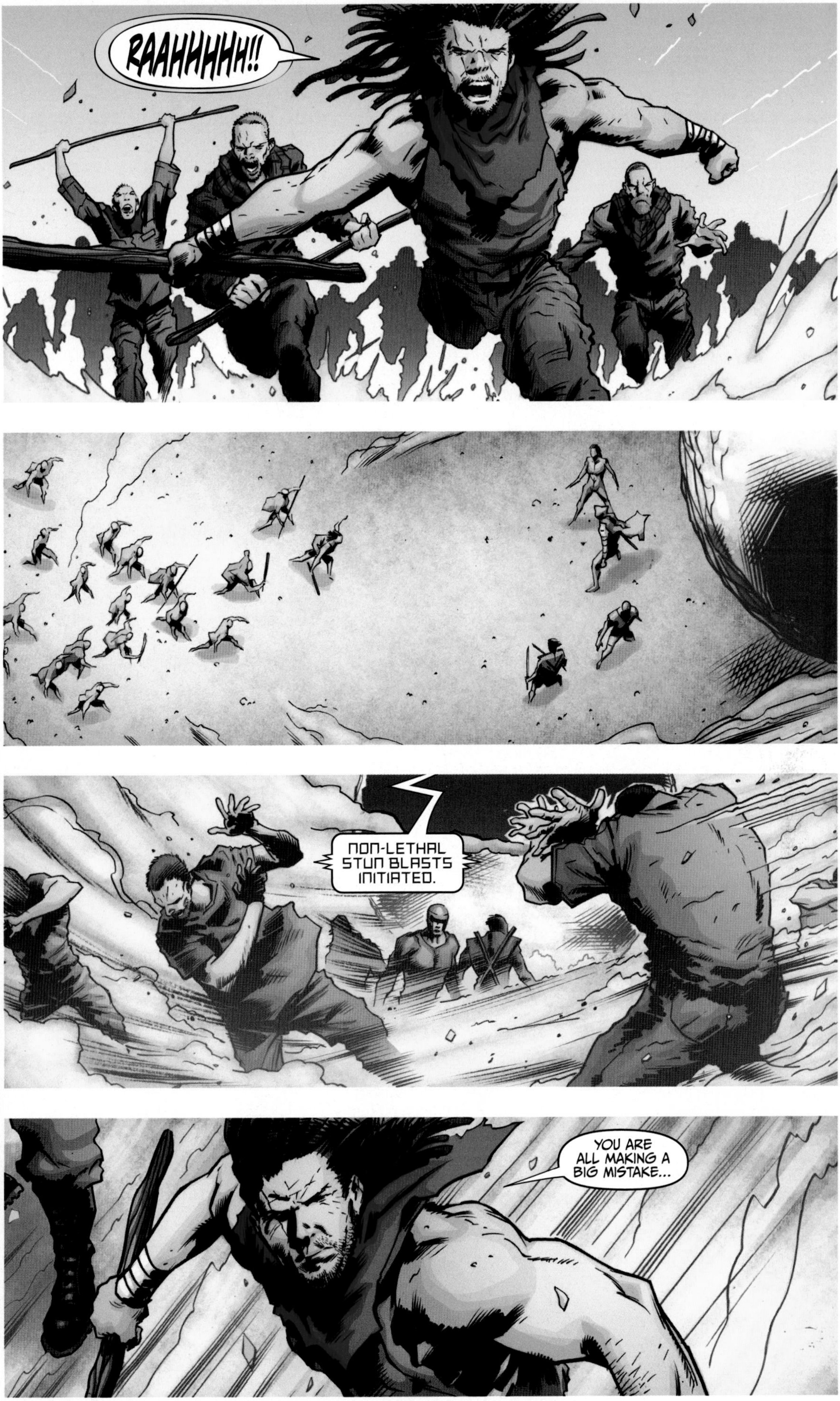
RAAHHHHH!!
NON-LETHAL STUN BLASTS INITIATED.
YOU ARE ALL MAKING A BIG MISTAKE...

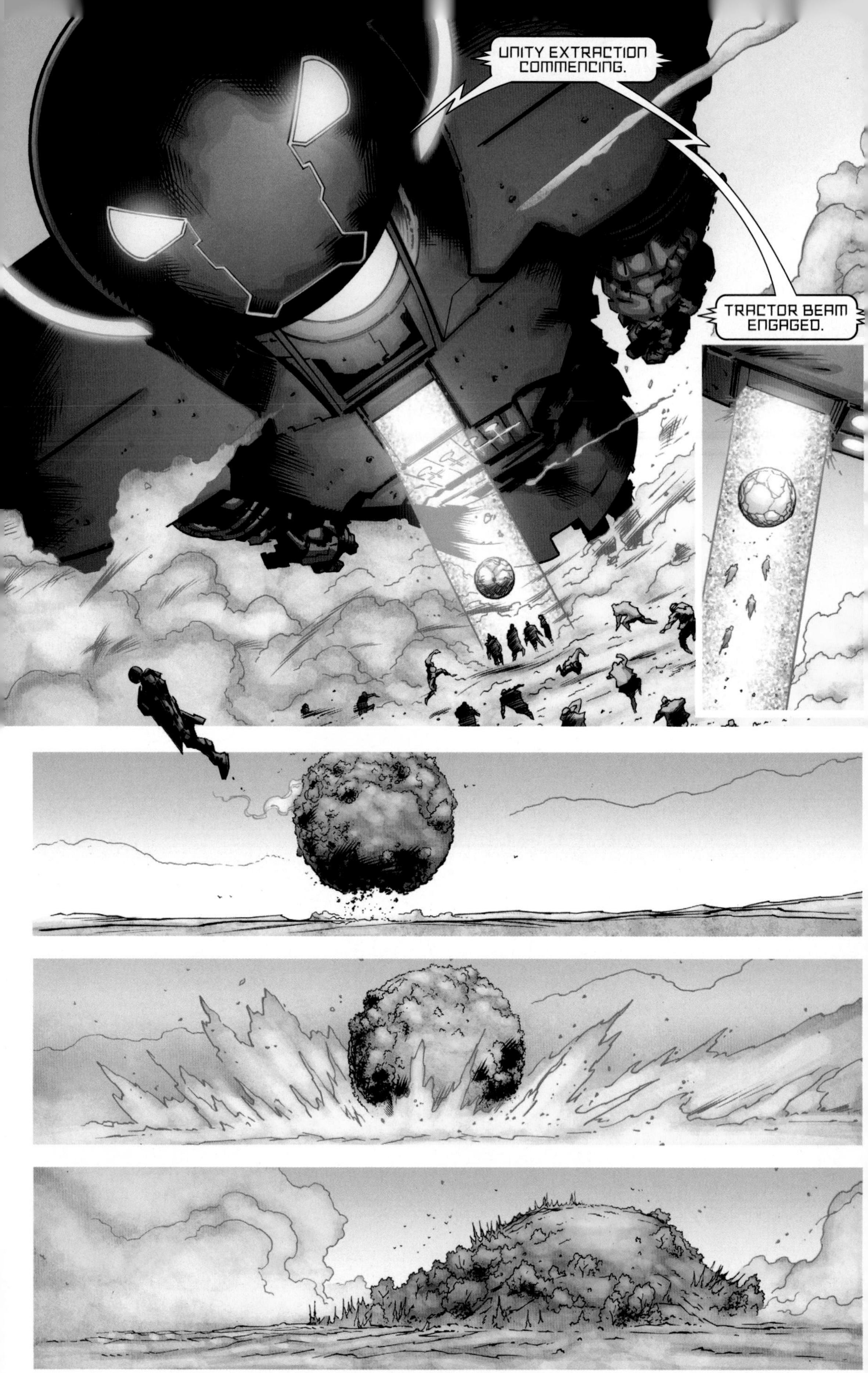
UNITY EXTRACTION COMMENCING.
TRACTOR BEAM ENGAGED.

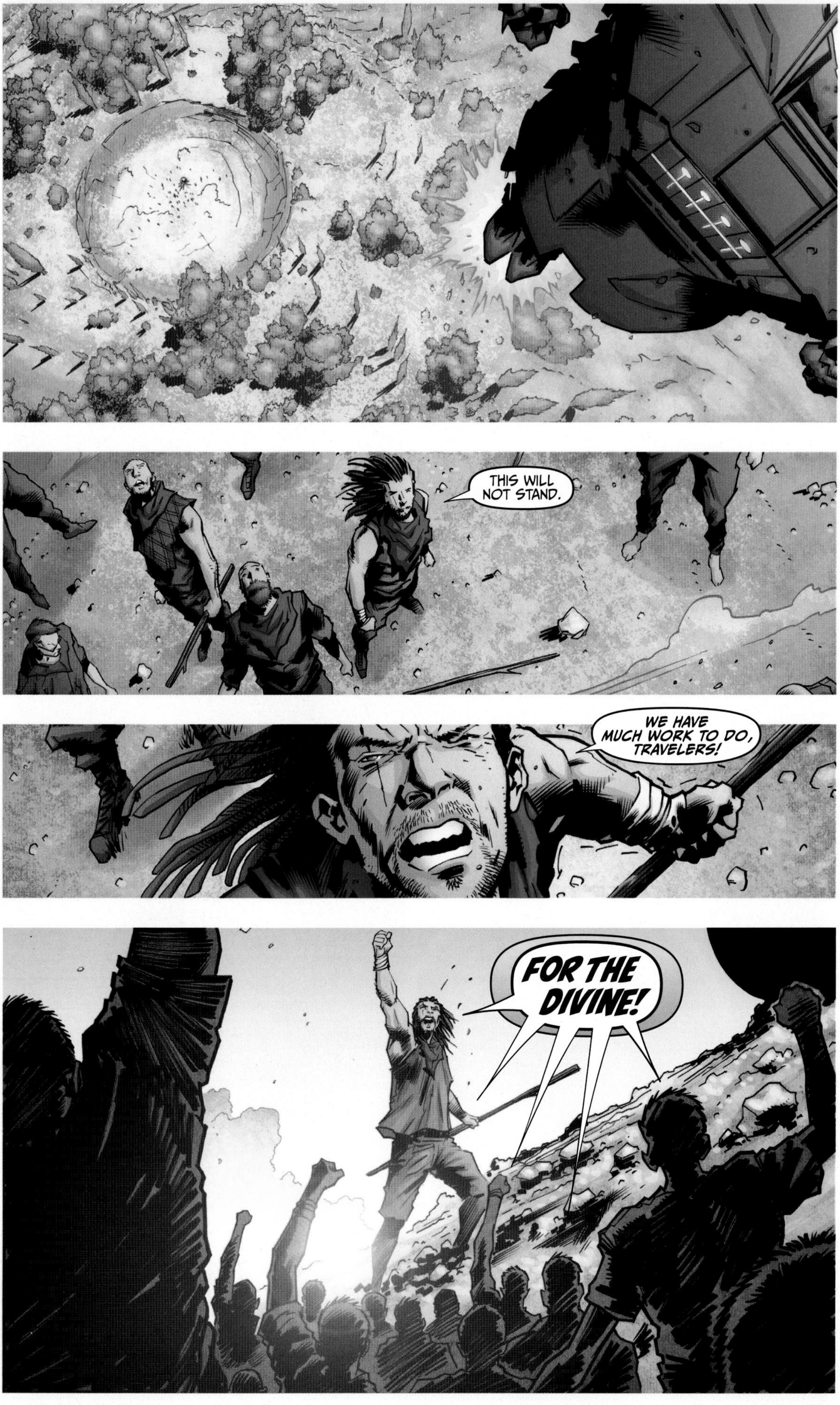
THIS WILL NOT STAND.
WE HAVE MUCH WORK TO DO, TRAVELERS!
FOR THE DIVINE!

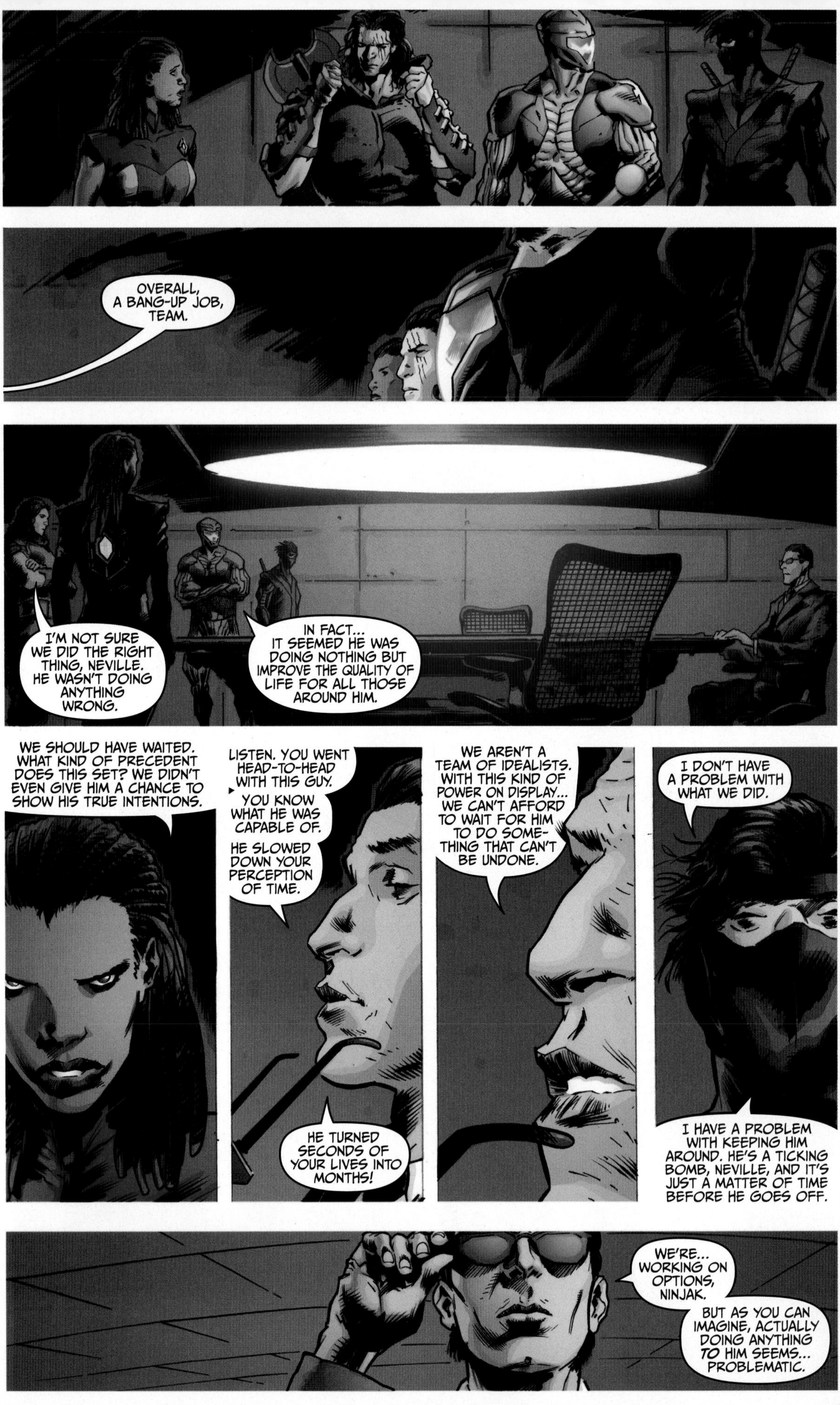
OVERALL, A BANG-UP JOB, TEAM.
I'M NOT SURE WE DID THE RIGHT THING, NEVILLE. HE WASN'T DOING ANYTHING WRONG.
IN FACT... IT SEEMED HE WAS DOING NOTHING BUT IMPROVE THE QUALITY OF LIFE FOR ALL THOSE AROUND HIM.
WE SHOULD HAVE WAITED. WHAT KIND OF PRECEDENT DOES THIS SET? WE DIDN'T EVEN GIVE HIM A CHANCE TO SHOW HIS TRUE INTENTIONS.
LISTEN. YOU WENT HEAD-TO-HEAD WITH THIS GUY.
YOU KNOW WHAT HE WAS CAPABLE OF.
HE SLOWED DOWN YOUR PERCEPTION OF TIME.
HE TURNED SECONDS OF YOUR LIVES INTO MONTHS!
WE AREN'T A TEAM OF IDEALISTS. WITH THIS KIND OF POWER ON DISPLAY... WE CAN'T AFFORD TO WAIT FOR HIM TO DO SOME-THING THAT CAN'T BE UNDONE.
I DON'T HAVE A PROBLEM WITH WHAT WE DID.
I HAVE A PROBLEM WITH KEEPING HIM AROUND. HE'S A TICKING BOMB, NEVILLE, AND IT'S JUST A MATTER OF TIME BEFORE HE GOES OFF.
WE'RE... WORKING ON OPTIONS, NINJAK.
BUT AS YOU CAN IMAGINE, ACTUALLY DOING ANYTHING TO HIM SEEMS... PROBLEMATIC.

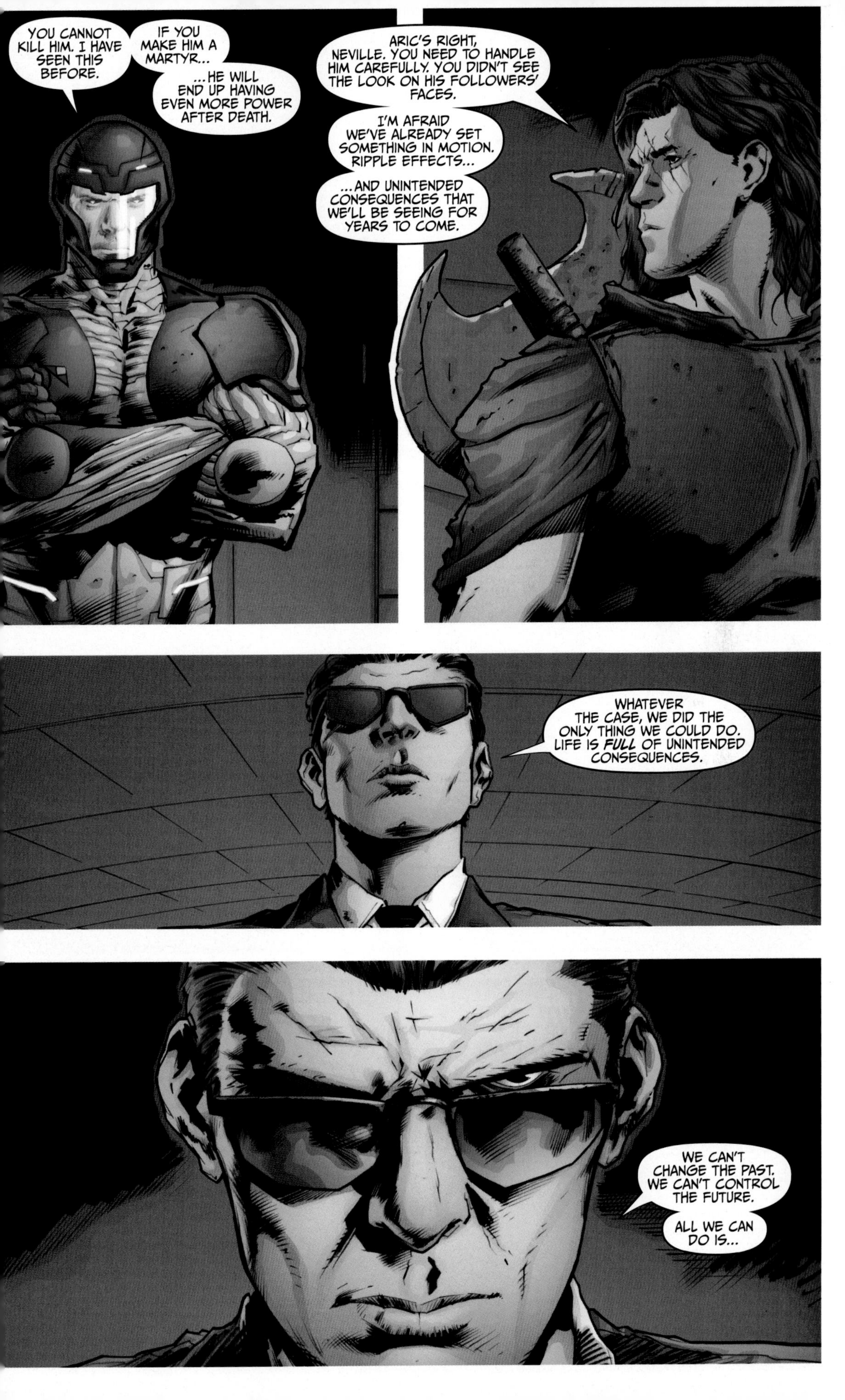
YOU CANNOT KILL HIM. I HAVE SEEN THIS BEFORE.
IF YOU MAKE HIM A MARTYR...
...HE WILL END UP HAVING EVEN MORE POWER AFTER DEATH.
ARIC'S RIGHT, NEVILLE. YOU NEED TO HANDLE HIM CAREFULLY. YOU DIDN'T SEE THE LOOK ON HIS FOLLOWERS' FACES.
I'M AFRAID WE'VE ALREADY SET SOMETHING IN MOTION. RIPPLE EFFECTS...
...AND UNINTENDED CONSEQUENCES THAT WE'LL BE SEEING FOR YEARS TO COME.
WHATEVER THE CASE, WE DID THE ONLY THING WE COULD DO. LIFE IS *FULL* OF UNINTENDED CONSEQUENCES.
WE CAN'T CHANGE THE PAST. WE CAN'T CONTROL THE FUTURE.
ALL WE CAN DO IS...

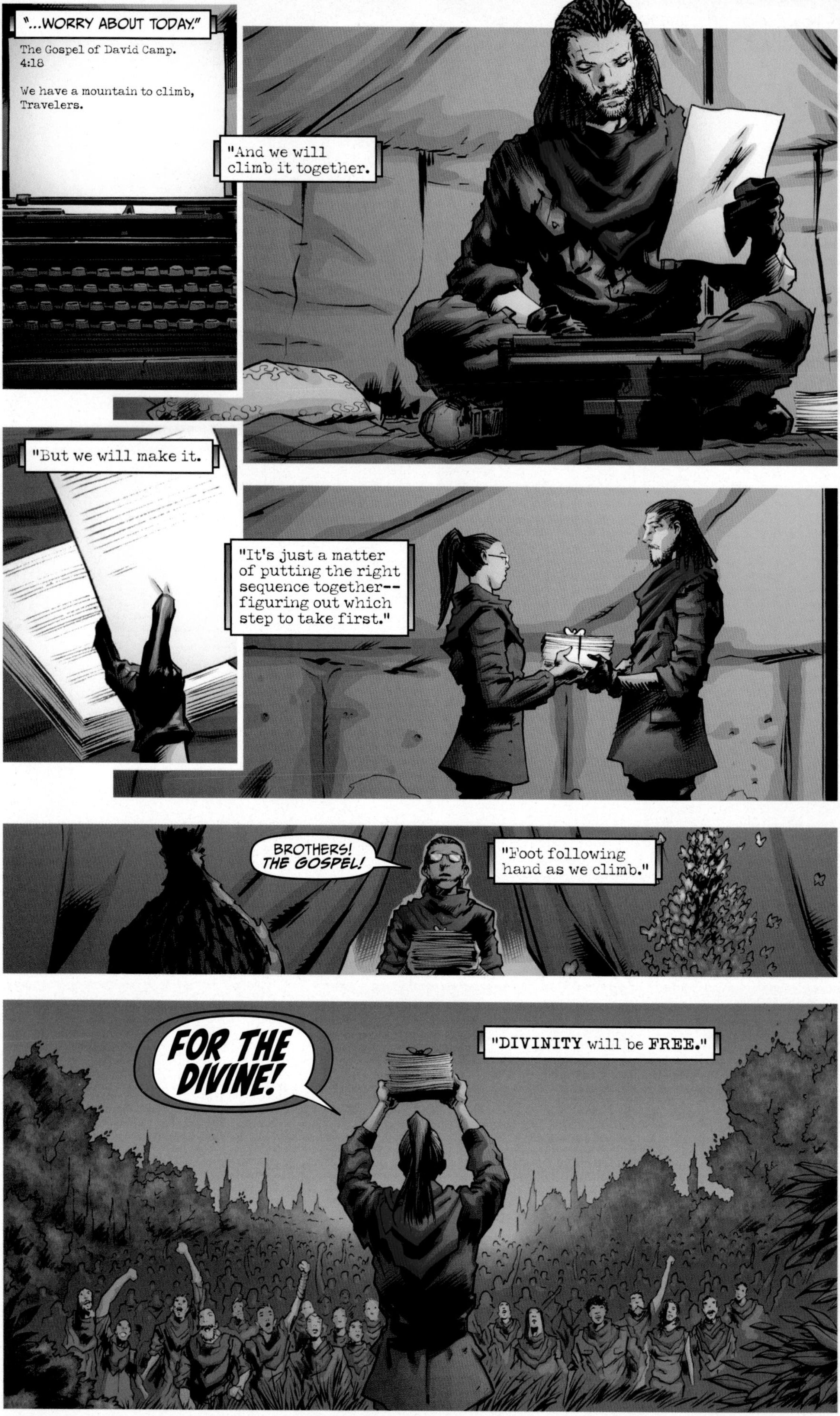
"...WORRY ABOUT TODAY."
The Gospel of David Camp.
4:18
We have a mountain to climb, Travelers.
"And we will climb it together.
"But we will make it.
"It's just a matter of putting the right sequence together--figuring out which step to take first."
BROTHERS! THE GOSPEL!
"Foot following hand as we climb."
FOR THE DIVINE!
"DIVINITY will be FREE."

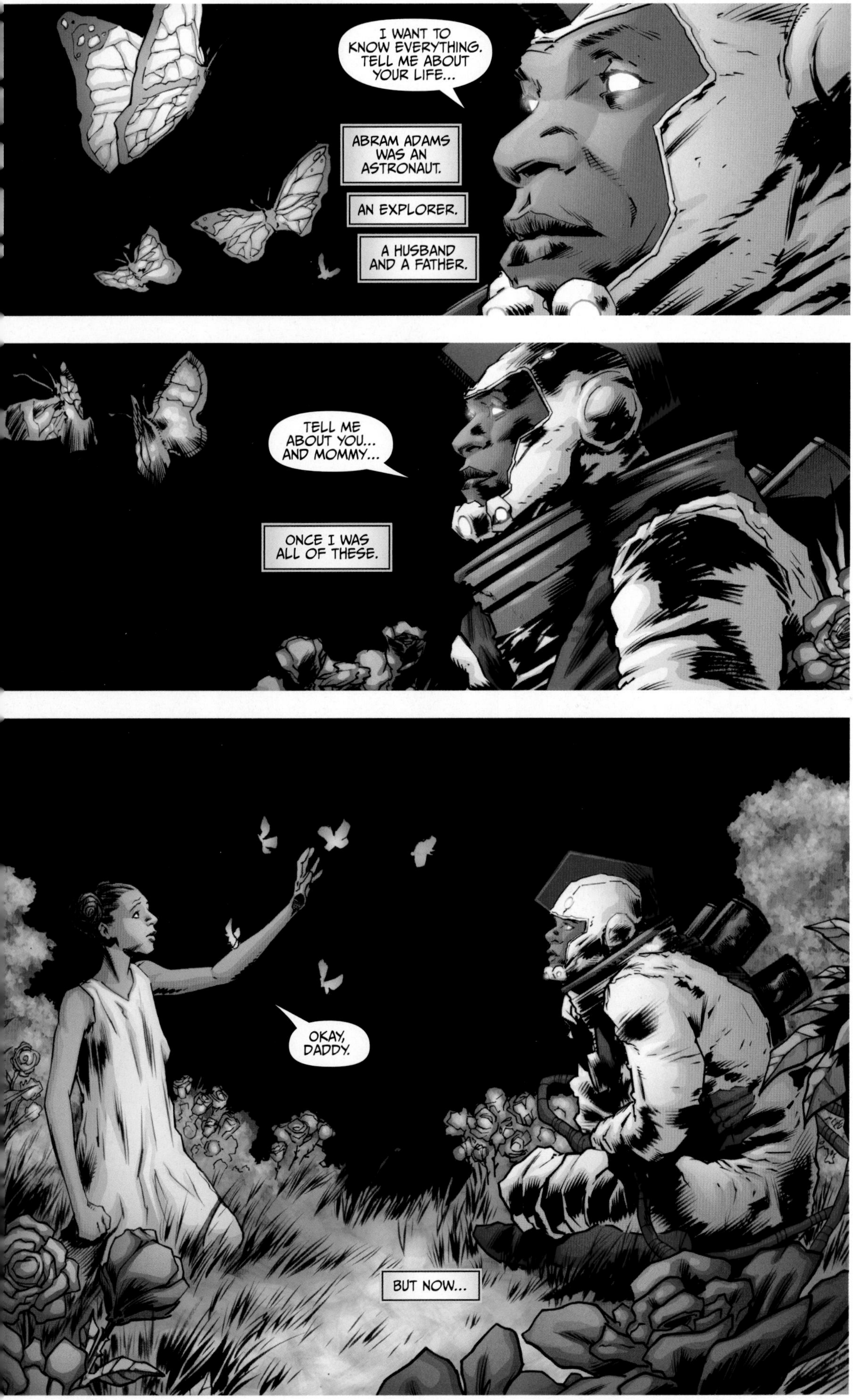
I WANT TO KNOW EVERYTHING. TELL ME ABOUT YOUR LIFE...
ABRAM ADAMS WAS AN ASTRONAUT.
AN EXPLORER.
A HUSBAND AND A FATHER.
TELL ME ABOUT YOU... AND MOMMY...
ONCE I WAS ALL OF THESE.
OKAY, DADDY.
BUT NOW...

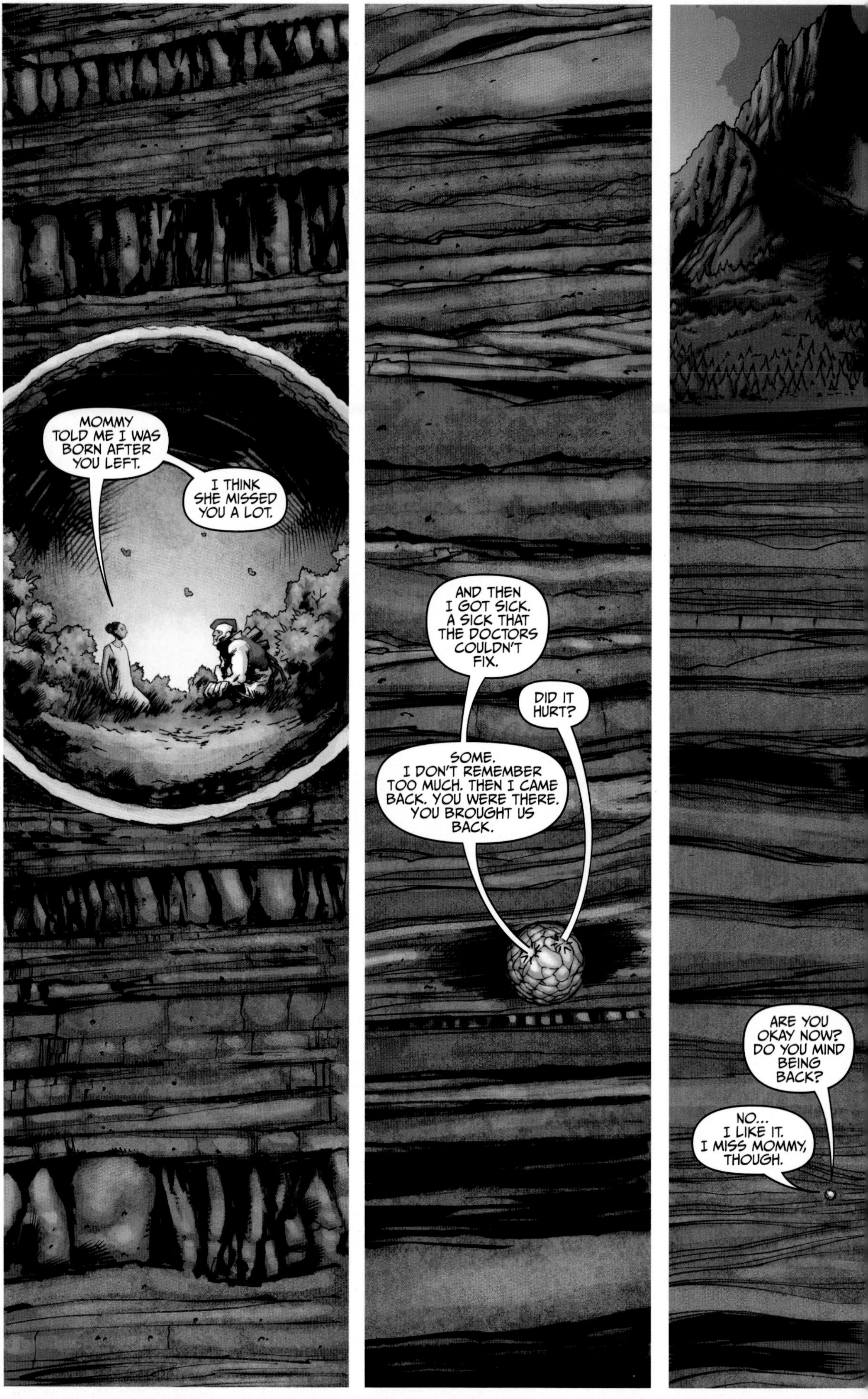
MOMMY TOLD ME I WAS BORN AFTER YOU LEFT.
I THINK SHE MISSED YOU A LOT.
AND THEN I GOT SICK. A SICK THAT THE DOCTORS COULDN'T FIX.
DID IT HURT?
SOME. I DON'T REMEMBER TOO MUCH. THEN I CAME BACK. YOU WERE THERE. YOU BROUGHT US BACK.
ARE YOU OKAY NOW? DO YOU MIND BEING BACK?
NO... I LIKE IT. I MISS MOMMY, THOUGH.

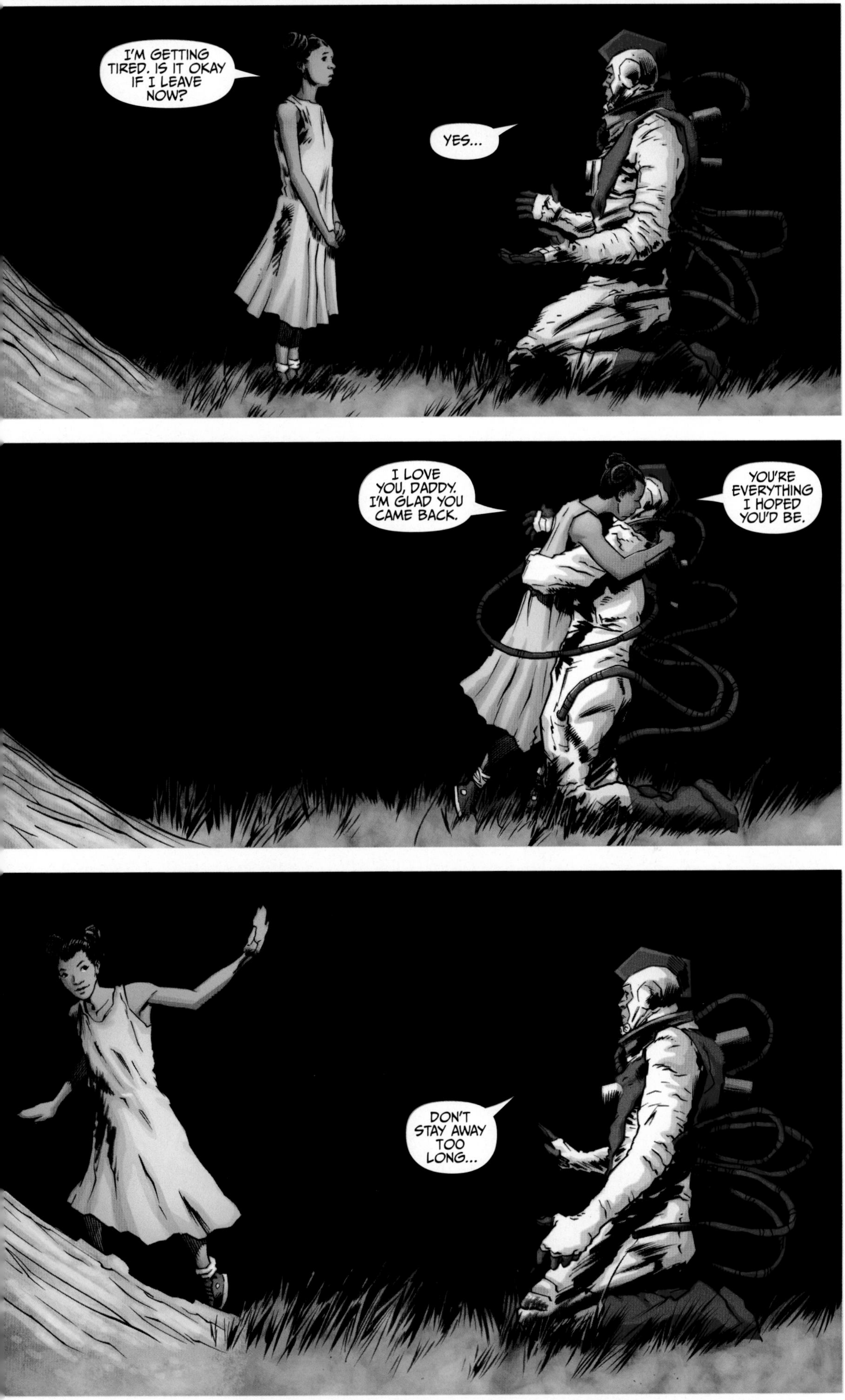
I'M GETTING TIRED. IS IT OKAY IF I LEAVE NOW?
YES...
I LOVE YOU, DADDY. I'M GLAD YOU CAME BACK.
YOU'RE EVERYTHING I HOPED YOU'D BE.
DON'T STAY AWAY TOO LONG...

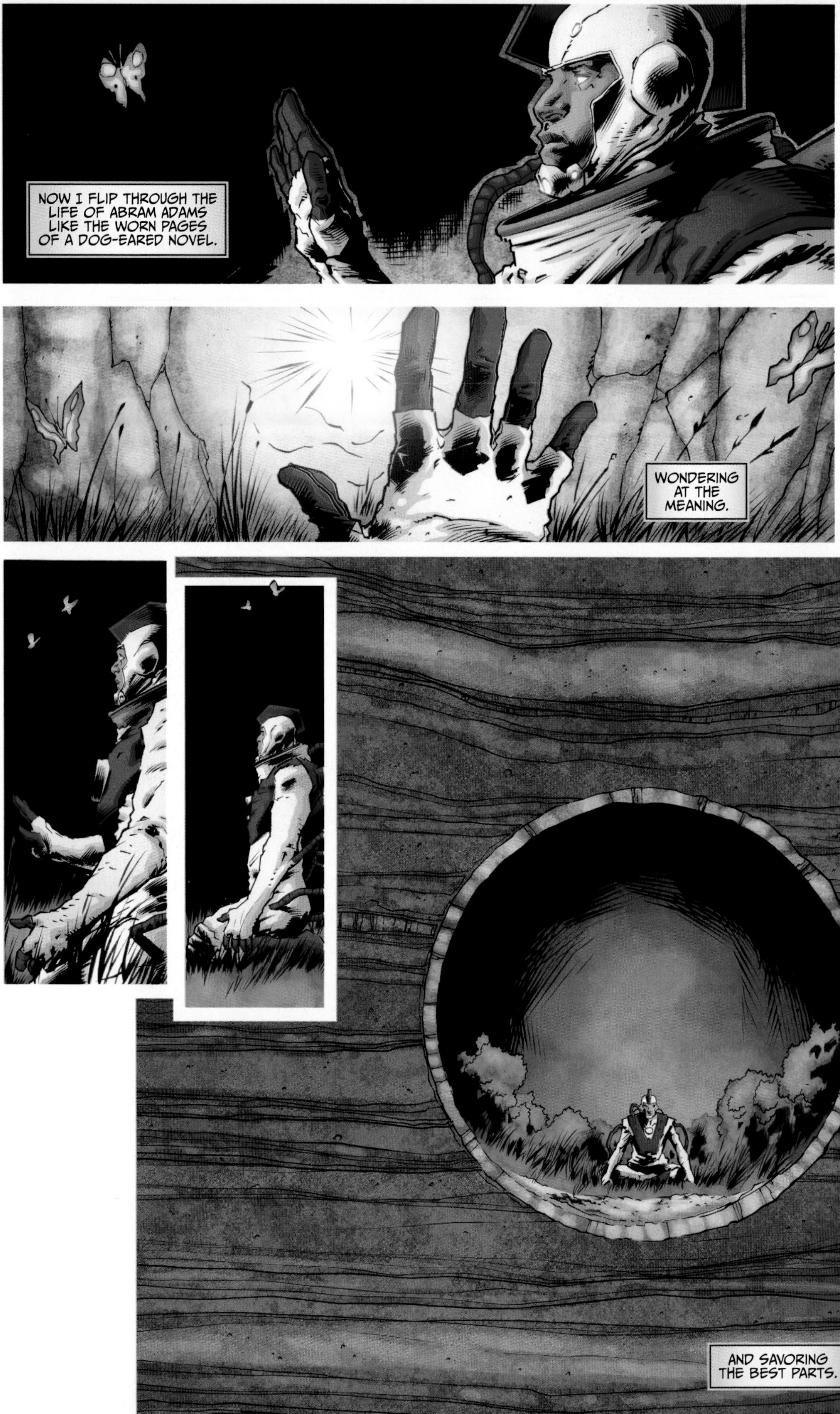

NOW I FLIP THROUGH THE LIFE OF ABRAM ADAMS LIKE THE WORN PAGES OF A DOG-EARED NOVEL.
WONDERING AT THE MEANING.
AND SAVORING THE BEST PARTS.

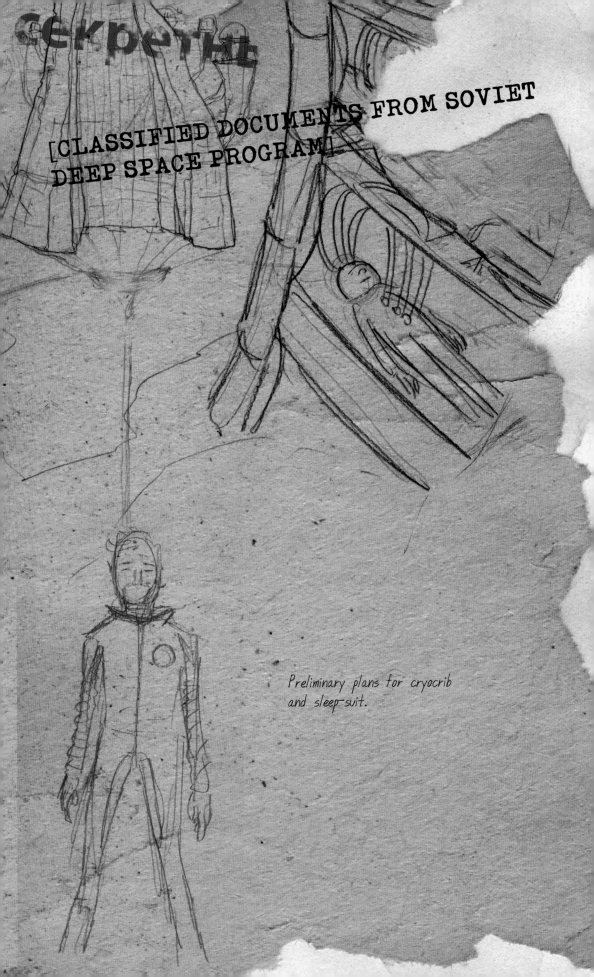

[CLASSIFIED DOCUMENTS FROM SOVIET DEEP SPACE PROGRAM]

Preliminary plans for cryocrib and sleep-suit.

секретный

Scouting report for potential training sites.

Valley of Death — Too inaccessible and lack of security.

Antarctica — Inhospitability is ideal. Isolation perfect for psychological training.

Siberia — Most likely location. Easy access. Remote areas should be isolated enough for psych training.

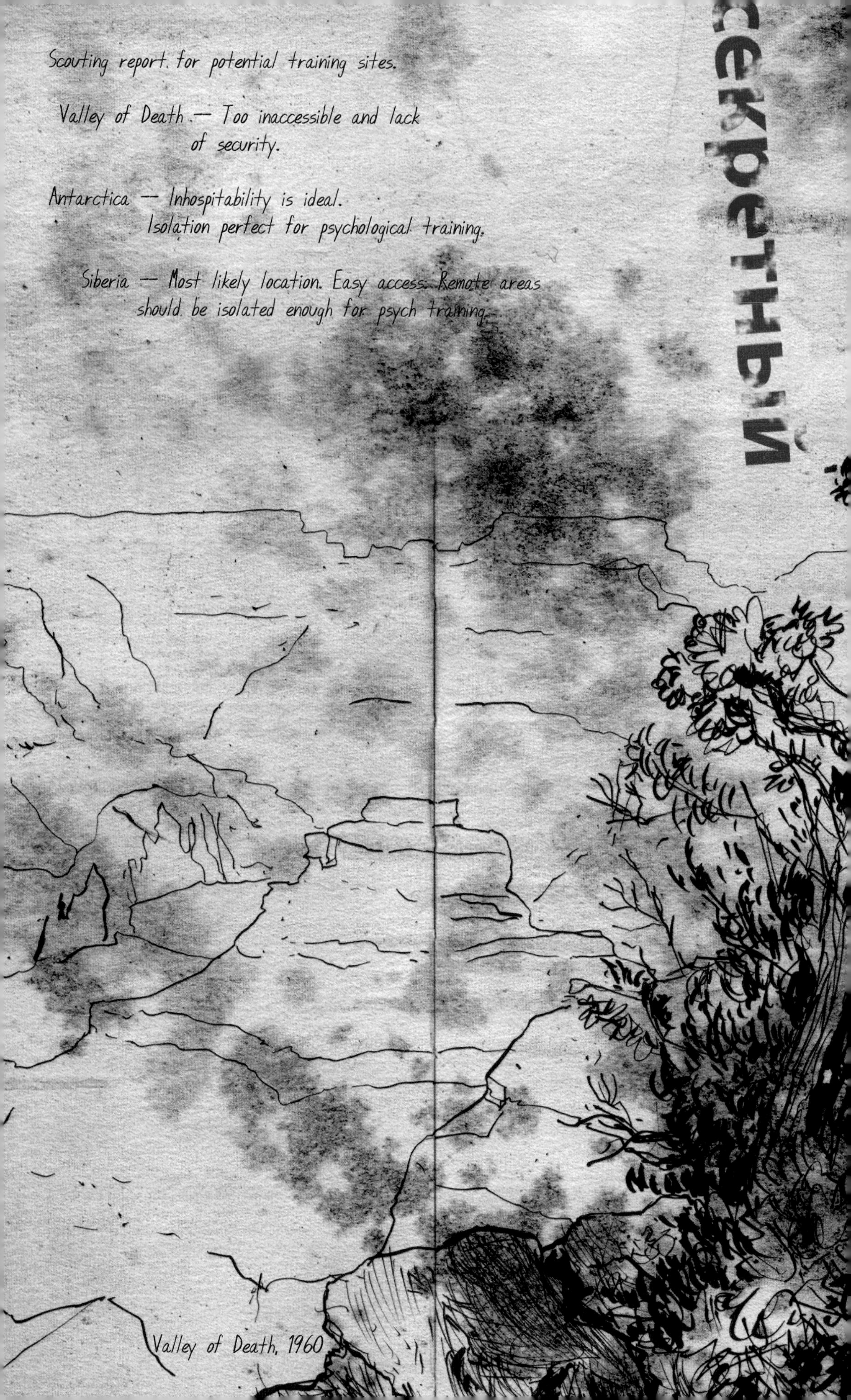

Valley of Death, 1960

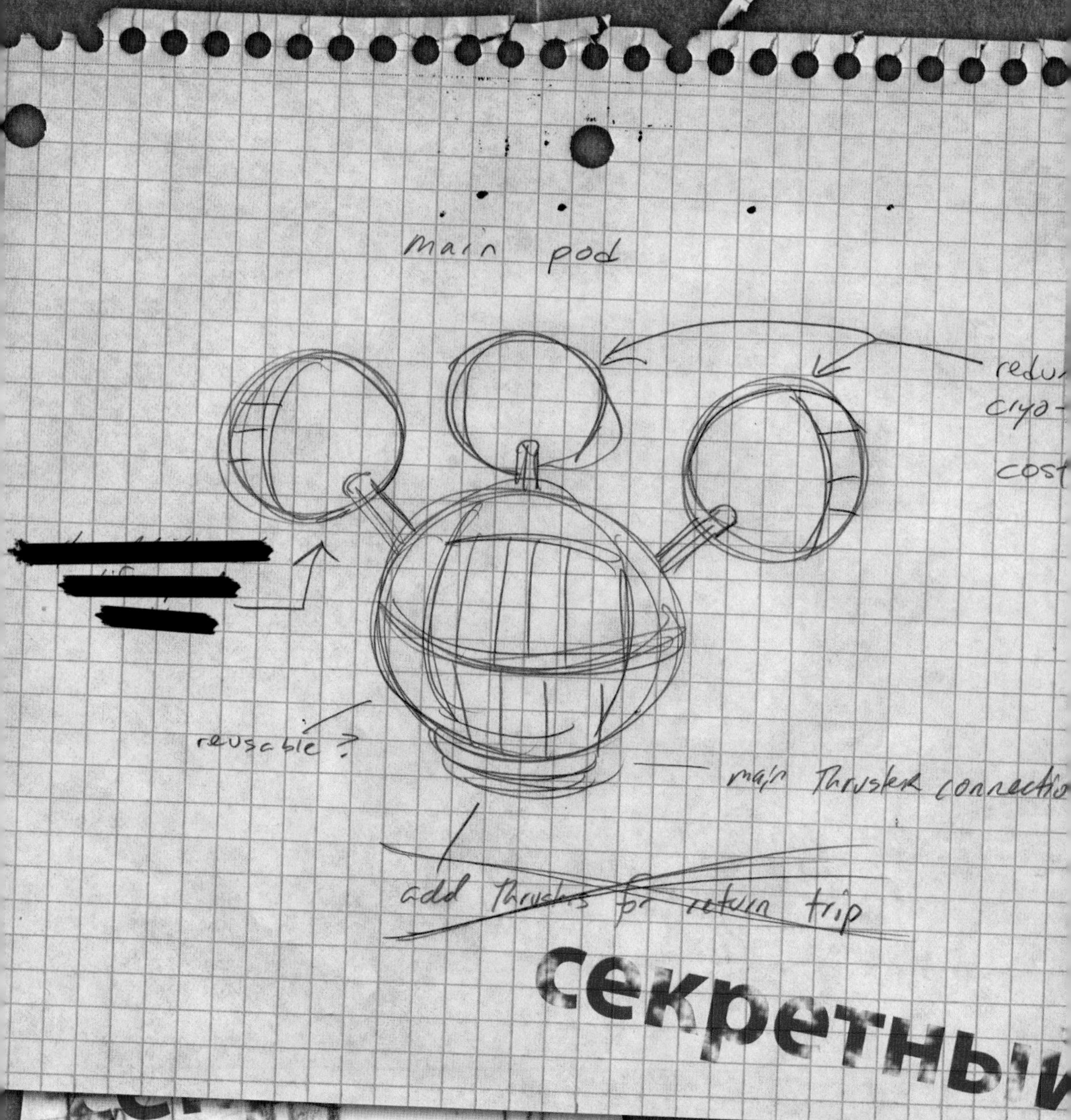
main pod
[redacted]
reusable ?
main Thruster
add Thrusters for return trip

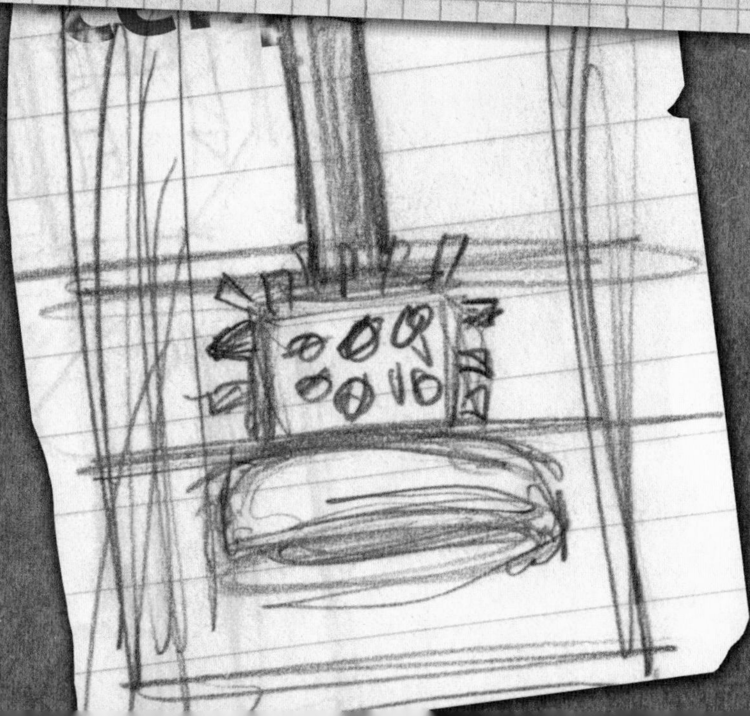

Preliminary final-stage pods. Able to accommodate [redacted]

Both designs include optional additional payloads that would allow for a return trip (if a return trip is necessary).

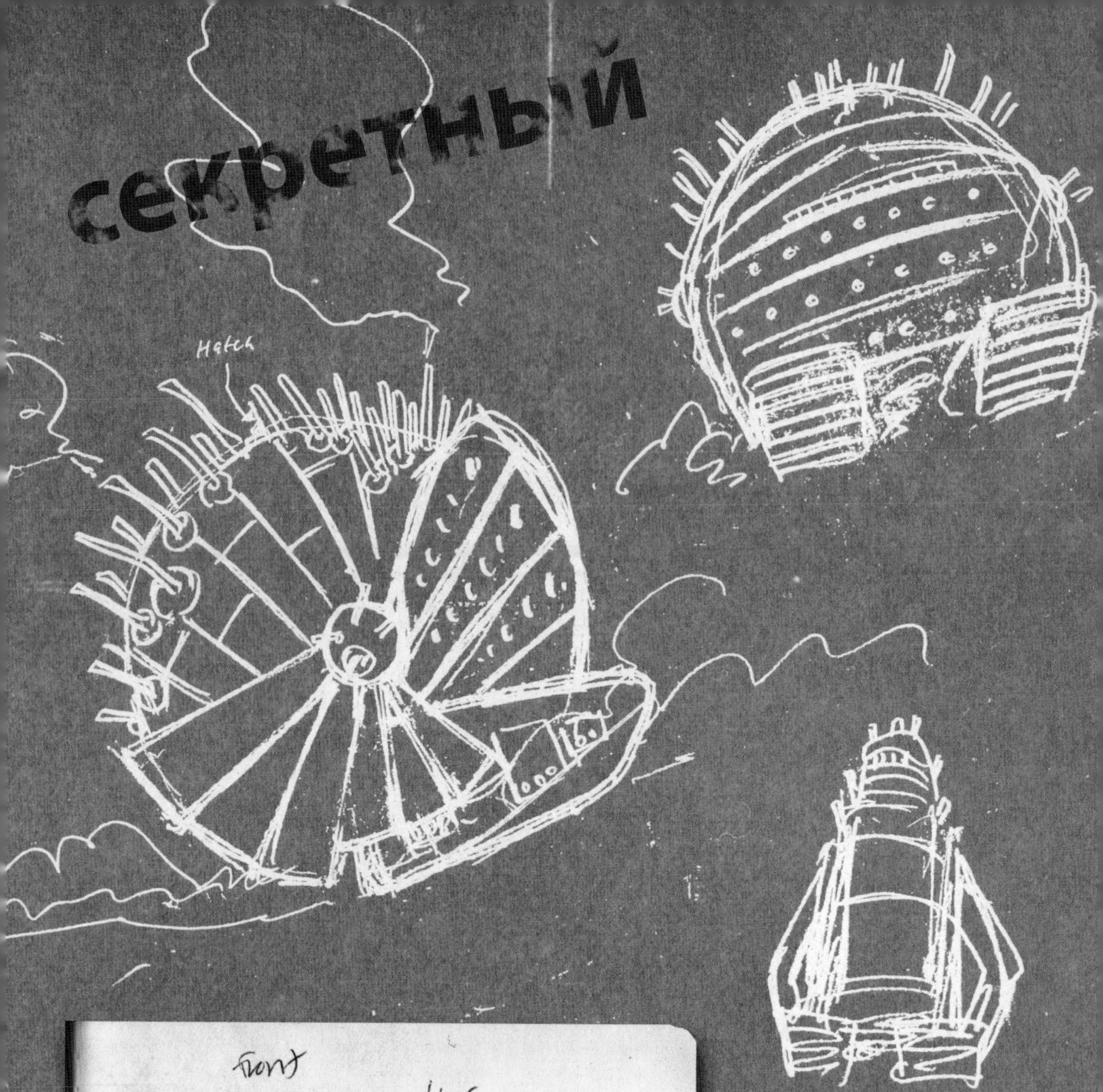
секретный
Hatch

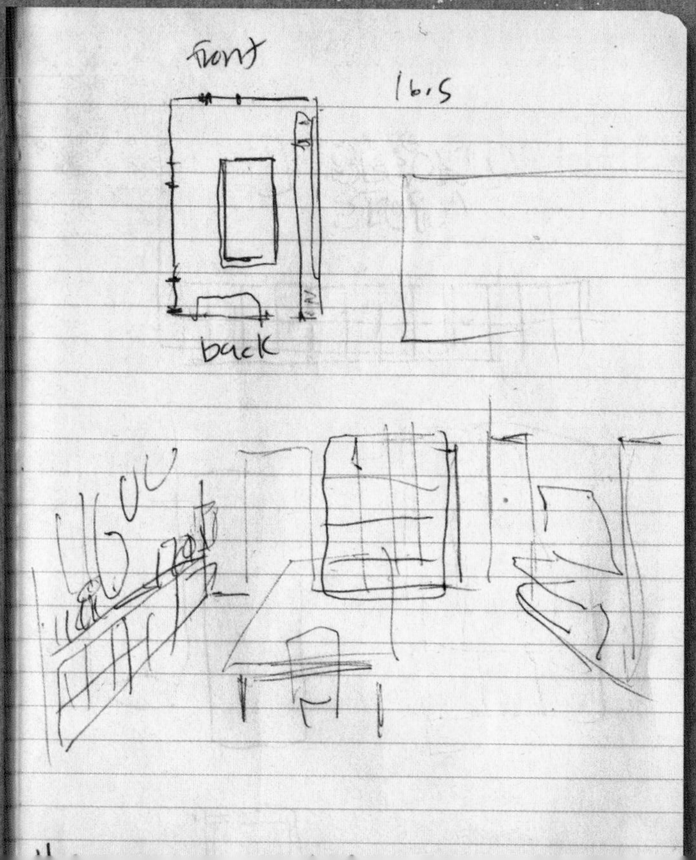
front
16.5
back

Additonal land-rover gear in the event of a succesful landing.

Includes [redacted] of [redacted]ear with the use of hydroponic station and solar panel reconfiguration.

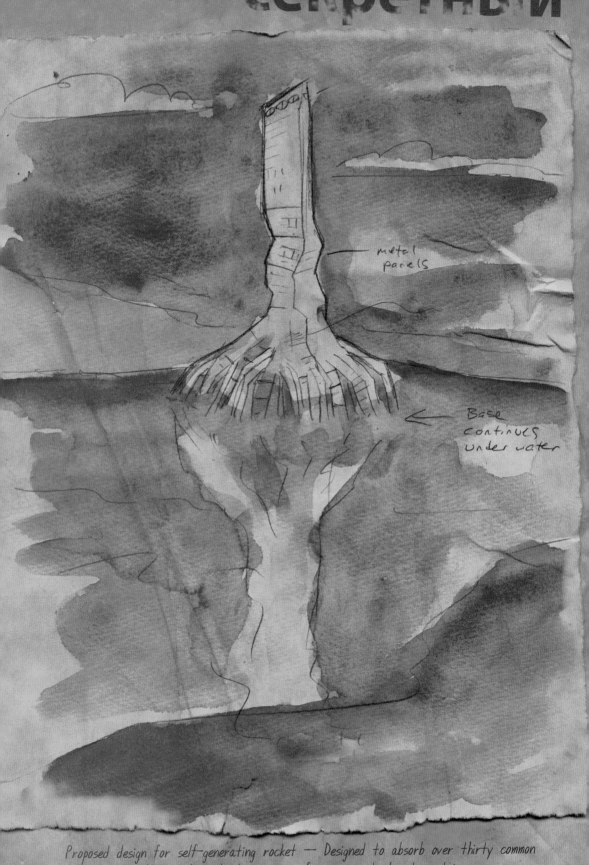

metal panels

Base continues under water

Proposed design for self-generating rocket — Designed to absorb over thirty common gases and minerals and store energy for an eventual return trip.

COMMENTARY

DIVINITY #2 COMMENTARY BY COLORIST DAVID BARON

PENCILS | INKS | COLORS

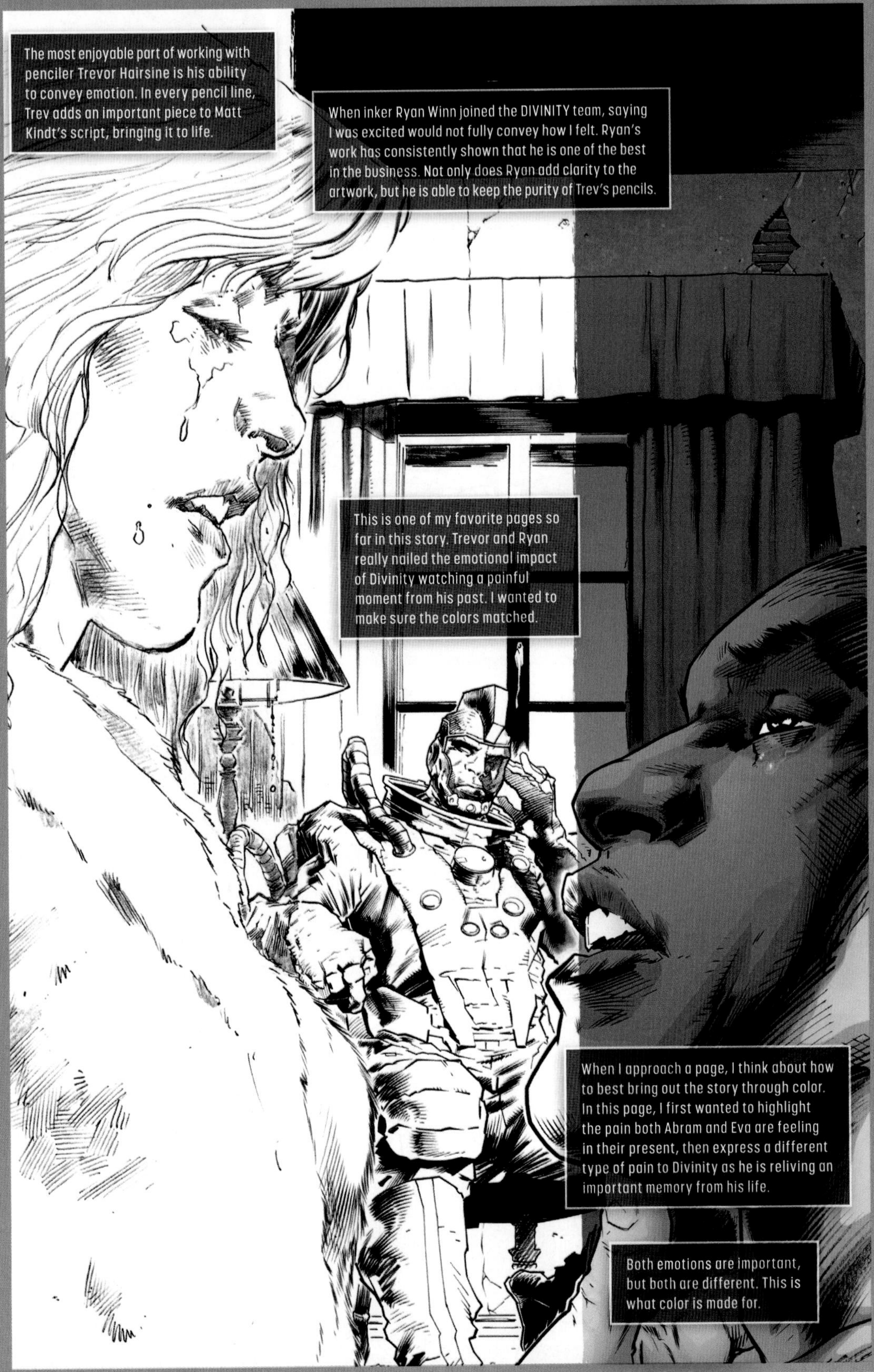

The most enjoyable part of working with penciler Trevor Hairsine is his ability to convey emotion. In every pencil line, Trev adds an important piece to Matt Kindt's script, bringing it to life.

When inker Ryan Winn joined the DIVINITY team, saying I was excited would not fully convey how I felt. Ryan's work has consistently shown that he is one of the best in the business. Not only does Ryan add clarity to the artwork, but he is able to keep the purity of Trev's pencils.

This is one of my favorite pages so far in this story. Trevor and Ryan really nailed the emotional impact of Divinity watching a painful moment from his past. I wanted to make sure the colors matched.

When I approach a page, I think about how to best bring out the story through color. In this page, I first wanted to highlight the pain both Abram and Eva are feeling in their present, then express a different type of pain to Divinity as he is reliving an important memory from his life.

Both emotions are important, but both are different. This is what color is made for.

GRAPHIC DESIGN BY DYLAN TODD

COLORS | INKS | PENCILS

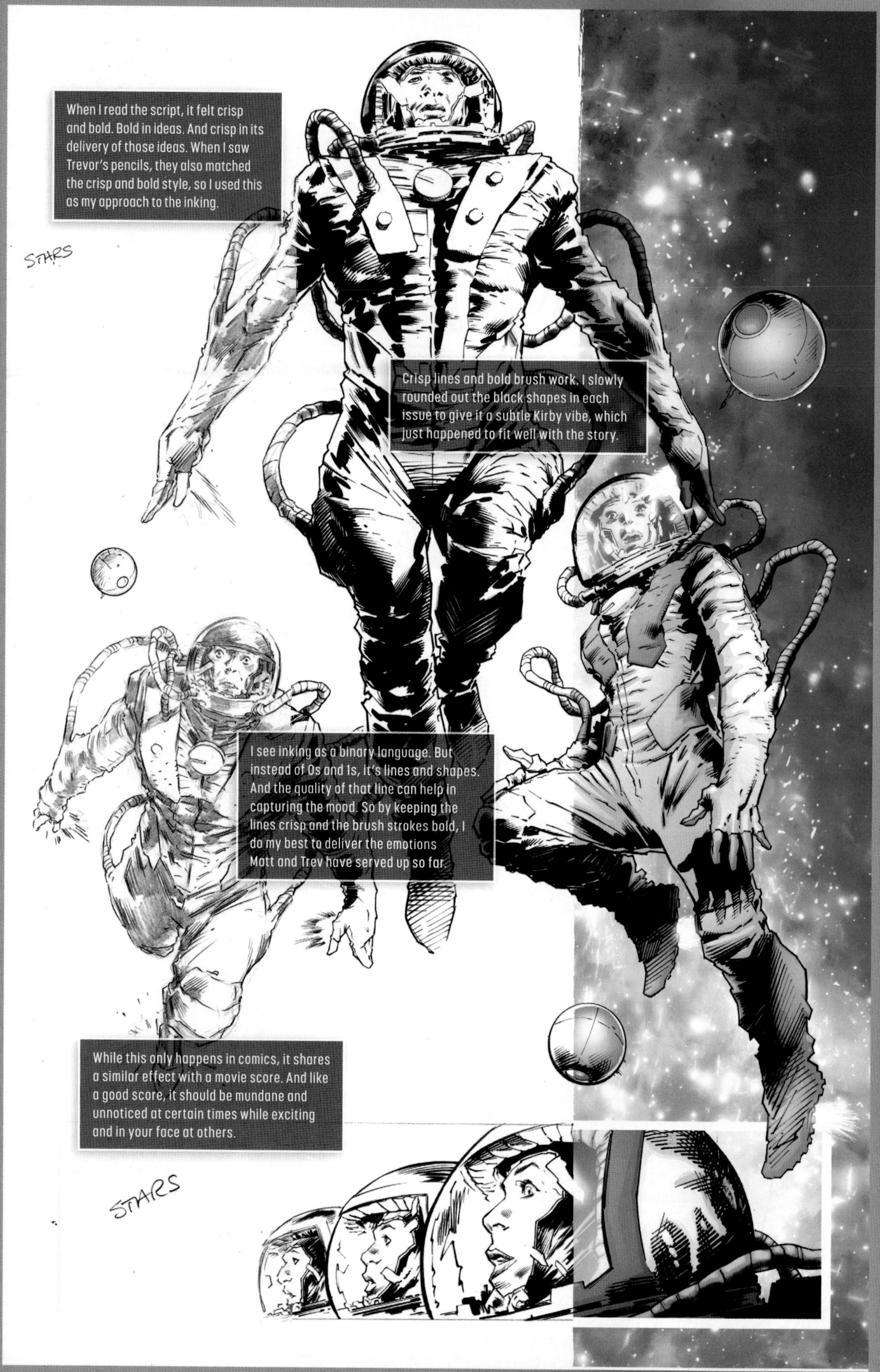
STARS
STARS

When I read the script, it felt crisp and bold. Bold in ideas. And crisp in its delivery of those ideas. When I saw Trevor's pencils, they also matched the crisp and bold style, so I used this as my approach to the inking.

Crisp lines and bold brush work. I slowly rounded out the black shapes in each issue to give it a subtle Kirby vibe, which just happened to fit well with the story.

I see inking as a binary language. But instead of 0s and 1s, it's lines and shapes. And the quality of that line can help in capturing the mood. So by keeping the lines crisp and the brush strokes bold, I do my best to deliver the emotions Matt and Trev have served up so far.

While this only happens in comics, it shares a similar effect with a movie score. And like a good score, it should be mundane and unnoticed at certain times while exciting and in your face at others.

PENCILS | INKS | COLORS

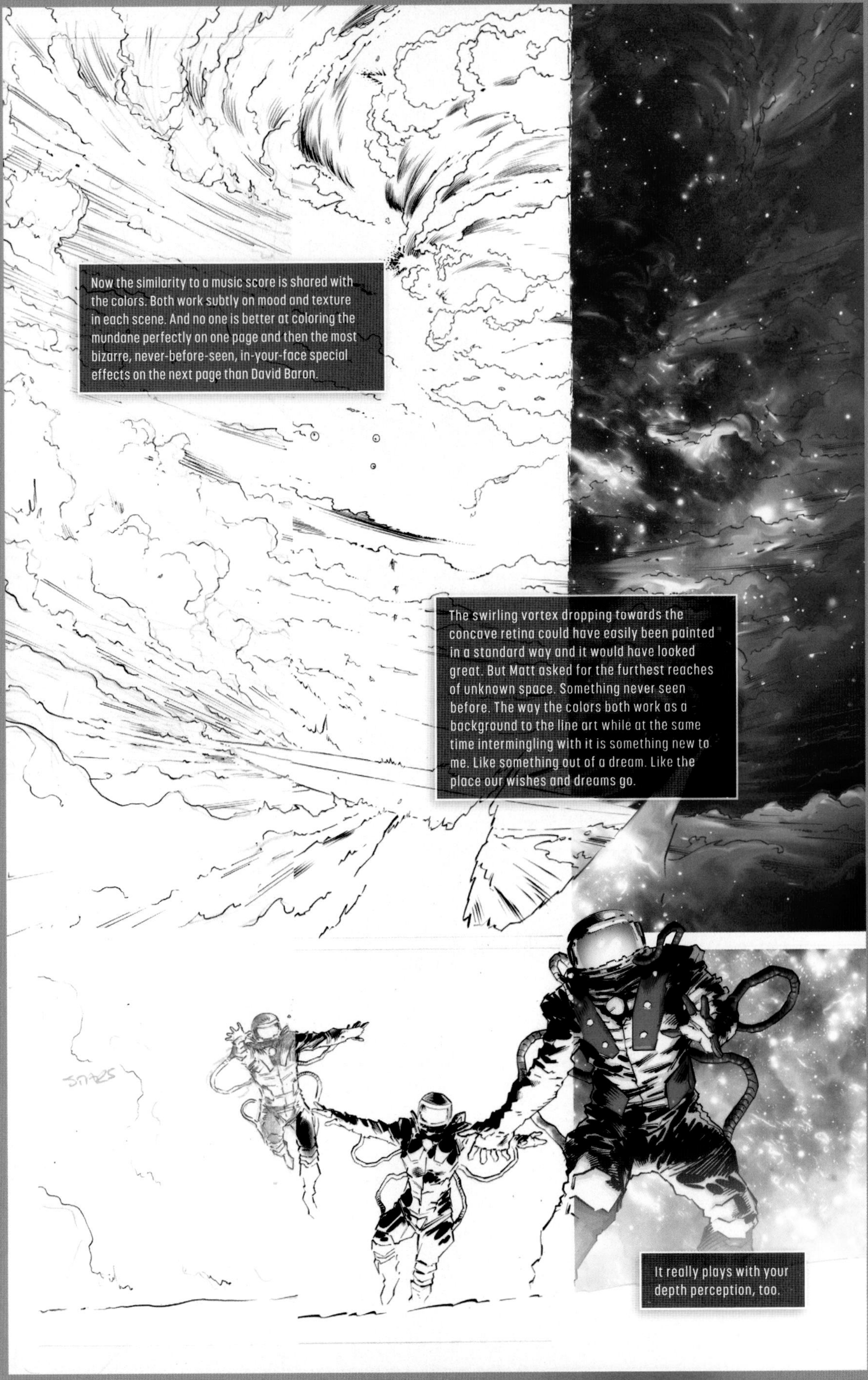

Now the similarity to a music score is shared with the colors. Both work subtly on mood and texture in each scene. And no one is better at coloring the mundane perfectly on one page and then the most bizarre, never-before-seen, in-your-face special effects on the next page than David Baron.

The swirling vortex dropping towards the concave retina could have easily been painted in a standard way and it would have looked great. But Matt asked for the furthest reaches of unknown space. Something never seen before. The way the colors both work as a background to the line art while at the same time intermingling with it is something new to me. Like something out of a dream. Like the place our wishes and dreams go.

It really plays with your depth perception, too.

PENCILS | INKS | COLORS

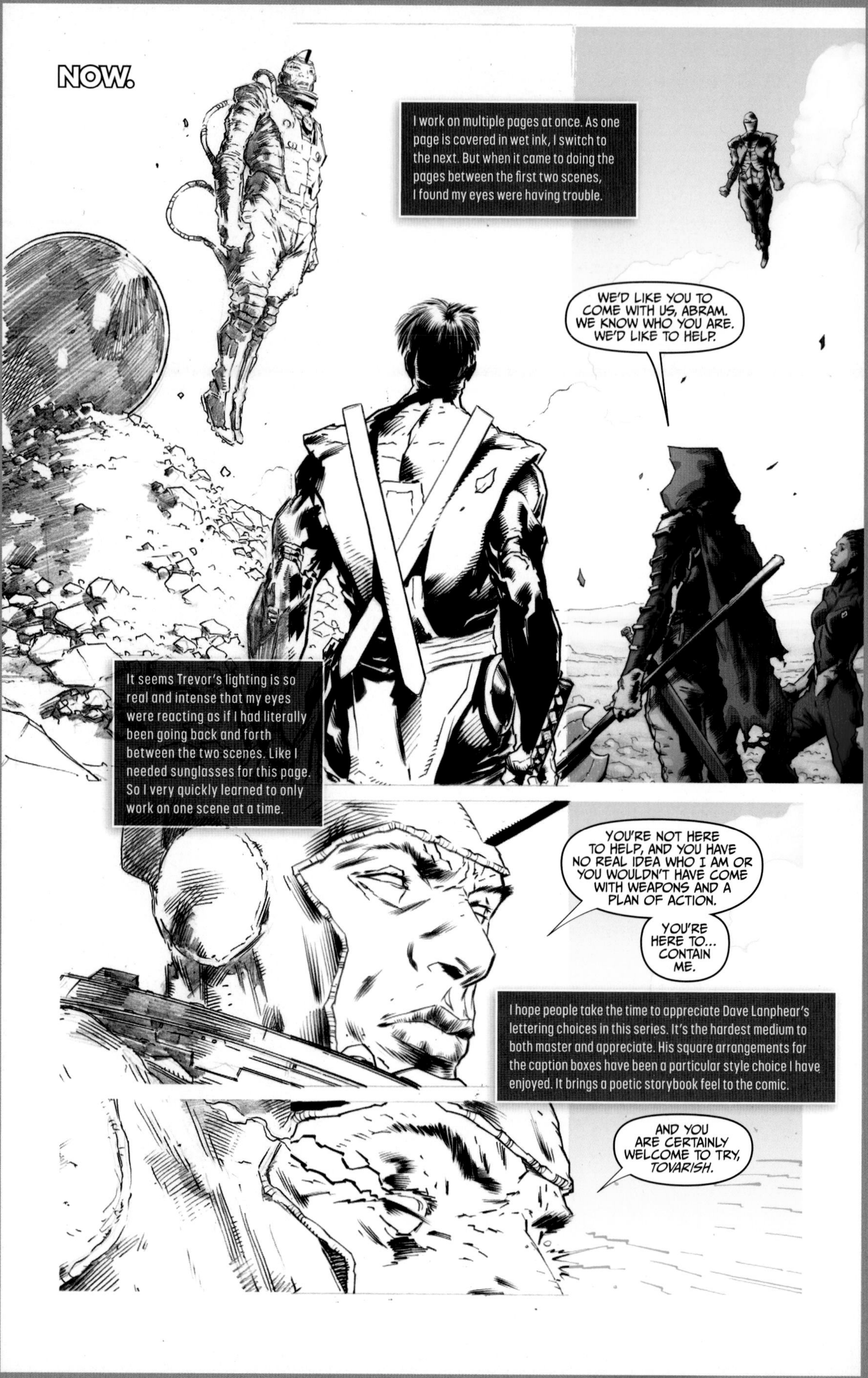
NOW.
WE'D LIKE YOU TO COME WITH US, ABRAM. WE KNOW WHO YOU ARE. WE'D LIKE TO HELP.
YOU'RE NOT HERE TO HELP, AND YOU HAVE NO REAL IDEA WHO I AM OR YOU WOULDN'T HAVE COME WITH WEAPONS AND A PLAN OF ACTION.
YOU'RE HERE TO... CONTAIN ME.
AND YOU ARE CERTAINLY WELCOME TO TRY, *TOVARISH.*

I work on multiple pages at once. As one page is covered in wet ink, I switch to the next. But when it came to doing the pages between the first two scenes, I found my eyes were having trouble.

It seems Trevor's lighting is so real and intense that my eyes were reacting as if I had literally been going back and forth between the two scenes. Like I needed sunglasses for this page. So I very quickly learned to only work on one scene at a time.

I hope people take the time to appreciate Dave Lanphear's lettering choices in this series. It's the hardest medium to both master and appreciate. His square arrangements for the caption boxes have been a particular style choice I have enjoyed. It brings a poetic storybook feel to the comic.

DIVINITY #4 COMMENTARY BY WRITER **MATT KINDT**

PENCILS | INKS | COLORS

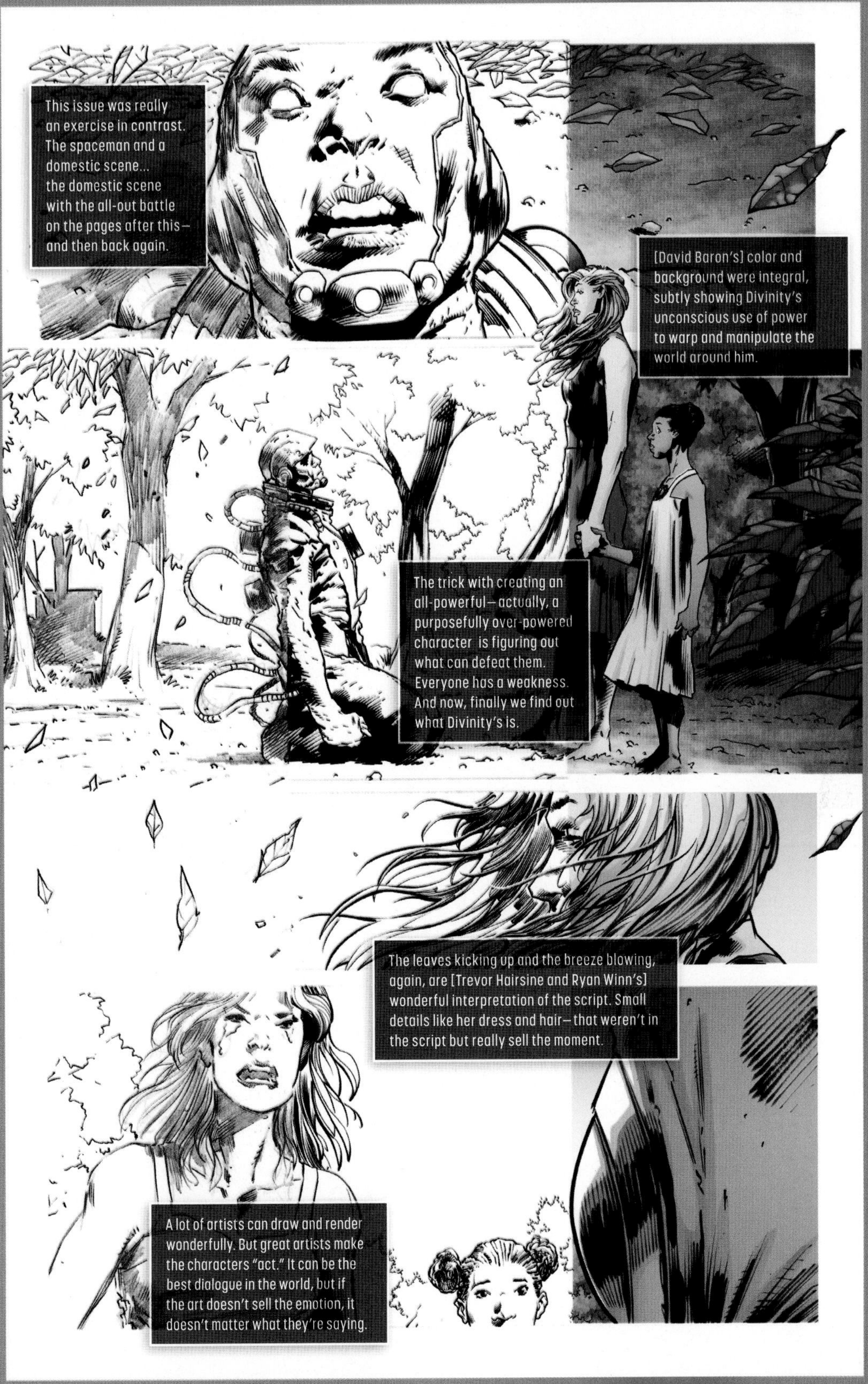

This issue was really an exercise in contrast. The spaceman and a domestic scene... the domestic scene with the all-out battle on the pages after this—and then back again.

[David Baron's] color and background were integral, subtly showing Divinity's unconscious use of power to warp and manipulate the world around him.

The trick with creating an all-powerful—actually, a purposefully over-powered character is figuring out what can defeat them. Everyone has a weakness. And now, finally we find out what Divinity's is.

The leaves kicking up and the breeze blowing, again, are [Trevor Hairsine and Ryan Winn's] wonderful interpretation of the script. Small details like her dress and hair—that weren't in the script but really sell the moment.

A lot of artists can draw and render wonderfully. But great artists make the characters "act." It can be the best dialogue in the world, but if the art doesn't sell the emotion, it doesn't matter what they're saying.

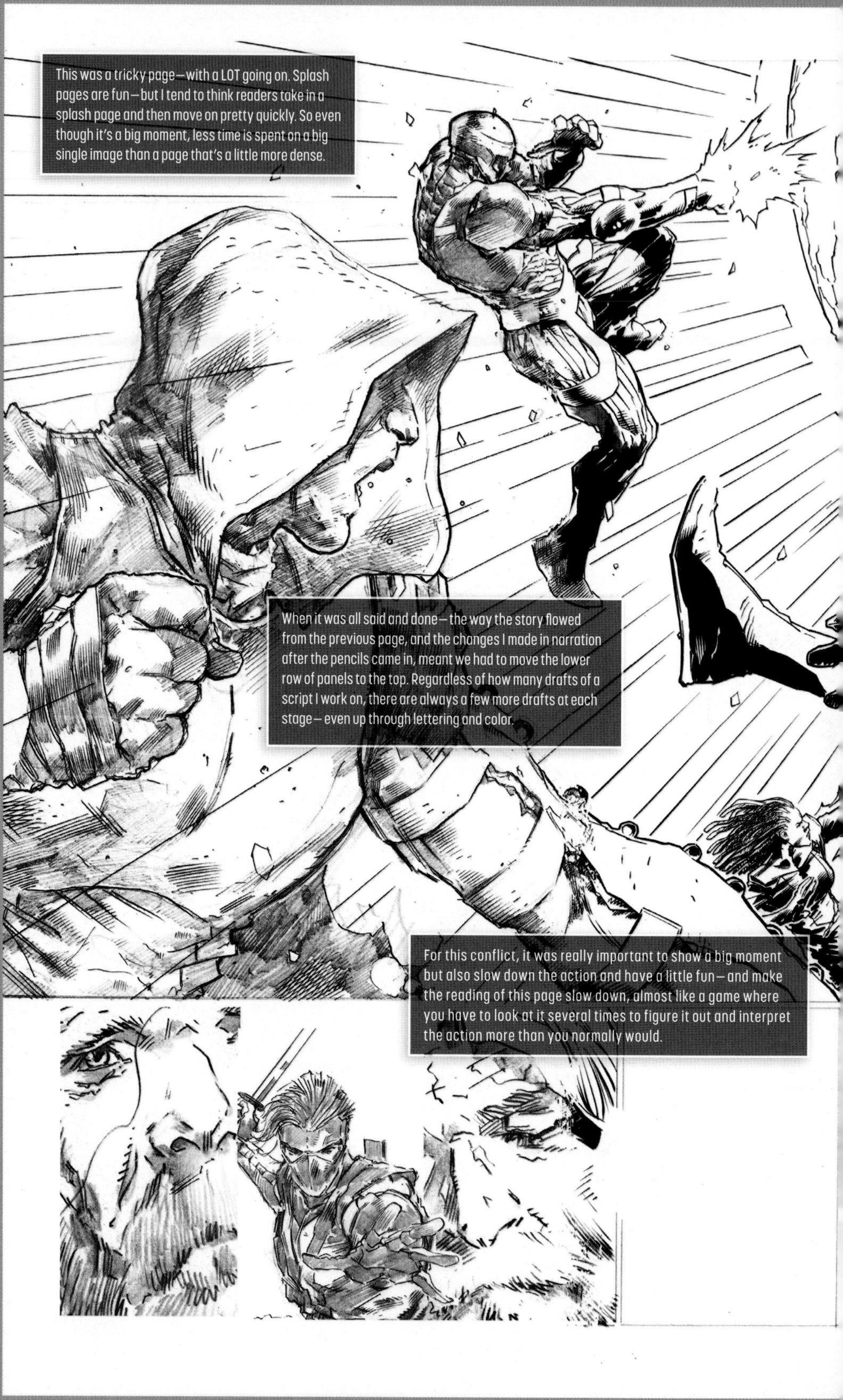

This was a tricky page—with a LOT going on. Splash pages are fun—but I tend to think readers take in a splash page and then move on pretty quickly. So even though it's a big moment, less time is spent on a big single image than a page that's a little more dense.

When it was all said and done—the way the story flowed from the previous page, and the changes I made in narration after the pencils came in, meant we had to move the lower row of panels to the top. Regardless of how many drafts of a script I work on, there are always a few more drafts at each stage—even up through lettering and color.

For this conflict, it was really important to show a big moment but also slow down the action and have a little fun—and make the reading of this page slow down, almost like a game where you have to look at it several times to figure it out and interpret the action more than you normally would.

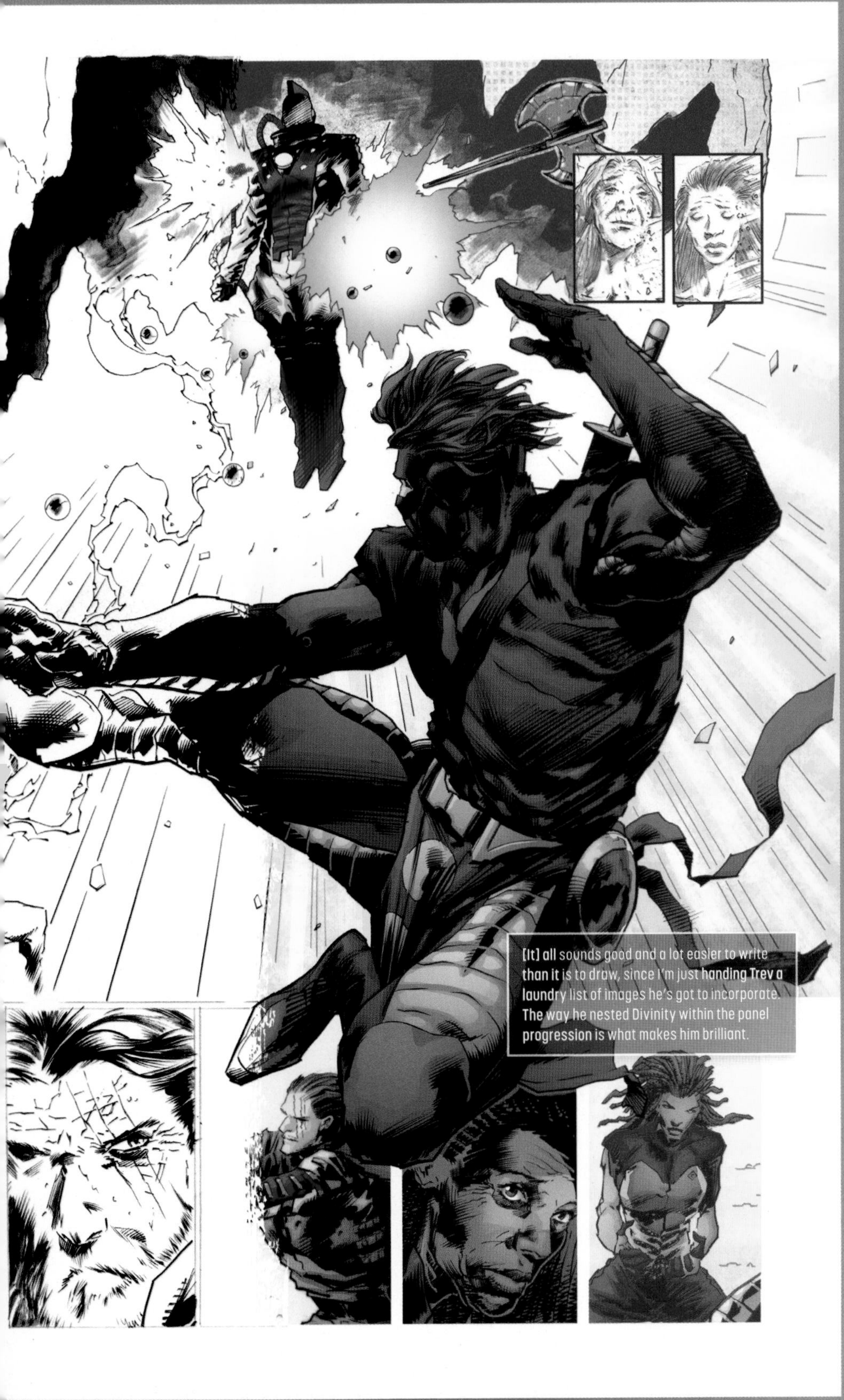

[It] all sounds good and a lot easier to write than it is to draw, since I'm just handing Trev a laundry list of images he's got to incorporate. The way he nested Divinity within the panel progression is what makes him brilliant.

PENCILS | INKS | COLORS

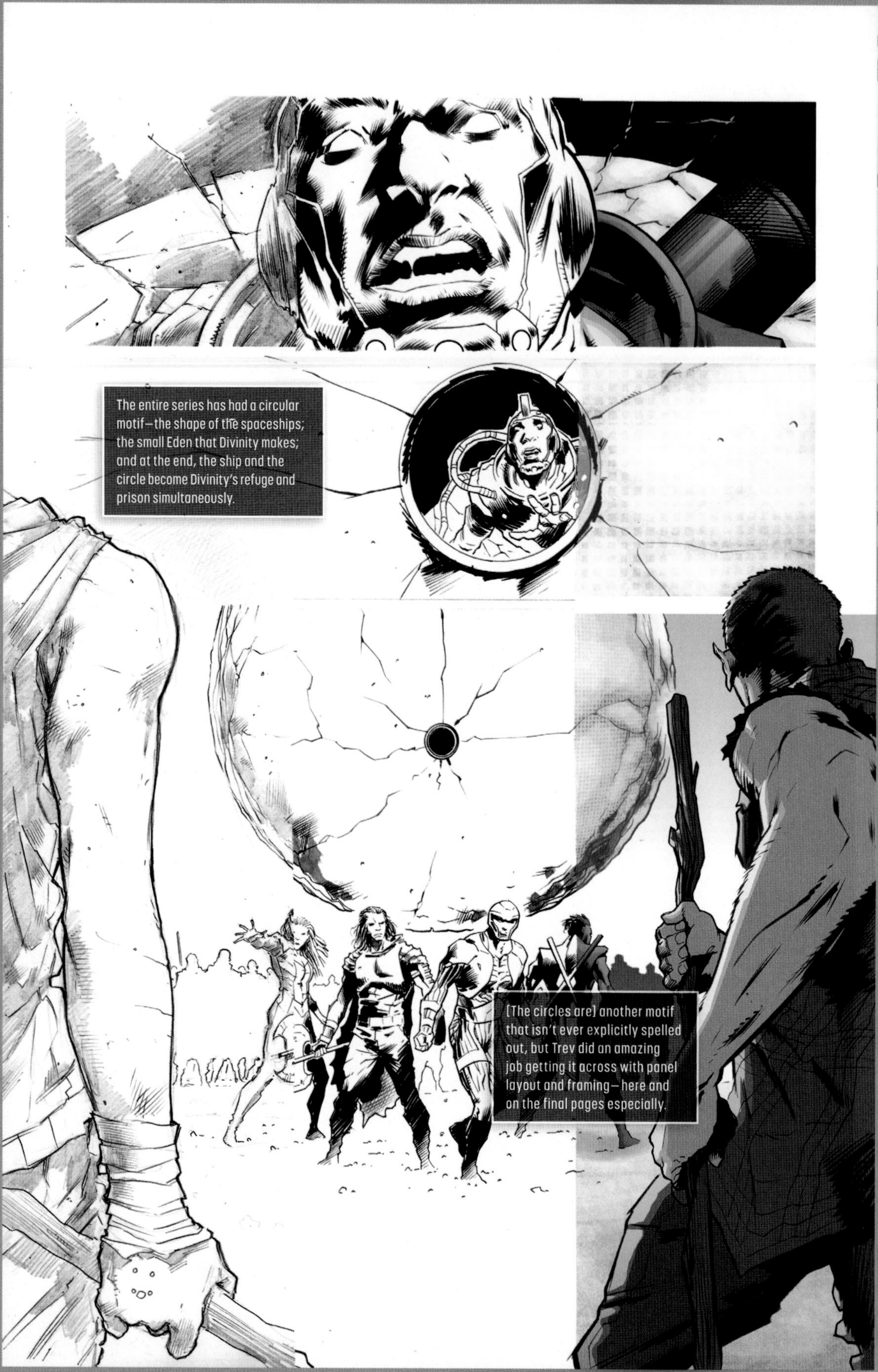

The entire series has had a circular motif—the shape of the spaceships; the small Eden that Divinity makes; and at the end, the ship and the circle become Divinity's refuge and prison simultaneously.

[The circles are] another motif that isn't ever explicitly spelled out, but Trev did an amazing job getting it across with panel layout and framing—here and on the final pages especially.

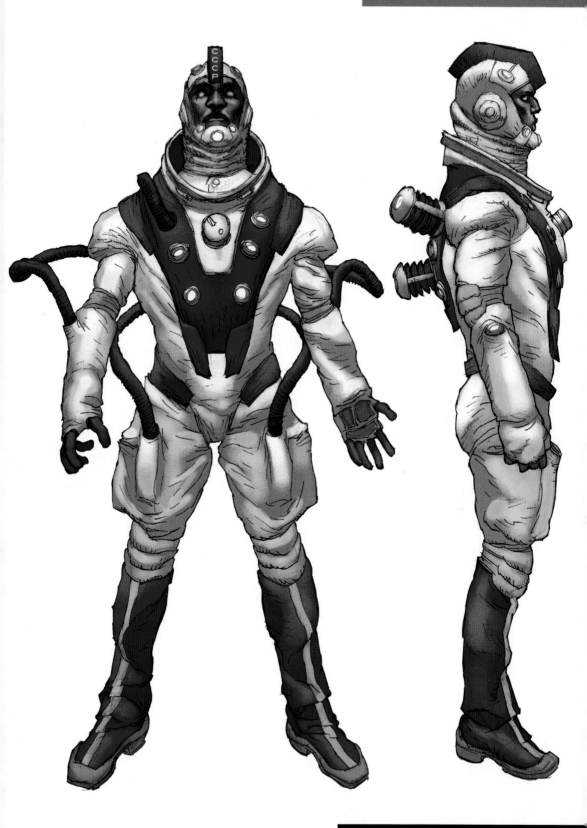

DIVINITY #1 CHARACTER DESIGN VARIANT
Cover by LEWIS LAROSA with BRIAN REBER

DIVINITY #4 VARIANT
Cover by BUTCH GUICE WITH BRIAN REBER

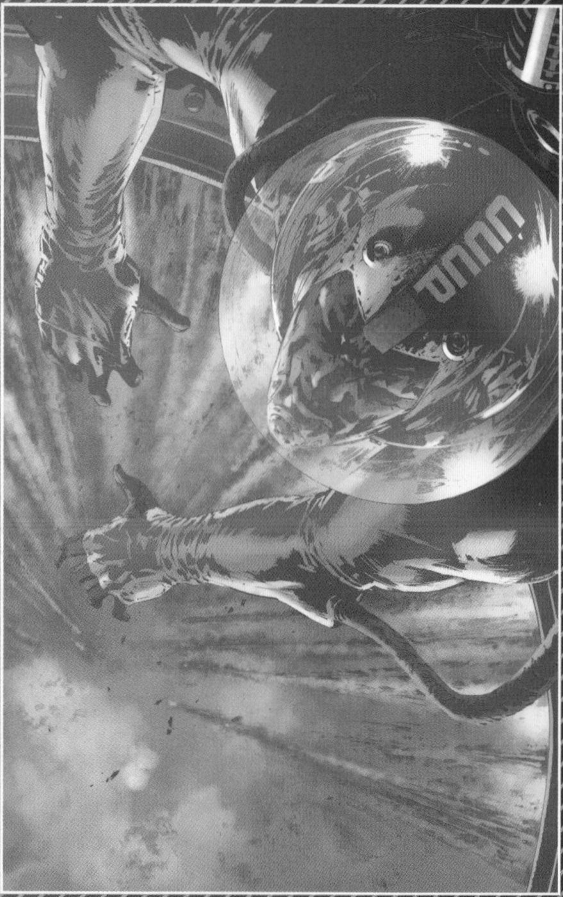
СССР

DIVINITY #4 VARIANT
Cover by RAÚL ALLÉN

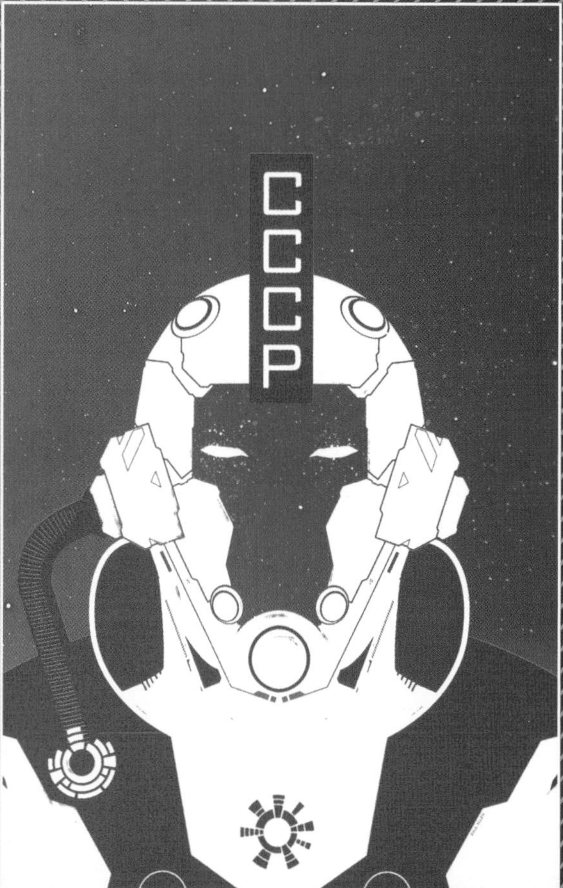
CCCP

DIVINITY #1, p.20
Pencils by TREVOR HAIRSINE
Inks by RYAN WINN

DIVINITY #2, p.14
Pencils by TREVOR HAIRSINE
Inks by RYAN WINN

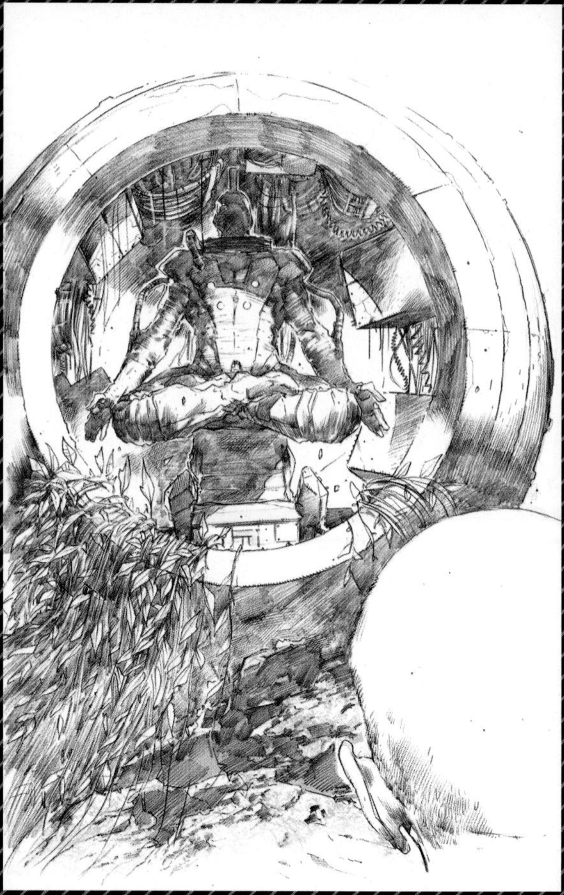

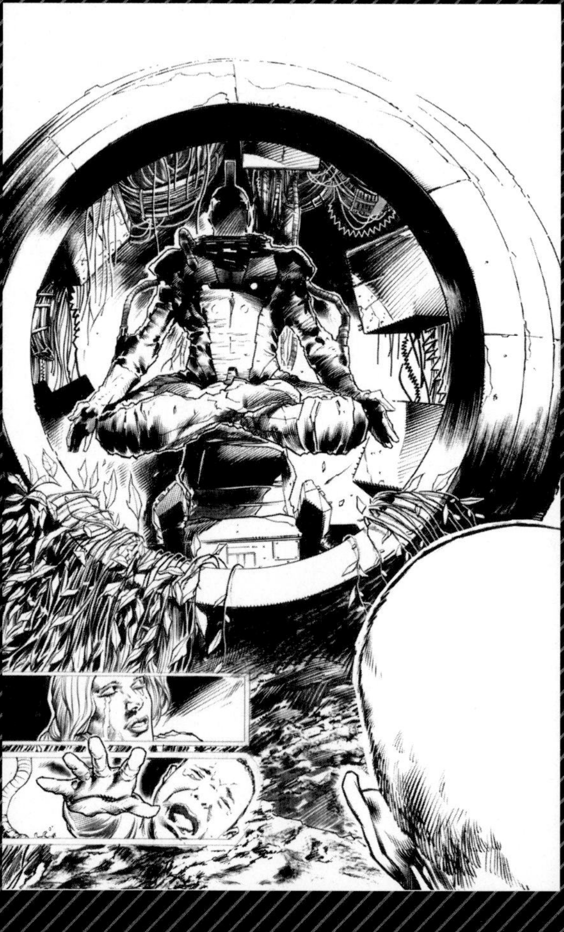

DIVINITY #2, p.19
Pencils by TREVOR HAIRSINE
Inks by RYAN WINN

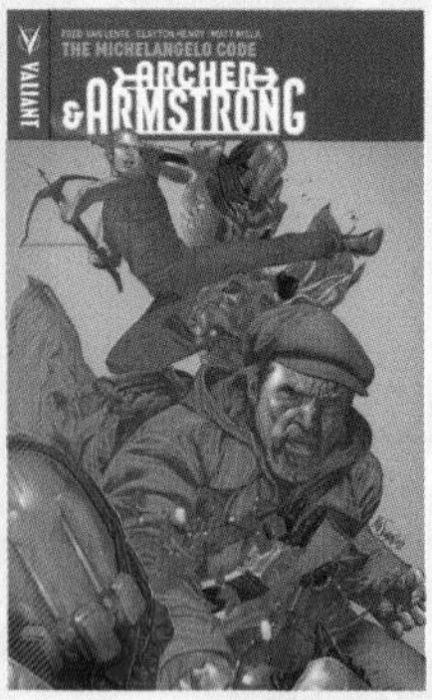
THE MICHELANGELO CODE
ARCHER & ARMSTRONG
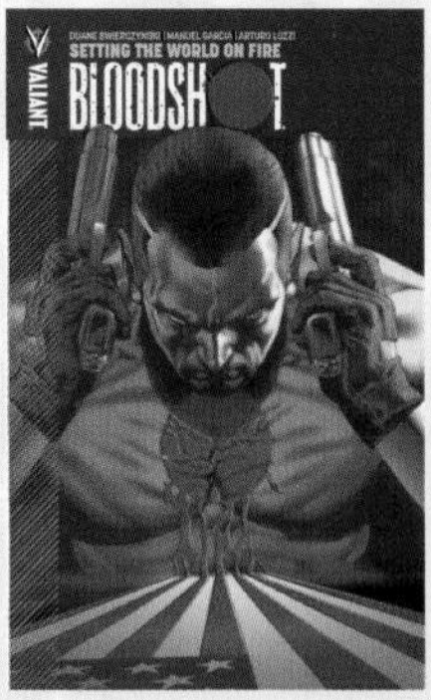
SETTING THE WORLD ON FIRE
BLOODSHOT
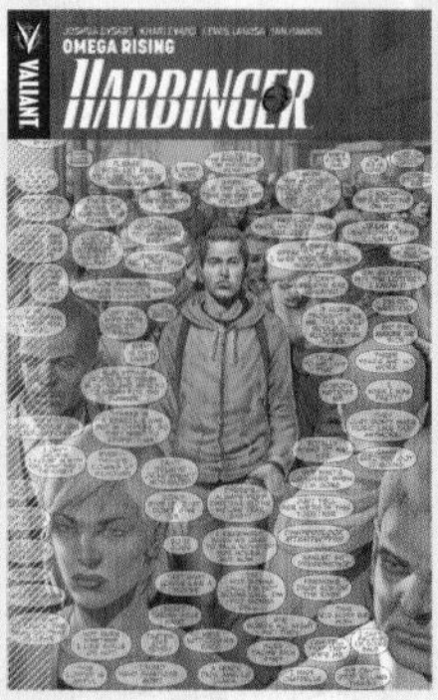
OMEGA RISING
HARBINGER
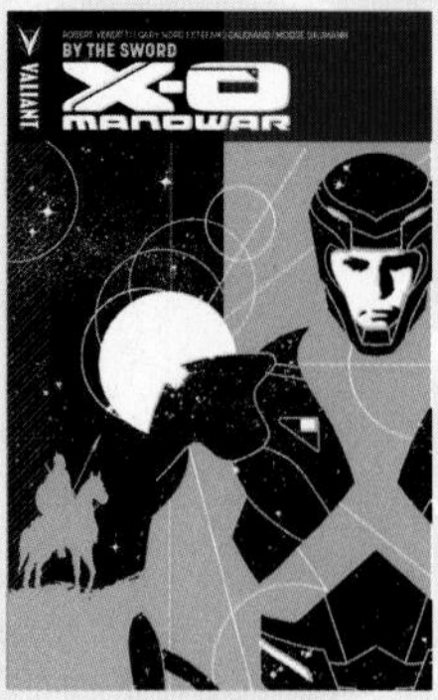
BY THE SWORD
X-O MANOWAR
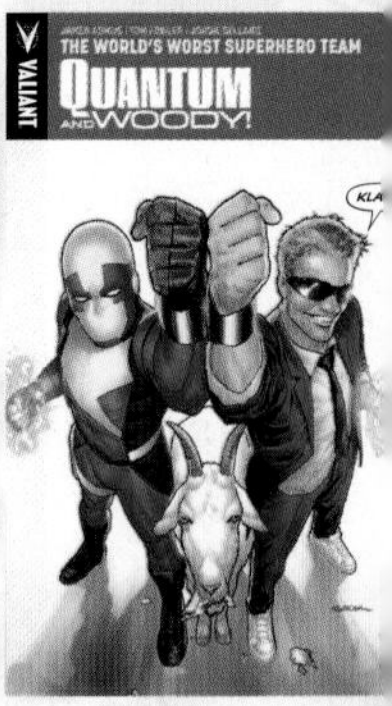
THE WORLD'S WORST SUPERHERO TEAM
QUANTUM AND WOODY!

ARCHER & ARMSTRONG

Volume 1: The Michelangelo Code
ISBN: 9780979640988

Volume 2: Wrath of the Eternal Warrior
ISBN: 9781939346049

Volume 3: Far Faraway
ISBN: 9781939346148

Volume 4: Sect Civil War
ISBN: 9781939346254

Volume 5: Mission: Improbable
ISBN: 9781939346353

Volume 6: American Wasteland
ISBN: 9781939346421

Volume 7: The One Percent and Other Tales
ISBN: 9781939346537

ARMOR HUNTERS

Armor Hunters
ISBN: 9781939346452

Armor Hunters: Bloodshot
ISBN: 9781939346469

Armor Hunters: Harbinger
ISBN: 9781939346506

Unity Vol. 3: Armor Hunters
ISBN: 9781939346445

X-O Manowar Vol. 7: Armor Hunters
ISBN: 9781939346476

BLOODSHOT

Volume 1: Setting the World on Fire
ISBN: 9780979640964

Volume 2: The Rise and the Fall
ISBN: 9781939346032

Volume 3: Harbinger Wars
ISBN: 9781939346124

Volume 4: H.A.R.D. Corps
ISBN: 9781939346193

Volume 5: Get Some!
ISBN: 9781939346315

Volume 6: The Glitch and Other Tales
ISBN: 9781939346711

BLOODSHOT REBORN

Volume 1: Colorado
ISBN: 9781939346674

DEAD DROP

Dead Drop
ISBN: 9781939346858

THE DEATH-DEFYING DOCTOR MIRAGE

The Death-Defying Dr. Mirage
ISBN: 9781939346490

THE DELINQUENTS

The Delinquents
ISBN: 9781939346513

DIVINITY

DIVINITY
ISBN: 9781939346766

ETERNAL WARRIOR

Volume 1: Sword of the Wild
ISBN: 9781939346209

Volume 2: Eternal Emperor
ISBN: 9781939346292

Volume 3: Days of Steel
ISBN: 9781939346742

HARBINGER

Volume 1: Omega Rising
ISBN: 9780979640957

Volume 2: Renegades
ISBN: 9781939346025

Volume 3: Harbinger Wars
ISBN: 9781939346117

Volume 4: Perfect Day
ISBN: 9781939346155

Volume 5: Death of a Renegade
ISBN: 9781939346339

Volume 6: Omegas
ISBN: 9781939346384

HARBINGER WARS

Harbinger Wars
ISBN: 9781939346094

Bloodshot Vol. 3: Harbinger Wars
ISBN: 9781939346124

Harbinger Vol. 3: Harbinger Wars
ISBN: 9781939346117

KICK ME
QUANTUM AND WOODY
BY PRIEST & BRIGHT
VOL 1: KLANG

VALIANT
BATTLE FOR NEW JAPAN
RAI

VALIANT
THE VALIANT

VALIANT
THE DEATH-DEFYING
DOCTOR MIRAGE

VALIANT
DIVINITY

インピリアム
MPERIUM

lume 1: Collecting Monsters
BN: 9781939346759

NINJAK

lume 1: Weaponeer
BN: 9781939346667

QUANTUM AND WOODY!

olume 1: The World's Worst Superhero Team
BN: 9781939346186

olume 2: In Security
BN: 9781939346230

olume 3: Crooked Pasts, Present Tense
BN: 9781939346391

olume 4: Quantum and Woody Must Die!
BN: 9781939346629

QUANTUM AND WOODY BY PRIEST & BRIGHT

lume 1: Klang
BN: 9781939346780

lume 2: Switch
BN: 9781939346803

lume 3: And So...
BN: 9781939346865

RAI

Volume 1: Welcome to New Japan
ISBN: 9781939346414

Volume 2: Battle for New Japan
ISBN: 9781939346612

Volume 3: The Orphan
ISBN: 9781939346841

SHADOWMAN

Volume 1: Birth Rites
ISBN: 9781939346001

Volume 2: Darque Reckoning
ISBN: 9781939346056

Volume 3: Deadside Blues
ISBN: 9781939346162

Volume 4: Fear, Blood, And Shadows
ISBN: 9781939346278

Volume 5: End Times
ISBN: 9781939346377

Ivar, Timewalker

Volume 1: Making History
ISBN: 9781939346636

UNITY

Volume 1: To Kill a King
ISBN: 9781939346261

Volume 2: Trapped by Webnet
ISBN: 9781939346346

Volume 3: Armor Hunters
ISBN: 9781939346445

UNITY (Continued)

Volume 4: The United
ISBN: 9781939346544

Volume 5: Homefront
ISBN: 9781939346797

THE VALIANT

The Valiant
ISBN: 9781939346605

VALIANT ZEROES AND ORIGINS

Valiant: Zeroes and Origins
ISBN: 9781939346582

X-O MANOWAR

Volume 1: By the Sword
ISBN: 9780979640940

Volume 2: Enter Ninjak
ISBN: 9780979640995

Volume 3: Planet Death
ISBN: 9781939346087

Volume 4: Homecoming
ISBN: 9781939346179

Volume 5: At War With Unity
ISBN: 9781939346247

Volume 6: Prelude to Armor Hunters
ISBN: 9781939346407

Volume 7: Armor Hunters
ISBN: 9781939346476

Volume 8: Enter: Armorines
ISBN: 9781939346551

Volume 9: Dead Hand
ISBN: 9781939346650

VALIANT
HARBINGER DELUXE EDITION 2

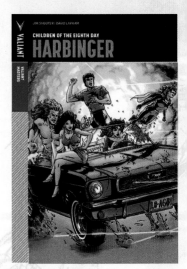

OMNIBUSES

Archer & Armstrong: The Complete Classic Omnibus
ISBN: 9781939346872
Collecting ARCHER & ARMSTRONG (1992) #0-26, ETERNAL WARRIOR (1992) #25 along with ARCHER & ARMSTRONG: THE FORMATION OF THE SECT.

Quantum and Woody: The Complete Classic Omnibus
ISBN: 9781939346360
Collecting QUANTUM AND WOODY (1997) #0, 1-21 and #32, THE GOAT: H.A.E.D.U.S. #1, and X-O MANOWAR (1996) #16

X-O Manowar Classic Omnibus Vol. 1
ISBN: 9781939346308
Collecting X-O MANOWAR (1992) #0-30, ARMORINES #0, X-O DATABASE #1, as well as material from SECRETS OF THE VALIANT UNIVERSE #1

DELUXE EDITIONS

Archer & Armstrong Deluxe Edition Book 1
ISBN: 9781939346223
Collecting ARCHER & ARMSTRONG #0-13

VALIANT
ARMOR HUNTERS DELUXE EDITION

Armor Hunters Deluxe Edition
ISBN: 9781939346728
Collecting ARMOR HUNTERS #1-4, ARMOR HUNTERS: AFTERMATH #1, ARMOR HUNTERS: BLOODSHOT #1-3, ARMOR HUNTERS: HARBINGER #1-3, UNITY #8-11 and X-O MANOWAR #23-29

Bloodshot Deluxe Edition Book 1
ISBN: 9781939346216
Collecting BLOODSHOT #1-13

Harbinger Deluxe Edition Book 1
ISBN: 9781939346131
Collecting HARBINGER #0-14

Harbinger Deluxe Edition Book 2
ISBN: 9781939346773
Collecting HARBINGER #15-25, HARBINGER: OMEGAS #1-3, and HARBINGER: BLEEDING MONK #0

Harbinger Wars Deluxe Edition
ISBN: 9781939346322
Collecting HARBINGER WARS #1-4, HARBINGER #11-14, and BLOODSHOT #10-13

Quantum and Woody Deluxe Edition Book 1
ISBN: 9781939346681
Collecting QUANTUM AND WOODY #1-12 and QUANTUM AND WOODY: THE GOAT #0

Q2: The Return of Quantum and Woody Deluxe Edition
ISBN: 9781939346568
Collecting Q2: THE RETURN OF QUANTUM AND WOODY #1-5

JAMES ASMUS | TOM FOWLER | MING DOYLE
KANO | JORDIE BELLAIRE | DAVE LANPHEAR
VALIANT
QUANTUM AND WOODY! DELUXE EDITION 1
MEH!

Shadowman Deluxe Edition Book 1
ISBN: 9781939346438
Collecting SHADOWMAN #0-10

Unity Deluxe Edition Book 1
ISBN: 9781939346575
Collecting UNITY #0-14

X-O Manowar Deluxe Edition Book 1
ISBN: 9781939346100
Collecting X-O MANOWAR #1-14

X-O Manowar Deluxe Edition Book 2
ISBN: 9781939346520
Collecting X-O MANOWAR #15-22, and UNITY #1-4

JIM SHOOTER | DAVID LAPHAM
VALIANT
CHILDREN OF THE EIGHTH DAY
HARBINGER
VALIANT MASTERS

VALIANT MASTERS

Bloodshot Vol. 1 - Blood of the Machine
ISBN: 9780979640933

H.A.R.D. Corps Vol. 1 - Search and Destroy
ISBN: 9781939346285

Harbinger Vol. 1 - Children of the Eighth Day
ISBN: 9781939346483

Ninjak Vol. 1 - Black Water
ISBN: 9780979640971

Rai Vol. 1 - From Honor to Strength
ISBN: 9781939346070

Shadowman Vol. 1 - Spirits Within
ISBN: 9781939346018

KEVIN VANHOOK | DON PERLIN
VALIANT
BLOOD OF THE MACHINE
BLOODSHOT
VALIANT MASTERS

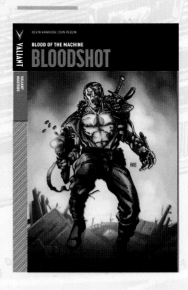

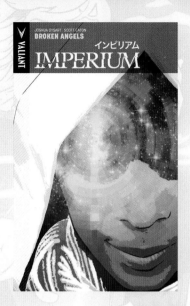

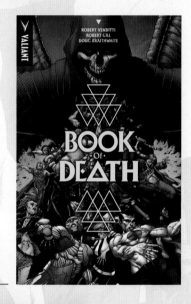

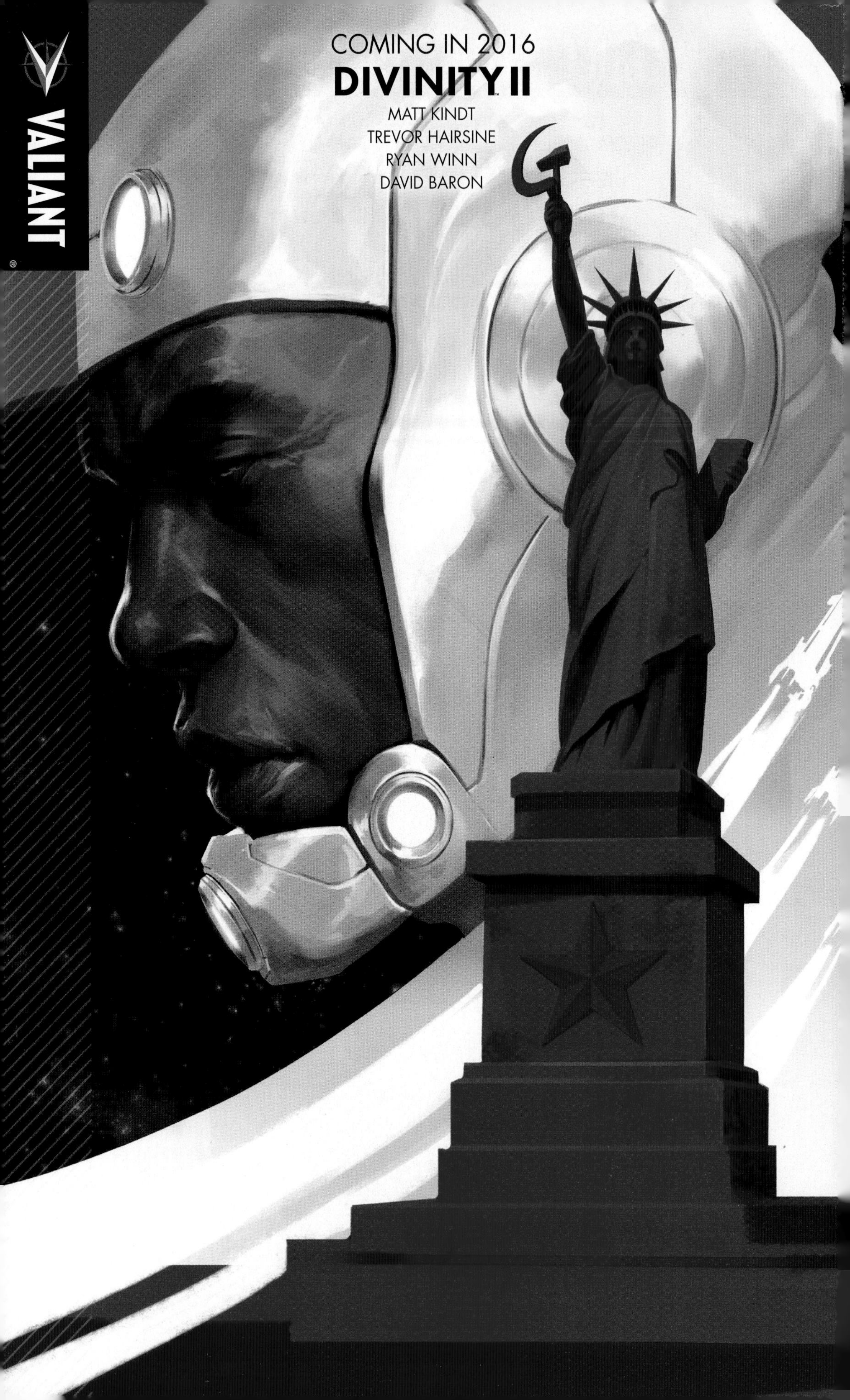

VALIANT®
COMING IN 2016
DIVINITY II
MATT KINDT
TREVOR HAIRSINE
RYAN WINN
DAVID BARON